I Love Lucy

I Love Lucy

THE
COMPLETE PICTURE HISTORY
OF THE MOST POPULAR
TV SHOW EVER

♥

Michael McClay

PHOTOGRAPHIC MONTAGES EDITED BY
DEANNA GAFFNER-McCLAY

Barnes
&Noble
BOOKS
NEW YORK

Copyright © 1995 by Michael McClay

This edition published by Barnes & Noble, Inc.,
by arrangement with Warner Books, Inc.

Interior design by Michaelis/Carpelis Design Associates Inc.

2001 Barnes & Noble Books

ISBN 0-7607-2756-2

Printed and bound in the United States of America

02 03 04 05 MC 9 8 7 6 5 4 3 2

KP

TO LUCILLE BALL AND DESI ARNAZ
AND
HOWARD MCCLAY

❤

CONTENTS

AUTHOR'S PREFACE

I watched with fascination as the woman reached out to grab the ledge, trying to keep herself from falling. The New York skyline loomed in the distance, and the huge, cement-pouring construction bucket holding her swayed dangerously across the expanse between the buildings. Wide-eyed with fear, she reached out with both hands as two men rushed onto the balcony to help her. One of them boosted himself onto the ledge and he managed to grab her hand, but the bucket swung out into space again, taking him with it. Clinging frantically to the outside of the bucket, he tried to hoist himself up into the safety of its concrete-spattered insides, his legs kicking wildly behind him as he pulled himself toward the lip. The woman's hands spidered down the length of his arms, trying to get a better grasp on his jacket. The bucket swung back and forth, back and forth, until the man couldn't take it anymore. "Get me out of here," he shouted. "I gotta go to the bathroom!!"

Loud peals of laughter broke out, and a voice yelled: *"Cut!"*

The man hanging onto the bucket was Milton Berle, the man on the ledge was Desi Arnaz, and the woman in the bucket was the most famous television star in the world.

Standing next to me, my father burst out laughing and I followed suit, along with the rest of the cast and crew. I figured it was okay to unstifle the laughter that had been building inside of me as the scene unfolded on Stage 9 of Desilu's Cahuenga Lot on that early morning shoot, late in the spring of 1959. There was no audience, since these last *Lucy-Desi Comedy Hours* weren't filmed in front of a studio audience.

I had never seen such red hair in all my nine years, and I watched raptly as the woman underneath it all came walking over in my direction, laughing that husky, wide-mouthed cackle that I would come to know so well over the years.

"Berle just can't keep it straight," she chortled. "Always gotta ad lib. Where's my smokes?"

"Here's mine, Lucy," said my father, pulling out his pack.

"Thanks, Howard," she said, lighting up.

He was about to introduce me when she looked around his shoulder and saw me staring up at her. "This must be Michael," she said, holding out her hand.

"H-h-h-ow do you do, Mrs. Ball," I stuttered.

"Lucy to you," she said, smiling. Those blue eyes looked deep into mine. "And it's not Mrs.—*Miss* Ball."

"I apologize..."

"It's okay, dear. The columnists still do that, don't they, Howard?" she said to my father, her publicist, a former *Los Angeles Daily News* columnist. She looked at me again and said, "My, you're a handsome little guy. Must take after your mother." She winked at my father and laughed. So did Dad.

The scene she had just played was from "Milton Berle Hides Out at the Ricardos," the first show of the ninth and final season of the *I Love Lucy* series. It was to be the beginning of the end of a television milestone. After the weekly half-hour series ended in 1957, Lucy and Desi had gone on to film thirteen *Lucy-Desi Comedy Hour* specials together. Two more would be filmed after this one, and then America's most famous couple would end their relationship for good. As a kid, I had no idea of what was going on in their personal lives at the time, but as far as I was concerned they were a happily married couple. It was my first visit to a soundstage, and I had finally met the woman who had made me laugh so much over the years.

After a few minutes of publicity talk between Lucy and my father, she went off to her dressing room, and we picked our way through a sea of cables over to Desi Arnaz and Milton Berle. Berle was holding court with Desi and producer Bert Granet, regaling them with a story of the farmer's-daughter-and-traveling-salesman variety. Their raucous laughter abruptly ended when I came within earshot. As my father introduced me to everyone, I suddenly felt a bit out of place.

Then Desi broke the ice and said to me, "Do you like miniature cars?"

"Of course," I said, surprised that someone knew that I did.

"Then come over here, *amigo*, I wanna show you somethin'." And as we walked away, he said to Berle, "Tha's a good one, Milton, but I already heard it from Buddy Hackett." Berle rolled his eyes. Putting his arm around my shoulder, Desi took me over to the miniature cars they had moving on the set to simulate the traffic below the ledge. He had the special-effects man show me how the cars worked, and I was enthralled.

Recalling that day in later years, I was stunned to realize that I'd spent the afternoon with three of the greatest icons from what has come to be known as the Golden Age of Television. Their lives had reached a pinnacle, and that era—along with the production of *I Love Lucy* itself—would soon pass into history.

In the thirty-six years since the last new episode of the half-hour series aired, on May 6, 1957, *I Love Lucy* has been playing almost continuously around the clock somewhere in the world. It's been estimated that *I Love Lucy* has been watched by over a billion people, and dubbed into dozens of languages, including Spanish, French, Portuguese, Italian, German, Dutch, Japanese and dozens of others. At any given time, it's being marketed in almost a hundred U.S. markets and in eighty countries. That makes it the most popular series in television history. When the show first went into reruns on CBS in 1959, the network needed to fill an empty slot in its summertime schedule. To the network's amazement, the ratings eclipsed most of the newly produced programming at the

This is the balcony scene in "Milton Berle Hides Out at the Ricardos," part of the Lucy-Desi Comedy Hour series in 1959. The author first met Lucy and Desi after this scene was filmed.

time. It was the first series that demonstrated how reruns could give new life to old shows and find new revenues for recycled programming.

This historic program also set the standards by which all subsequent sitcoms have been measured. The techniques for sitcom production were created by the *I Love Lucy* staff and—except for camera technology advancement—the procedure for filming or taping television sitcoms has not essentially changed since that original team created them.

Lucy, Desi and the rest of the talent responsible for the show had no idea it would be a hit of any kind, much less become a classic. Neither did my father, who went to work for Lucy and Desi in 1958, just two years before the last hour-long episode of *I Love Lucy* became history. During the next two decades, *I Love Lucy* and their Desilu Studios would become an integral part of our family life. Though many of my formative years were spent watching their antics on television along with millions of others, I also had the opportunity to be a part of the Desilu family from the inside. Frequent field trips to the studio increased my enchantment with the production process. When I went to work in Desilu's mailroom at the age of sixteen during summer vacations, I never considered my job at the studio any kind of work.

In the years after *I Love Lucy* had stopped production and the principals had gone on to other projects, Lucy and my father talked about putting together a book about the show. At first it wasn't really a serious idea, but public response to the series over the years had been so overwhelming that—as time went on—Lucy felt her fans deserved a lasting tribute to the show that had so profoundly changed her life, the history of television and the world of American popular culture, both here and abroad. She wanted viewers to be able to relive the series in a book.

Lucy placed in my father's custody the complete record of the show, including all her reflections and observations and all the photographs shot while the program was in active production. Early in the 1980s, Lucy and my father had finally reached the stage where they were talking to publishers and had finally settled on a format for the book. In addition to my principal responsibility for the syndication of *Here's Lucy* at Lucille Ball Productions at the time, I had participated in some of the archival research for the book, but I was never aware at the time of the immense volume of material. My father had already begun the writing process, and had assembled all the source material that Lucy had given to him, when fate intervened to change the course of everyone's life. On the front steps of the Samuel Goldwyn Studios, Howard McClay suffered a coronary and died on the morning of December 9, 1981, at Cedars-Sinai Hospital in Beverly Hills. He was carrying with him some of the materials which now comprise a portion of this book.

Lucy and I agreed to shelve the project for a few months, but we never got back to it again. My career took a different path, though while I was deep in the development of the promotion and publicity launch campaign for *Entertainment Tonight* in 1982, I would think often of the book and resolve to work on it—perhaps someday. It wasn't until 1988 that I was able to start working on it again. I had never completely looked through all the materials, and I was astonished to find that photos and negatives for nearly every

The author's father, Howard McClay, coordinates a publicity camera setup with Lucille Ball during the filming of "Lucy Goes to Mexico." He was Lucy's publicist from 1958 until his death in 1981.

episode of the show were virtually intact. Apparently many of them had never been used, and I called Lucy to let her know. She never answered the call. Two days later, on April 26, 1989, she suffered a ruptured aorta and—like my father—also died at Cedars-Sinai. Out of respect, I put the project on hold again. Then early in 1991, I called Lucie Arnaz. Now, more than ever, I was determined to finish the book as a tribute to her mother's memory. Perhaps the sons and daughters could pick up the torch.

I told her I wanted this book to be not only the definitive pictorial look at the series, but a tribute to the hundreds of talented people who were involved in the making of the show. But most of all, it was Lucille Ball's and Howard McClay's wish for this book to be a special gift for the millions who loved Lucy and Ricky and Fred and Ethel. Graciously, she agreed to cooperate with me on it.

There have been many biographies of Lucille Ball and Desi Arnaz, and much has been written—both fictional and factual—on the *I Love Lucy* phenomenon. What has been missing from that bookshelf is what made the show—and makes this book—so special: the images.

The *"I Love Lucy"* book represents the distillation of the thousands of photographs that Lucy left in the care of my father. It draws from the world's largest collection of *I Love Lucy* photos, over twelve thousand original production negatives from the 179 episodes of the entire half-hour series from 1951 through 1957— the most complete pictorial representation of the series in existence, all shot in high-resolution 4 x 5 Speed Graphic camera format. What makes this archive even more valuable are the negatives. No other book or publishing project can tap into the original camera negatives which comprise this extraordinary collection of stills.

Though there is enough archival material to reenact almost

every scene from nearly every single show, I've decided to focus on the most beloved and best-remembered episodes, with detailed pictorial highlights of each one, accompanied by in-depth synopses and analyses, as well as anecdotal glimpses behind the scenes. These thirty-five episodes represent a consensus of critics, fans and the surviving creators of the series. Of course, everyone has their favorite *I Love Lucy* episode, but most fans will find their own choices among them. What I hope you will experience in reading this book is the closest thing to a live performance on paper.

I have also taken a new look at the history of the show and its principals. With the volumes of written material on the subject of Lucille Ball, Desi Arnaz, Desilu and the series, I have chosen to concentrate on the essence of the phenomenon and avoid the minutae, with fresh insights based on personal interviews with a variety of people who worked on the show.

For the real Lucyphile, at the back of the book, I've compiled a complete "TV-ography" of the entire series in numerical episode sequence.

I have also included an additional treat. Though *I Love Lucy* was photographed in black and white, and most of the production stills were shot that way, you will find in this book a plentiful assortment of color photographs that were also taken during production. Not tinted or color-computer enhanced, these are original color photographs, none of them ever published before—nor have most of the black-and-white photos been published, not even in newspapers or magazine articles when the shows first aired.

The world continues to love Lucy and Desi. Television will never see their kind again. So turn the page and return to a simpler time, a time that's never far away. The memories and images live on your television and in these pages.

INTRODUCTION BY LUCIE ARNAZ

I think it's fair to say that no single shared experience has ever brought more laughter to more people than a forty-year-old black-and-white television series called *I Love Lucy*. Still playing in reruns around the world, it's simply the most watched TV show in history. Quite an extraordinary feat when you consider that it was a daffy redhead, her unknown Cuban husband and their frumpy neighbors who were at the heart—and soul—of this unique phenomenon. But the remarkable chemistry between the foursome known as the Ricardos and the Mertzes was unrivaled in the world of television comedy. Show after show, year after year, their impact on viewing audiences everywhere on earth still continues to resonate. Lucy and Ricky, Ethel and Fred not only succeeded, they endured. The humor of the show, the situations, both comical and poignant, are universal and timeless—the very reasons why old fans remain so faithful and new ones keep discovering the show.

Two years ago, when I was putting together home-movie footage for the television production of *Lucy and Desi: A Home Movie*, I realized and understood, perhaps for the first time, that the phrase "I Love Lucy" summed up not only my parents' relationship, but their entire life. For all their hopes, plans and dreams for a happy future were wrapped up in that TV sitcom. Not only was it a wonderful showcase for my mother's matchless comedic gifts, and a great vehicle for my father's charm and musical talents, it was also intended to provide them both with something they lacked, something they desperately needed and wanted: a way to stay together. They were a passionately adoring and loving couple whose show-business careers took them on different paths and kept them apart. Long separations from one another were taking an early toll on their married life, so finding a way to work together meant saving their marriage. This was the main reason for the genesis of *I Love Lucy*.

They also knew that if they were together more of the time, they would be able to make their other dream come true: starting a family. Both my parents had come from unhappy backgrounds, filled with adversity and childhood trauma. My mother's early life, laced with tragedy and poverty, paved the way for her ambitious career goals in later years, and for her relentlessly hard work in pursuit of them. My father's family fled from Cuba, and once in exile, especially after his parents had separated, Desi suffered a sense of isolation and rootlessness, and it made him yearn all the more for a stable family life.

After my parents met, fell in love and got married, they bought a ranch in Chatsworth that reminded my father of the *ranchos* he knew in Cuba. They called it "Desilu," and it became for both of them the first real beginning, a foundation on which to build the lifestyle they had always wanted for themselves. In fact, their years at the Desilu ranch, with its livestock, its dogs and cats, fruit and vegetable gardens and all the refurbishing projects that were undertaken, were the most idyllic in their lives together.

But while the ranch was a fun-filled, happy refuge from the disappointments and setbacks of show business, their careers still continued to keep them apart. There they were, both struggling separately for success and yet wanting so much to be together. Because of the scarcity of Latin film roles, my father was on the road a great deal, performing with his band—in truth, entertaining nightclub audiences was what he preferred to do. It was during these separations that telephone arguments between my parents grew into the more serious misunderstandings and impasses that almost led them to a divorce in the mid-forties. And then, in 1947, when Lucy was starring in *Dream Girl* in summer stock and Desi was planning a surprise romantic rendezvous with her, a near-brush with tragedy changed the course of their lives. A bus carrying my father's band crashed, and if he hadn't been on his way to meet my mother, he would have almost certainly been killed. This event had a profound effect on them: they were now determined to keep their marriage intact, and they even renewed their wedding vows in a Catholic church ceremony.

After my mother's success on the old radio show *My Favorite Husband*, she harbored an intense desire to perform in front of a live audience. Her kind of clowning and comedy talent thrived on the sound of real people laughing uproariously at her antics. And so a pilot for *I Love Lucy* finally came to fruition. But her biggest battle with the networks and sponsors wasn't trying to sell the show, but insisting that my father play opposite her in the TV series. She won that round and, as they say, "the rest is history." Things happened rather quickly after that: within a month of the network's approval for the pilot, my mother became pregnant with me, and after I was born, they started filming the TV series. At last, the Arnazes would be a family, both off and on the screen. Immense good fortune and renewed hope for marital happiness seemed to be at their doorstep.

Happy endings and "perfect" families, however, are the stuff of movie fantasy. We can only work *toward* achieving these goals, knowing that the journey is all. But despite the inevitable problems of a family life lived far more publicly than privately—with people rapping on our front door several times a day, asking, "Is she home?" or pulling the grass out of our lawn for souvenirs—and despite the pain that I often felt when I was growing up, and the pain my parents inflicted on one another—there were, of course, wonderful and memorable times. It wasn't until I began viewing those old home movies, though, that I really saw—and what a revelation it was—this fun-loving, joyful, playful, happy couple who were my mother and father.

Once the series started airing, what followed began to change the face of television, and with it, the lives of my parents. Unprecedented wealth, power and international fame were now on the horizon. Ironically, when they were newlyweds, Lucy and Desi were seventy-five-dollar-a-week contract players at RKO. Little could they have possibly imagined that seventeen years later, after the incredible success of *I Love Lucy*, they would be able to *buy* the entire RKO studio they had once worked for! Desilu was no longer just the name of their Chatsworth haven, it now meant Desilu Productions, an entertainment empire.

My brother arrived during the second year of the show, and I know there were thousands of letters from viewers who had nothing but praise for the way in which *I Love Lucy* treated the birth of a baby; an event in those days that was considered a highly sensitive subject for television—almost taboo. Once again, the personal impact that the show had on people was astonishing. Men and women opened up their hearts to my parents, writing letters that said things like, "You saved my marriage," or "If he can take it, so can I," or "We both can tell you love each other."

As success grew, so did our family lifestyle: there were three beautiful homes, expensive vacations, lavish parties. But though the surroundings became more luxurious, my parents still wanted to keep things "homey" and down-to-earth. Even Desilu Productions was run as though it were one big family. In fact, I'm sure that's why, to this day, the people who worked directly for my parents have such loving memories. I've been told time and time again that the years at Desilu were the best of their lives. My mother and father even got involved in the planning of company picnics—big family affairs with softball games, relay races and tons of food. Everyone had a great time, and probably nobody more than Lucy and Desi.

Although my parents had become America's best-known and most admired married couple, and although the television Ricardos always arrived at a happy ending each week, life at the Arnaz home was definitely no longer as joyful as it had been in the years before their wildest dreams were realized. The work ethic ruled both my parents' lives—they were simply at their happiest when they were working. My mother used to say, "The more you do, the more you *can* do," and my father was, at this point, not just costarring with her every week, but running a television studio and handling all their various other projects, including movies, TV shows and commercials. And he ran it all brilliantly. Not only was he an astute businessman, but also an uncannily good judge of comedy. His executive vice president once remarked, "Desi was very good at knowing what worked and what didn't—especially for Lucy. We had the biggest studio in town, and most of that was due to Desi's drive and shrewd business savvy. What an achievement." This was the prevailing conviction of those who knew and worked with my father, but he himself invariably felt it was Lucy who got the accolades—he was merely the tail wagging the dog. He never realized how much he was truly respected for all the innovative things he did, both in the creation and day-to-day running of Desilu Studios.

Our family life soon began straining at the seams. The more my parents worked and were away from my brother and me, the higher the level of stress and anxiety at home. And, of course, in those days, you rarely talked about domestic problems or sought help to resolve them. People were even reluctant to own up to the reasons for the conflicts in the first place. As my brother, Desi, once aptly put it, "Just like other families, we had problems, and part of the problem was admitting there were problems." And, so, with all the enviable comforts and pleasures that my parents' success brought to my brother and me, it also brought us a great deal of unhappiness. Success can often become its own trap: the more you have of it, the more you want. Theirs was a mistaken belief that producing more shows, making more money, buying more property, accumulating more possessions, would somehow take the place of time not spent with the family, of commitments not kept to the children because of the demands being made on the parents.

Although this was all quite hard for me to deal with when I was growing up, it turned out to be the best lesson I could have learned by the time I had children of my own. In retrospect, I don't think I could have otherwise ever known both the enormous difficulty and tremendous importance of balancing career and domestic life. I feel I had to go through the experience to realize that there are no easy answers, no shortcuts, and that "being there" for your children, emotionally and physically, is simply crucial to their sense of security, trust and self-worth.

I also know that it wasn't only work that made it hard for both my parents to create a strong bond with my brother and me. Much of it had to do with their own painful formative years—especially my mother's. She never really had a childhood. She had to be an adult so early on because her own mother was gone a great deal of time. This unfortunate part of her past, coupled with the fact that she worked so hard and so intensely all her life, is what put distance between her and us when she was raising her own family. A dear friend of hers once said, "Lucille Ball's first love is her work." But I also believe that it was those very years of her childhood—unhappy and grindingly poor—that forged her into the woman who was destined to give to the world such an abundance of joy and laughter.

My parents' divorce took me many years to make peace with; I kept thinking my mother and father would somehow, someday, get back together. But whatever their ultimate heartbreak, and whatever personal and professional crises they created, suffered, survived or were undone by, through it all they remained companions in spirit and, to the rest of the world, an utterly lovable, remarkably talented, incomparably funny couple who created a show upon which an entire sitcom industry was built, and which still, to this day, has no equal.

That is why I want so much to share their legacy with you through the pages of this very special book. In text and pictures, candidly and more comprehensively than ever before, *I Love Lucy* has been beautifully brought to life by Michael McClay. With its inside story of the show, and its mint-condition still photographs of the entire series, many of them never before seen, it is the definitive portrait of the program and the people behind it. And no one but Michael could have put it together more lovingly, because it began as a project conceived by my mother and Michael's father, Howard McClay, her longtime publicist. Before their mutual dream could be realized, both of them passed away, so it has been left up to their children to complete the work and fulfill its purpose: giving you the chance to relive, and share with friends and family, your favorite episodes of *I Love Lucy*, in all their hilarity and delightful madness. I truly believe that these days, perhaps more so than at any other time in our history, the gift of laughter is the greatest gift of all. So please consider this book our heartfelt gift to you and yours.

My Love,
Lucie Arnaz

I LOVE LUCY

Lyric by
HAROLD ADAMSON

Music by
ELIOT DANIEL

There's a cer-tain coup-le that I know_____ They're strict-ly love birds,_

_ a pair of tur-tle dove birds. He's a guy who wants the world to

know_____ So ev-'ry day_____ you'll hear him say._____

Song continues on page 116

A Historical Perspective

The Jester and the Troubadour

Lucy.

Few people have a monopoly over a name, and Lucille Ball was one of them. Anywhere in the world where *I Love Lucy* is seen—and that's just about everywhere—the name "Lucy" can only mean one person.

And Desi owned his name as much as Lucy owned hers. The two are inseparable.

To understand the phenomenal impact of *I Love Lucy*, one has to understand the personal relationship of Lucille Ball and Desi Arnaz, and how the dynamics of their marriage were responsible for the creation of the show, and for its success.

One also has to understand the American psyche. It's the quintessential American success story. A young girl born to a humble background, aspiring to greatness, and an immigrant youth whose family fled political persecution and a uncertain future, meeting and falling in love, becoming one of the best-known couples of the twentieth century.

Lucy, the small-town Yankee gal whose grit and gifts allowed her to persevere until she found her calling and her life after the age of forty. Glamorous, yet unpretentious; a heartwarming presence on-screen, yet personally aloof; a genius comic performer who was intensely serious in her personal life; brutally blunt, yet able to exhibit astounding thoughtfulness. One of her executives once described her as a woman who "had a heart of steel encased in a velvet glove."

Desi, on the other hand, was born to wealth, lost it all, and as a young entertainer turned on his charm and rhumba'd his way into America's nightclubs—and into Lucille's heart. He was vain,

Few people in history can claim exclusivity with their given names. Lucy and Desi belonged to this elite club.

yet humble; a man of excessive appetites who loved simplicity; warm and loving, yet at times violently confrontational; a clearheaded problem-solver who couldn't solve his own inner problems; a man who insisted on the truth, yet was unfaithful to his own marriage vows. A close associate of Desi once described him as a "magnificent booming thundercloud with lightning and bright rays of sunshine filtering through."

To understand the legacy of *I Love Lucy*, the complex and mercurial relationship between Lucille Ball and Desi Arnaz must also be understood. And to understand their relationship—what made it work and what ultimately ruined it—one has to understand where they came from, and what made them the people they were.

Lucy was three and a half when this picture was taken, not long before her father died of typhoid. When her mother gave her the news, sparrows were feeding in the kitchen window. For the rest of her life Lucy hated pictures of birds.

IT STARTED IN JAMESTOWN

Laughter was a commodity hard to come by in Lucille Ball's early life. Born on August 6, 1911, in Jamestown, New York, she was only four when her father died of typhoid fever, and four years later, Lucille's mother DeDe married Ed Peterson, a factory worker whose unfortunate shortcomings included drinking and gambling. When Ed's work took him on the road, DeDe followed him, but he insisted that Lucille and her brother, Fred, move in with his parents, who were stern disciplinarians. Lucy's independent nature made her a frequent runaway, so DeDe sent the two children to live with Lucille's beloved grandfather Frederick C. Hunt in Celoron, a small town near Jamestown where he had worked variously as a mailman, a wood turner and a hotel manager. Her footloose ways continued, but she would usually wind up staying at some acquaintance's house before coming home after a few hours away.

It seemed that the only time Lucy was really happy was when her grandfather would take her, her brother and their cousin Cleo to vaudeville on Saturday nights. "He was a devotee, and we loved it, too," she recalled. "All I know is that

This is the first studio portrait of Lucille Ball, taken at eight months, when her mother DeDe turned eighteen and was living with her parents in Jamestown, New York.

Lucy's beloved grandfather, Frederick C. Hunt, was Lucy's surrogate father after the death of her real father when she was four. The inscription on the photo reads: "To My Lucille from Daddy."

I wanted to make people laugh." One of only two girls in a small high school, she staged an amateur production of *Charley's Aunt* in the fall of 1926, and "felt for the first time the wonderful feeling that comes from getting real laughs on a stage. I not only played the male lead but sold the tickets, swept up the stage afterwards and turned out the lights. It was a great success. At twenty-five cents a ticket, we made twenty-five dollars and gave all of it to the ninth grade for a class party. The success of the show encouraged me to get into as many musical and dramatic offerings as I could."

At the age of fifteen, she left Celoron and her mother helped enroll her in the John Murray Anderson–Robert Milton Dramatics School, considered one of the finest of its kind on Broadway. Thought exceedingly shy and self-conscious, she began her long apprenticeship. After only twelve months of study, she heard a discouraging litany that would echo through her life for the next several years: she was told bluntly that her talent was minimal and she should consider looking for a new profession.

Lucy returned to Celoron, rejoined her high school classmates and resumed such mundane pursuits as dating, cheerleading and the usual teenage jobs: soda jerking at the Walgreen's Drug Store in Jamestown and hawking hot dogs at the Celoron amusement park. She often put on some kind of performance for her customers, but management didn't appreciate her antics.

In the summer of 1927, while supervising a small target match during her brother Fred's birthday party, Grandpa Hunt allowed a girl who was inexperienced in the handling of firearms to fire a round that accidentally hit a neighborhood boy, who wound up paralyzed below the neck and died five years later. Even though the judge ruled it an accident, he ordered Grandpa to pay the medical bills and legal expenses. It was an experience from which he never quite recovered. In order to fulfill the ruling of the court, the family had to sell their house in September of 1928.

By the time this modeling photo was taken of a seventeen-year-old Lucy in 1928, she had begun her difficult apprenticeship years, trying to break into the New York show-business scene.

This devastating blow would have a telling effect on Lucy's life. From that day forward, she harbored a deep mistrust of the legal system, and was deathly afraid of guns. But this setback also gave her the incentive to try New York again. For the next six years, she would pay some heavy dues in learning her craft. New York was not a friendly city to Lucy in those days, so she commuted back to Jamestown between long intervals of unemployment. Acting seemed an impossible dream, so she tried a brief but equally disappointing effort to make a living as a Broadway showgirl. Soon, however, she found herself regularly employed as a model.

She learned to look and move with elegance and grace. She also gained firsthand experience in observing the celebrities and high-society women of the day. In between her changes of long, slinky evening gowns and suits, she was cramming a stockpile of information on dress, style, attitude

By 1931, Lucy had reached the pinnacle of the fashion modeling world for celebrated designer Hattie Carnegie.

After an illustrator submitted his 1931 illustration of Lucy to an advertising agency, she became a "Chesterfield Girl."

In 1933, at twenty-one, Lucy (far right) arrived in Los Angeles with a contingent of prospective "Goldwyn Girls."

and acting that would serve her well in the coming years.

A debilitating bout with rheumatoid arthritis kept her in bed for many months while she was a model for the prestigious Hattie Carnegie Salon. Her first modeling break came when she became one of the 1933 "Chesterfield Girls" who appeared on signs and billboards for that cigarette from coast to coast. This fame, along with a chance meeting with showgirl agent Sylvia Hahlo in front of the Palace Theater, set her on a course to Hollywood. Hahlo needed one more girl for a troupe she was sending to California to work for Sam Goldwyn. Lucy appeared in the 1933 Goldwyn movie *Roman Scandals* (with Eddie Cantor) and signed a contract with Columbia Pictures in 1934.

Though Columbia would later cancel the contract due to cutbacks, she slowly earned a positive reputation, and was soon able to send for her family, who moved out to California to stay. A small but memorable role in the Fred Astaire and Ginger Rogers film

*A*mong these aspiring starlets, *Lucy* was the one with her legs wrapped around the donkey in this publicity shot for *Roman Scandals*.

*L*ucy performed slapstick humor with the irrepressible Eddie Cantor in *Roman Scandals*. "To me it was an education—getting my foot in the door," she said.

Roberta led to a long contract with Radio-Keith-Orpheum or RKO, where she put in her days mostly as a contract player, first as an extra, then in a variety of small roles. The Ginger Rogers–Katharine Hepburn film, *Stage Door,* was her most important work, where she portrayed a wise-cracking Broadway hopeful. Though she had appeared in nearly forty films by the end of 1939, she never quite achieved top-line star status.

In December of that year, while Lucy was on an RKO promotional tour in New York for the film *Five Came Back,* one of the studio executives advised her to see the hit Lorenz Hart Broadway musical *Too Many Girls*, which RKO had just recently purchased for the screen. The studio brass hinted that she would be in it and was being groomed for "A" roles. Unfortunately, while performing a publicity skating stunt at Rockefeller Plaza, she slipped on the ice, and spent the next ten days in a hospital. She was still in bed when friends came into her room and raved about the young Cuban singer in *Too Many Girls* whose looks and talent were sending the ladies into a dither. His name was Desi Arnaz.

When Lucy was able to hobble around enough to get to the show, she couldn't take her eyes off Desi. Even many years later she could recall the mesmerizing effect he had on her. During the performance, whenever he would speak, she remembered breaking into her characteristic belly laugh, finding his onstage antics completely irresistible: "He was not only thrilling but funny. What a combination!" When the show was over, she couldn't wait to go to the La Conga nightclub where Desi was appearing nightly after the show. But he was off that night, and the meeting would have to wait seven months.

Desi arrived in Hollywood in June of 1940 to repeat his Broadway role in the movie ver-

Lucy's portrayal of a Parisian model in the 1935 picture Roberta led to an RKO contract.

Lucy's role in 1937's Stage Door was a breakthrough that allowed her to demonstrate her flair for comedy. Ginger Rogers (left) was a close personal friend.

sion of *Too Many Girls*. During a preproduction lunch at the RKO commissary, Desi was with director George Abbott, who had directed him on the stage and was set to direct the film as well. Lucy was on a break from *Dance, Girl, Dance*. She sauntered over to the duo, passed idle conversation with Abbott and walked on. She had just finished filming a catfight scene with costar Maureen O'Hara, and looked a mess.

"I was wearing a slinky gold lamé dress slit up to my thigh, and I also had a fake black eye," remembers Lucy. "Because of my

When Desi saw Lucy bedecked in this getup during the filming of Dance, Girl, Dance, their unbridled romance began. Said Desi at the time: "Wotta hunk o' woman!"

appearance, I'm sure he was not impressed. I was impressed with him, though, and I must admit that I fell in love with Desi—wham, bang—in about five minutes."

An hour or so later, it was Desi's turn to be impressed. He was rehearsing with Abbott at RKO's Lila Rogers Theater when Lucy came in after showering and changing her clothes. She looked so completely different that he didn't recognize her at first, and when he finished his number, he uttered his now classic line to the pianist, "Wotta hunk o' woman!"

They hit it off immediately, dueling verbally right from the start. Even with the friendly put-downs and the corny come-ons, the electricity had been turned on, and they knew this was the start of something special.

THE PRINCE OF SANTIAGO

Desi, the son of Desiderio Arnaz II, told Lucy that he had grown up in his native Cuba hearing tales about queens and kings of Spain who had bestowed land and wealth on his ancestors. Desi's great-great-grandfather Don Manuel Arnaz had settled in southern California more than a century before, and owned the land which is now part of Beverly Hills, the Wilshire district and much of the San Fernando Valley. The name Ventura—familiar throughout southern California—had come from Desi's great-great-grandmother.

Desi's father, he said, was elected mayor of Santiago, Cuba's original capital city, and at twenty-nine, he was by far the youngest politician on the whole island. Desi's mother, the attractive socialite Dolores de Acha, was also reared in an atmosphere of wealth and power. Her father, Alberto, had been one of the founding partners of the Bacardi Rum company.

Desi was born a year after his father's marriage, on March 2, 1917, in Santiago. With all the advantages that had come along with his birthright, it's no wonder that Desi would be somewhat spoiled as a youngster. He even admitted to Lucy that he was a "fathead." Though he performed various chores on one of his father's three farms, he lived in a world filled with toys, bicycles, horses, maids, speedboats, beach houses, summer skin-diving off private family island resorts and a wide range of other diversions that most Americans—much less Cubans—never experienced.

In 1923, the year his father was elected mayor of Santiago, Cuba, six-year-old Desi posed in his treasured sailor outfit.

But the winds of change would alter not only the history of Cuba but the fortunes of the Arnaz family as well. In the summer of 1934 Fulgencio Batista rallied the army against the corrupt Machado regime, and all of the officials associated with his power structure—including Desi's father—were rounded up and thrown into jail. Desi witnessed the heartbreaking destruction of his home when angry mobs descended on the Arnaz property, watching helplessly as the family pets and livestock were ruthlessly slaughtered. It was a chilling memory that would haunt him for the rest of his life. After Desi's father was released from prison, the family quickly booked passage for him to Miami, and Desi followed three months later.

This formal study of Desi Arnaz was taken at the time he formed his own band, which opened at the Waldorf-Astoria on December 30, 1937.

Playing forward on the St. Patrick's High School basketball team in Miami, Desi is the second from right, behind his best friend, Al Capone, Jr., an irony that would come full circle when Desilu produced The Untouchables twenty-three years later.

Though America was a refuge, life was a struggle. Desi's father managed to start a tiny import business that specialized in providing tiles for builders. Then, in 1936, an Arnaz family friend from Cuba introduced Desi to the owner of a small rhumba band at the Roney Plaza Hotel, which was considered the leading resort in Miami Beach. He was looking for a Cuban who could sing and play the guitar.

Desi's band days began: he joined the Siboney Septet at the Roney Plaza, and one evening not long afterward, Xavier Cugat, the world's leading Latin bandleader, happened to be sitting at a table watching the show. Cugat called Desi over after his set, auditioned him the next day, and offered him a job. Desi said yes, and after finishing high school, he joined Cugat's band. Within a year he

In his Broadway debut, Desi portrayed the Cuban football heartthrob Manolito in the 1939 Broadway Rogers and Hart musical, Too Many Girls.

Lucy and Desi share an intimate moment backstage at the Roxy Theater, November 30, 1940. They had been married that afternoon in Greenwich, Connecticut, and returned by police escort to a waiting audience of almost six thousand, who showered them with rice.

had gone about as far as he could with Cugat, and so he left to form his own band, which debuted on December 30, 1937, in Miami. It was a slow start, until, one night, he introduced the then-unknown conga line at Mother Kelley's in Miami. It became an overnight sensation, and conga fever swept America. By the time Desi and his band reached New York, the fever had spread with him, and soon Broadway was conga crazy. It was in the summer of 1939 that lyricist Lorenz Hart approached him to star as the Latin love interest in his new musical, *Too Many Girls*. His double duty as a Broadway performer in the early evening, capped by a late-night gig at New York's La Conga Club with his band, brought him overwhelming

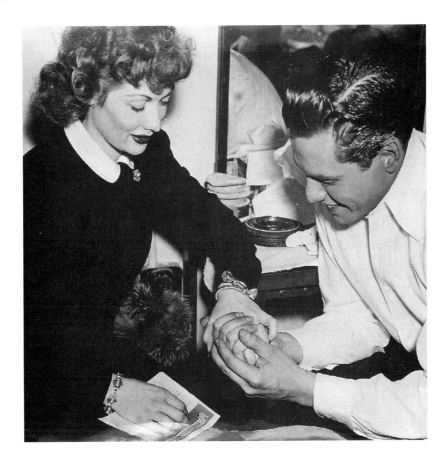

Shortly after their wedding, the newlyweds admire Lucy's wedding ring backstage at the Roxy, November 30, 1940. Lucy's right hand rests on their marriage certificate.

popularity—enough for Hollywood to take notice and invite him to reprise his role in the RKO movie.

The rest, as the saying goes, is show-business history. The day Desi met Lucille Ball in rehearsal for that film in 1940 was the beginning of a relationship that would forever change the face of entertainment. They spent the next several months pursuing each other between their various professional obligations, until they couldn't wait any longer, and made their relationship official, exchanging wedding vows in front of a justice of the peace at the Byram River Beagle Club in Greenwich, Connecticut, on November 30, 1940. One of the most famous couples of the twentieth century could now call themselves "husband and wife."

DESILU: A RANCH AND A MARRIAGE

It was soon afterward that they purchased a five-acre ranch in Chatsworth in the San Fernando Valley for about eighteen thousand dollars. A cozy, romantic place, it included a large ranch house, a swimming pool, a barnyard and stables. They named it "Desilu."

In spite of their passionate love for one another, there were deep differences between them. Lucille's rootless upbringing, coupled with her arduous road to Hollywood, which had taught her to be strong and self-reliant, clashed with Desi's privileged youth and smoother rise to celebrity. He was a romantic who lived for the moment, while Lucy was a levelheaded realist who never lived beyond her means. Desi was also the product of a predominantly male culture, in which a man's word was almost law and the woman's only role was wife, mother or mistress—not an independent-minded career woman. He understood this intellectually, but his early years in Cuba had colored both his perceptions and his male-female attitudes.

For now, however, the physical and emotional attraction between the couple dominated their relationship. And she admitted that she sensed a vulnerability in Desi that appealed to her.

The Arnazes discuss their future on the veranda of the Desilu ranch, their new home in Chatsworth, where they shared some of their happiest moments as a couple.

"Beneath that dazzling charm was a homeless boy who had no one to care for him, worry about him and love him. And I wanted him and only him as the father of my children."

Lucy and Desi began transforming their Desilu ranch into a real home. Desi knew how to cook, and he taught Lucy a number of his favorite Cuban dishes, many of them prepared with vegetables grown in their own garden. They raised chickens and received a pair of calves as a gift, but the livestock never wound up on the dinner table—they became pets, along with their five

This idyllic moment in a cornfield between the campesino and his Yankee bride would be the first of many at their San Fernando Valley ranch.

The "pardners" get ready for chores behind their corral on the Desilu spread in 1941.

dogs and ten cats. In short, life on the Desilu ranch was idyllic.

Lucy and Desi even worked together to help develop his film career in the hope that it would provide more time together. Favorable audience reaction to Desi in *Too Many Girls* had prompted RKO to place him under a three-picture contract, so he stopped touring with his band and concentrated on making movies. As time went on, though, he found that roles for thick-accented Latins were sparse, so he took elocution classes to diminish his accent, and Lucy took an active role in developing his acting skills. But a far more serious and complex problem was Desi's pride: he came to feel that he was being forced on the Hollywood community to humor his wife.

Their relationship was complicated further in 1941 when Lucy fell ill and discovered she was pregnant. The couple's joy turned to sorrow when she suffered a miscarriage. This was a different but more fundamental blow to Desi's masculinity. As the last male in

Lucy worried that the hard-edged character she played in 1942's The Big Street *was "too bitchy, too crude." But it turned out to be the finest dramatic role of her motion picture career.*

his family, he felt that the perpetuation of the Arnaz name rested on his shoulders, so this was a devastating ordeal. "I was sick with disappointment," he said years later, "but I felt that things would work out. As the months would turn into years, though, we were worried that there would be no next time."

One of the final setbacks came at a premiere one evening soon afterward. Desi had spent the entire afternoon washing and waxing his Buick convertible in order to make an impression at the star-studded event. Everything went well, until an attendant called for "Lucille Ball's car, please," within earshot of the couple. Barely containing his rage, he got into the car and as he drove off down Hollywood Boulevard, he blew his stack, vowing, "That's it! I'm leaving this goddamn town and getting a job!"

Desi reassembled the band and went back on the road. In that arena, he felt he was the master of his world. He didn't have to have his wife find work for him; it fed his thirsty Latin pride, and it completely satisfied his overwhelming need to perform. During the long separations while Desi was on the road in the forties, the couple communicated almost entirely by phone for months on end. Both suffered from bouts of jealousy: Desi's accusations about Lucy's relationships with her leading men were groundless, but her suspicions about Desi's fidelity were painfully well founded. Philandering was commonplace for virtually every touring band. Desi maintained that he truly loved her, but Lucy felt that he worked at their marriage only intermittently.

She did manage to join him on tour in New York while he was headlining in a musical revue, *Havana Holiday*. Lucy and Desi ran into a booking agent who suggested that they might pair up for an upcoming live appearance at Loew's State on Broadway. At first the

Though Lucy played opposite Red Skelton in Du Barry Was a Lady, these two great clowns hadn't yet developed much of a rapport, and they didn't "click" as a team.

In the mid-forties Lucille Ball was dubbed "Technicolor Tessie" because her coloring was the most difficult to photograph and light.

As the member of a doomed patrol in World War II, Desi's improvised death scene in <u>Bataan</u> won him an acting award.

idea stunned them, but it soon began to make sense. Though she had no intention of giving up her film career, the idea of working in front of an audience with her husband appealed to her, so they accepted the challenge and began working up an act during a stay in Palm Beach. It was while they were there that Pearl Harbor was attacked by the Japanese, and while they intended to go on with the date, they knew that the war would have an impact on their lives.

They opened on January 1, 1942, one of four acts sandwiched between screenings of the Jeanette MacDonald film, *Smilin' Through*. Desi did several of his popular songs, and after Lucy joined him for some soft-shoe duets, they finished with Lucille mimicking his oversexed style. As much as they enjoyed this outing—despite her bouts with stage fright—it was short-lived because of Lucy's motion picture commitments and the uncertainty brought about by World War II. But it gave them enough confidence to feel that, given the right circumstances, they might be able to combine their careers in some way.

After his third film for RKO was released—the flag-waving *The Navy Comes Through*—Desi's contract wasn't renewed. But he knew he'd soon be playing the same role in real life. He still wasn't a U.S. citizen, but as a resident, Desi was eligible for the draft. In the meantime, he joined the Hollywood Victory Committee and traveled around the country entertaining the men in uniform.

Most of the films Lucy was making during this period were routine programmers, with the exception of *The Big Street* with Henry Fonda, which was considered probably her finest dramatic role as a crippled showgirl. She went on to land a prestigious MGM contract, but she was trapped in Hollywood and couldn't join her husband on the road. So she prevailed upon Louis B. Mayer to offer Desi a contract in order to help keep him closer to home. Mayer agreed, but no roles surfaced, so Desi took off on short-hop USO tours. Lucy had to resign herself to the situation,

Lucy plunged into the war effort in a 1944 San Francisco War Bond parade with (left to right): Dorothy Merritt, Betty Hutton, Greer Garson, Mickey Rooney and Judy Garland.

Celebrating her thirty-fifth birthday with director Eddie Sedgwick and Buster Keaton, Lucy said, "They were the first to really sit me down and teach me about slapstick comedy."

and threw herself into her work. Though her singing was dubbed in *Du Barry Was a Lady* (with Gene Kelly and Red Skelton), she proved she could handle musical comedy and was subsequently cast in *Best Foot Forward*. While she was teamed with Ann Sothern in *In Thousands Cheer*, Mayer finally cast Desi in a dramatic role. His deathbed scene in *Bataan* raised a few eyebrows and made Hollywood take notice. It might have been a breakthrough motion picture for him, but Uncle Sam finally intervened, and in May 1943 Desi was drafted into the army.

Lucy starred with George Sanders and Sir Cedric Hardwicke in a 1947 film noir thriller, Lured, her last free-lance assignment before signing a contract with Columbia Pictures.

Between films Lucy began to carve out a second career for herself by performing on the radio, starring on *Philip Morris Playhouse*, *Burns and Allen* and *Kraft Music Hall* with Bing Crosby. She also did her part in a variety of war-drive-related activities. Desi, meanwhile, was organizing entertainment shows for the army, using his and Lucy's influence to snag stars for guest appearances. Word began to get around about his abilities as a producer, and he was put in charge of staging events for the army's Birmingham Hospital in the San Fernando Valley. Lucy, of course, was thrilled to have him stationed right between the studio and the Desilu ranch. Though she was under a $2,500-a-week contract, Mayer wasn't using Lucy at the time, so she threw herself into fund raising activities for Desi's hospital.

It seemed like an unbelievable stroke of luck for the two of them to be living so close together. Unfortunately, Desi proceeded to make personal use of the starlets Lucy was providing for the various shows and functions he was producing. When word got back to her, she tried to reciprocate by dating other men—like MGM contract players Peter Lawford, Scott McKay and Robert Mitchum—but her efforts to make Desi jealous were unsuccessful, so she filed for divorce in September 1944. When she moved out of the Desilu ranch and retained a lawyer it finally got his attention. A devout Roman Catholic, Desi was genuinely distraught and, in an effort to reconcile their differences, he invited her out to dinner the day before she was scheduled to appear in court.

They went out to the ultra-trendy Mocambo that evening, to the shock of many who saw them acting like newlyweds on the dance floor. It was an evening that ended in a truly memorable night of passion. Much to Desi's amazement, Lucy got dressed the next morning and proceeded with her court appearance—then went straight back to him at her apartment, thereby nullifying her divorce. She had made her point.

By the time the war was over, Lucy, at the age of thirty-four, was beginning to lose roles to up-and-coming actresses. MGM had used her for a total of eleven weeks from 1944 to 1945, and finally dropped her option. In the remaining years of her MGM contract, she spent countless hours talking shop with director Eddie Sedgwick and Buster Keaton, from whom she learned both the art and the craft of classic comedy, which she would put to use later in her career. For the next couple of years, she freelanced until she landed a contract with Columbia Pictures.

In 1948, Desi was performing with his band at Hollywood's trendy Ciro's—part of his ongoing effort to get bookings in L.A. and remain close to Lucy.

Out of the army by now, Desi had hit the road again with his band, but these out-of-town engagements were still contributing to further marital disharmony. He tried to book as many gigs as possible on the West Coast, but his nonexistent film career was no match for his $12,000-a-week road work.

This situation would have continued indefinitely if it hadn't been for a fateful bus accident with Desi's band. While Lucy was appearing in Detroit in *Dream Girl*, Desi left his band in Madison, Wisconsin, and flew for a surprise one-night romantic rendezvous with her. The next day he planned to take a plane to Akron, Ohio, where a chartered bus would have driven his band the night before. A phone call in the middle of the night jarred them out of their sleep, informing them that the bus had crashed. Although several members of the band sustained critical injuries, no one was killed. But the part of the bus that sustained the most damage was where Desi would have been sitting. The couple took this as a serious omen—it brought them closer together at a time when they needed it. Their professional and personal lives were now fated to unite.

"MY FAVORITE HUSBAND"

Lucy was willing to try anything that would stabilize not only her profession but her marriage. It was then that the CBS West Coast director of network programming, Harry S. Ackerman, offered her a new radio program, *My Favorite Husband*. Radio was in decline, and the networks looked to television as the future of their business. As Ackerman told Lucy, "If a show is successful on the radio, we can transfer it to television."

My Favorite Husband, based on characters in the book *Mr. and Mrs. Cugat*, by Isabelle Scott Rorick, revolved around the travails of Liz and George Cugat, a very normal, middle-class couple from Minneapolis. Liz was a dizzy, scheming wife who gets into relatively minor but vexing scrapes that make life challenging for her long-suffering husband, a banker played by Richard Denning. The social milieu was genteel, and her schemes—albeit eccentric—were not so outrageous that they defied logic or credibility.

Bob Carroll, Jr., and Madelyn Pugh (now Pugh-Davis), a young CBS writing team, had submitted a spec script for *My Favorite Husband* to Ackerman. He liked it and bought it, and when the show's original writers returned to their chores on *The Adventures of Ozzie and Harriet*, Ackerman replaced them with Carroll

The success of radio's My Favorite Husband, with co-star Richard Denning, paved the way for I Love Lucy. Lucy played a scatterbrained housewife much like Lucy Ricardo.

Remarried on June 17, 1949, after almost nine years of matrimony, the couple pose for a portrait in front of Our Lady of the Valley Church in Chatsworth, flanked by Best Man Ken Morgan (left) and director Eddie Sedgwick.

and Pugh. Self-admitted greenhorns when it came to writing for a major star like Lucille Ball, both Madelyn and Bob were thrilled at this opportunity, but they would have to quit their staff jobs to do it, and if the show flopped, they would be out of work.

"We didn't have any experience in running a show, and we were terrified," Madelyn recalls. A firm hand was needed to make the whole thing work, and the show seemed to be headed for trouble until Ackerman hired radio writer-producer Jess Oppenheimer to produce, direct and function as head writer on the show, in October 1948. Oppenheimer had a long history of guiding creative teams and handling big-star egos such as Fanny Brice on *Baby Snooks*, Fred Astaire on *The Packard Hour*, Eddie Cantor on *The Chase and Sanborn Hour*, and *The Jack Benny Program*.

"Jess directed, produced, pulled the whole thing together, and put everyone on a schedule," says Madelyn. "He got us to work a week ahead, and really got the whole cast and crew settled down. He was a godsend." In addition to taking charge, Oppenheimer gradually began to revamp the program. He also reworked Lucy's role into a daffier, broader character—much closer to the Lucy Ricardo who would soon appear on television.

With Jess at the helm, the show settled into a routine, picked up General Foods as a sponsor, and thus began one of television's most important writing collaborations. It was a good time to hone their craft in the relative ease of the somewhat "rural" environment of radio.

The show was performed in front of a live studio audience. "This wasn't just actors in front of microphones reading their lines," recalls Bob. "Performers were in costume, and it was very much like theater." It also provided Lucy with her first regular gig that involved feedback from a live audience, and she found the experience exhilarating. So did the audience. Something magic and electric happened when Lucille began to work in front of them, and she began hitting performance levels that were missing from any of her previous film work. "She absolutely bloomed in front of an audience," said Ackerman.

TELEVISION LOOMS

With the show's continued success from 1948 to 1950, talk about translating *Husband* to television had begun brewing, and it was Harry Ackerman who spearheaded the move. Lucy saw the possibility of a television series as an opportunity to not only take her radio success to another level, but as an ideal way to mesh career and marriage into one convenient package: by working with Desi on the same show.

It was during this period that he asked her to renew their marriage vows, this time in a Catholic church ceremony. After eight stormy years of marriage, this was a way to validate his intention to patch up their long-standing differences. Desi also vowed to inaugurate a stay-at-home policy, to give up his cross-country tours with the band and try to concentrate on bookings closer to Los Angeles.

Lucy immediately began campaigning to include Desi in the television package of *My Favorite Husband*. Of course, the show's principal character relationship, as written, wouldn't lend itself to Desi's conspicuous Latin dialect and tempera-

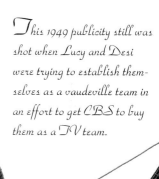

This 1949 publicity still was shot when Lucy and Desi were trying to establish themselves as a vaudeville team in an effort to get CBS to buy them as a TV team.

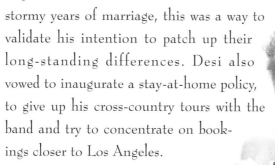

ment. That would remain the principal stumbling block for the network brass, and the Arnaz's tenacious agent, Don Sharpe, met with much resistance. "Some of the New York executives thought Lucy had lost her marbles," Jess Oppenheimer remembered. "One of them said, 'Who would believe her married to a wop?'" One of Lucy's most oft-quoted comments came in answer to that reaction: "What do you do mean, nobody'll believe it? We *are* married!"

THE VAUDEVILLE GAMBIT

In order to get CBS to agree, Lucy and Desi officially formed Desilu Productions in the spring of 1950. Next, they dusted off their old, early-forties vaudeville routine, in which Desi played straight man to Lucy's burlesque comic clown. By 1950, vaudeville was a shadow of what it once was. But Lucy and Desi saw the fading medium as a way to demonstrate their viability as a performing team.

This time they prevailed on Bob Carroll and Madelyn Pugh-Davis to give more structure to their act, and to provide fresh dialogue. Lucy also tapped the talents of her old MGM friends, Buster Keaton and director Eddie Sedgwick, to help them hone their slapstick skills, while the internationally renowned Pepito, "The Spanish Clown," supplied them with a special xylophone and a Rube Goldberg type of cello. They broke in the act with Desi's band in San Diego, San Francisco and an assortment of army camps. Word spread through the circuit, and six months of engagements materialized. The tour was cut short, however, when Lucy discovered she was pregnant and flew back to the ranch in Chatsworth. Due to her previous miscarriage, they didn't want to risk any complications, but she suffered another one on July 27.

Lucy and Desi's 1950 vaudeville skit—with the cello and the "saxo-vibro-trumpa-phonavich"—was eventually adapted into a memorable episode of I Love Lucy: "The Audition."

TEST PATTERN: THE PILOT DEAL

When Ackerman was promoted from chief executive of West Coast programming to executive in charge of production for CBS radio and television, Lucy found in him a powerful executive to champion her cause. Knowing her need to stabilize their marriage with projects that kept them in close proximity, Ackerman offered Desi his own radio program, *Your Tropical Trip*. "CBS didn't want to lose her," Ackerman remembers. "And they realized that Lucy had something special going with audiences." Even though it wasn't certain that she and Desi would be right together, the network wanted to make it clear that it respected Desi, too. The show went on as planned in January 1951 and Desi continued hosting it for most of that year.

After Lucy had recuperated from the miscarriage, the couple revived their vaudeville act and, after a disappointing stand at San Francisco's Paramount Theater, returned home. She was then offered a major role in Cecil B. DeMille's *The Greatest Show on Earth*. At any other time, this would have been a career-changing opportunity, and her most important motion picture part in years. But she was still under her Columbia Pictures contract and had to get Harry Cohn's permission to do the picture. She pleaded with the acerbic mogul but—in typically malicious Cohn fashion—he sent her a script for a turban-and-scimitar potboiler, *The Magic Carpet*. He was sure she would turn down this role for the opportunity with DeMille, thus breaking her contract and saving Columbia the $80,000 she would have to have been paid for the role.

In the midst of all this turmoil, Lucy and Desi discovered that she was again pregnant. This was the last development they expected, and they brainstormed over their options. *The Magic Carpet* was scheduled to go before the cameras almost immediately, while with the extended production of *The Greatest Show on Earth*, her pregnancy would make it impossible for her to take the part. Her part

Harry Ackerman, CBS director of West Coast programming, was the prime mover in getting I Love Lucy on the air.

in *Carpet*, however, would take little more than a week or two to film, and Cohn would have to pay her the $80,000. Without mentioning her pregnancy to anyone, they finally decided to turn down the DeMille offer, take *The Magic Carpet*, and fulfill her contract with Cohn. After she had completed his film and fulfilled her contract, he was furious when he found out about her pregnancy. "Why, you bitch," he hissed at her. "You screwed me, didn't you?" DeMille was more philosophical, and told Desi later, "Congratulations, Mr. Arnaz. You are the only man who has ever screwed his wife, Cecil B. DeMille, Paramount Pictures and Harry Cohn at the same time."

During this fall of 1950, agent Don Sharpe managed to stir up interest in a series for both of them at the rival network, NBC, which still held long-term grudges about CBS president William Paley's penchant for stealing talent such as Jack Benny and Edgar Bergen and shows such as *Amos 'n' Andy* from NBC. NBC's reasoning was that Lucille Ball had certainly proved herself successful in the sitcom format with *Husband* and with her film-career name recognition and her husband's marquee value as a nightclub performer, plus his recording contract with RCA, they made an attractive package. This interest from NBC made Paley finally realize that there was nothing CBS could do that would rival the bonds of love between them.

Three months into her pregnancy, during the holiday season between Christmas and New Year of 1950, CBS abruptly okayed the television sitcom that Lucy, Desi, Don Sharpe and Harry Ackerman had been lobbying for: with Desi portraying her husband. The name for the show hadn't even been selected, but it now seemed at last that their dreams would soon be realized.

Replacing an up-and-coming comedian named Johnny Carson to placate Lucy, CBS president William Paley signed Desi to host a 1950 musical TV quiz show, Your Tropical Trip.

THE "I LOVE LUCY" PILOT

After Lucy's successful *My Favorite Husband* radio outing, she insisted that Jess Oppenheimer take on the same role as producer and head writer of the pilot, as well as any subsequent series, with Bob Carroll and Madelyn Pugh-Davis as writers. Though Oppenheimer was two years into his five-year CBS contract, he negotiated an ownership deal in the show for his services. That percentage would cause some problems in the future, but with the potential of television still unknown, it would prove to be a very lucrative deal over the ensuing years. Ackerman agreed.

Fortunately, the creative interplay had long since been firmly established between the three writers, and that helped the team formulate the script without the usual get-acquainted period. Using the foundation of a pragmatic husband pitted against a scatter-brained wife, they developed the premise of a working husband who loved his wife in spite of her outrageous antics. Ackerman recalled the obstacles vividly: "We had been asking ourselves what to do with

The pilot for I Love Lucy—originally entitled The Lucille Ball-Desi Arnaz TV Show—would follow the basic Lucy theme: while Ricky's trying to get ready for a performance, Lucy needles her husband to include her in the act. The pilot was broadcast on March 2, 1951.

In the pilot, Desi portrays Ricky Ricardo's immediate precursor, bandleader "Larry Lopez."

As Lucy prepares to audition, bandleader Lopez asks: "Are you going to play that thin'?" "What thin?" she retorts.

Lucy gets set to play a Rube Goldberg cello in the comic finale of the I Love Lucy pilot. This plotline would be recycled as episode number 6, "The Audition," where Lucy substitutes her act for a sidelined burlesque clown.

a comedian and a Cuban orchestra leader. Finally, after much discussion, Jess said he thought he had the answer: 'I think we should deal with a lady who is always trying to get into the act.'"

In contrast to the previous concept of a highly successful bandleader, Desi's role was rewritten to be a marginally successful Cuban bandleader whose job situation was not unlike most working Americans—with a boss (owner of the Tropicana), who needed to be managed and cajoled for pay raises, and a wife. Lucy was written as an average housewife, but one who fancies herself a talented performer.

Much of their vaudeville routine was reconstructed around a pilot premise that had Lucy horning in on her husband's nightclub act. It was a thin plot, but it was well designed to showcase her brilliant comedic skills and the obvious chemistry between her and Desi.

The kinescoping of the pilot took place at Studio A at Columbia Square, the network's West Coast radio and television division headquarters on March 2, 1951—Desi's thirty-fourth birthday. Lucille was four months pregnant at the time, and spent

most of the performance in a bathrobe and pajamas to conceal her condition. But the show was performed with no serious complications, and followed precisely the plotline that Oppenheimer had sketched.

Selling the Pilot

It was sometime during this period that the title was finally locked in. No one lays claim to the idea of titling *I Love Lucy*, but it was a brilliant and diplomatic way to give Desi top billing. "People would know that the 'I' was Desi," Lucy later reflected. "And then, how could you go wrong with 'love' in the title?"

Jess Oppenheimer's son, Gregg, illuminates the subject further: "The title *I Love Lucy* appeared on the pilot program, which opened with three hand-held title cards which read 'Lucille Ball and Desi Arnaz...IN A NEW COMEDY SERIES... *I Love Lucy*.' The title was selected by my father from many suggestions a few days before the pilot was kinescoped, just in time for an artist to paint it on the title cards. No one has ever stepped forward to claim credit for the title, *I Love Lucy*, but, according to Lucy, it may have been my father's idea. When he passed away in 1988, Lucy observed, 'He put the word "love" in our title, and for that I will be forever grateful.' Of course, she may just have been referring to the fact that he was the one who *selected* the title *I Love Lucy*. So it is still a mystery."

Everyone who saw the kinescope recognized the potential of the show, but Madison Avenue was not overwhelmed. After six intensive weeks, Don Sharpe had nearly worn out his shoes shopping it to the agencies. The president of the Biow Agency, Milton H. Biow, finally took a liking to it and one of his clients—the tobacco giant Philip Morris—agreed to commit the nearly one million dollars required to sponsor the program for a season.

Just then a crisis erupted: no one had mentioned to Milton Biow that Lucy and Desi planned to do the show from Los

Angeles, not New York. When Jess Oppenheimer casually mentioned that fact to him in a phone conversation, Biow blew his top, voicing strong opposition to any West Coast production. He feared that if the show was kinescoped on the West Coast and rebroadcast via that inferior recording process, it would be unacceptable for East Coast viewers.

A tempest brewed that was picked up by the trade press and threatened to shake the whole deal apart. Then, during a series of mid-May meetings in Hollywood, Sharpe and Ackerman came up with the solution: "If you don't like kinescope, how about film?" said Sharpe. Added Ackerman: "We can give you a live look to it—but on film." So the next logical step was to produce live studio audience reaction on film.

Lucy breaks from rehearsal to talk with Karl Freund, the Academy Award-winning cinematographer she prevailed upon to light the show.

Ackerman called Martin Leeds—who at that time was a CBS West Coast programming executive—and asked if he had seen the "locked camera" system developed by production pioneer Jerry Fairbanks. Soon, through a CBS association, independent production manager Al Simon was contacted. He told Leeds that cameras could be put on dollies for their proposed show. "Hire Simon!" Leeds told Desi. Of course, the technique was adopted, refined and became the cornerstone of the entire sitcom industry. It hasn't changed to this day.

Desi told CBS that he could put together a unit that would produce a live show and put it on film. CBS's reaction was "We can't do that. The unions won't let us." Desi said: "I *can* do that," and he proceeded to take on the responsibility of producing his *own* show for broadcast on CBS. Thus did the Desilu dynasty begin.

The decision to film the show solved one problem, but created a new one. What remained was the question of money. The original deal called for each episode to be budgeted at $20,000 to $25,000. With the use of film, it was feared that costs could go way over budget, and they did go up. While both sides of the corporate fence were willing to contribute enough to collectively approach the figure, there remained a $5,000 difference that neither was willing to put up.

The solution came when Don Sharpe suggested Lucy and Desi each take a $1,000-a-week salary cut for the first year—but they added one important proviso: CBS would have to give them a hundred-percent ownership of the show. The network agreed, in order to get the project started—and Desi gained a priceless asset he would use in a few years to become a very wealthy man. And it was the consummation of this deal that created the television syndication marketplace that would survive to this day. Don Sharpe—one of the most forgotten people who was instrumental in getting the show on the air—proved an invaluable source in finding solutions to monumental problems.

Desi was beginning to exercise his business acumen, and it would come to full flower over the next several years. "All he had ever managed was a sixteen-piece Latin band, and now he had to rent and equip a studio and assemble the team to produce thirty-nine weekly shows," said Lucy.

With the expanded responsibility of producing its own show, the Desilu team was about to develop into a total production unit, requiring full staffing and a raft of other below-the-line costs. Months of preparation lay ahead, and during that summer of 1951, the pieces would eventually fall into place.

CHAPTER TWO

THE FIRST SEASON

1951 to 1952

I LOVE LUCY: OPENING SHOT

"We were an eager and innocent crew," recalled Oppenheimer, "embarking on a trip in a medium of which we knew nothing. We all knew that Lucille Ball's glowing talent was the one irreplaceable ingredient which served as a base for the show. The rest must be credited to a group, not an individual. Every decision was made by consensus, after many hours huddled in consultation with everyone concerned. We were a happy group, with everyone's opinion respected, and we had no inkling of the high-flying success that lay ahead."

There are fallacies that have persisted over the decades with respect to the production of *I Love Lucy*. One is that it was the first network sit-com shot on film. It wasn't. *Amos 'n' Andy* holds that distinction, though it wasn't filmed in front of a live studio audience. And the much-touted "three-camera technique" used on *Lucy* was actually introduced on NBC's 1947 to 1948 series *Public Prosecutor*, produced in NBC's New York film department.

With a multiple-camera technique refined by production manager Al Simon, the next stumbling block was to light *I Love Lucy* so that every show would have a consistent quality never before attempted for television. When film was chosen as the medium of delivery, Lucy insisted on contacting Karl Freund, one of the best-known and most respected cinematographers in Hollywood. When the con-

The Ricardos bridged the gap between entertainment glitz and American family life in the fifties.

Lucy and Ricky's show business lives allowed I Love Lucy to explore outlandish, exaggerated stoylines without losing believability.

Lucy Ricardo's face resembled a clown's, which brought a universality and a timelessness to the role.

cept of the show was explained to him, he didn't believe it could be done—filmed in front of a live studio audience and like a stage play. But the challenge intrigued him, and he devised a system of lighting that would keep the illumination evenly balanced over the entire set. There were no individual light changes other than those accomplished by general dimming. Lights were suspended from a maze of catwalks which kept the power cables off the floor, allowing cameras virtually total freedom of movement without a break in action.

Marc Daniels, one of the few directors who had been exposed to three-camera work in live television, was fresh from New York, with a background in live theater. He had come out to the West Coast about six months before *I Love Lucy* was to go before the cameras. Called to meet Desi, Oppenheimer and Harry Ackerman to discuss the possibility of his directing *I Love Lucy*, he was hired on the spot.

CREATING LUCY AND RICKY RICARDO

The world of Lucy and Ricky was a masterstroke of conception. It effectively and believably bridged the gap between the glitter of show business and the real world of 1950s American family life. The Ricardos represented identifiable social stereotypes, and the close proximity of the entertainment world to their lives provided a premise that allowed excursions into outrageous theatrical situations that were grounded in reality.

They displayed distinctly different mannerisms and physical characteristics, yet performed as perfect partners and foils for each other's intrigues. They even looked like their personalities. Lucy and Desi were an incongruous combination of Yankee gumption and Latin bravura. Lucy Ricardo had every bit the clown face: red hair piled on her head like a circus wig, big blue eyes and fair skin with lipstick drawn like a clown's mouth, all giving her the look of a female jester. And Ricky, with his pompadoured, jet-black hair and his expressive eyes set in a suavely handsome face, was reminiscent of an amalgam of several characters from the

Lucy Ricardo is a portrait of the American mid-century housewife—a woman with no power or validation for aspirations beyond the kitchen.

Ricky Ricardo came from a long line of theatrical characters rooted in the commedia dell'arte Italian theater— with Latin overtones.

commedia dell'arte tradition of Italian theater.

Lucy's character was a product of the times, much like the real Lucy, but she did exhibit a streak of independence that baffled the Latin *machismo* of both Desi and of Ricky, the character he played. Yet there was a vulnerable quality in both Ricardos that couldn't be dismissed. In spite of the shenanigans and the marital chicanery that permeated their relationship, there was never any act or verbal dueling that suggested a lack of respect or smacked of meanness.

In *Honey, I'm Home,* a book analyzing the American sitcom, author Gerard Jones sums up Lucy Ricardo this way: "She is the self-embodiment of female energy with no valid outlet. She is the mid-century American woman with no job, no power, no reinforcement for her aspirations. She is a comic demon called forth from the boredom and frustration of an entire generation of housewives. She is what happens when a woman is allowed to go to college, tantalized with career possibilities, asked to give all to war-work, and then told to retreat to the kitchen."

Jess Oppenheimer: "Lucy is a stagestruck schemer with an overactive imagination who finds herself in embarrassing situations."

Jess Oppenheimer describes the Lucy character as "impulsive and scatter-brained and a stage-struck schemer with an overactive imagination, who often jumps to the wrong conclusions and as a result finds herself in embarrassing situations. To Lucy, life is a series of contests between her and her husband, and she is determined to win."

There was an intensity in the dynamics of their relationship that had never before been explored in any domestic situation com-

"Lucy Ricardo's existence," said producer Jess Oppenheimer, "is a series of contests between her and her husband, and she is determined to win."

Whatever prank Lucy perpetrated on Ricky, he still loved her.

edy, including radio. Ricky was not the typical bland, self-assured husband, but a combustible combination of cockiness and stubborn authority mixed with a fiery Latin temperament tinged with vanity—and a hilarious accent. But whatever capers Lucy Ricardo perpetrated on her husband, he still loved her. He realized she was eccentric, but their love for one another was never in question.

LUCY'S CHARACTER TRAITS

Many of the great comics of our time have a set of standard shticks and gimmicks that help identify and thereby ingratiate themselves to the viewing public. Lucy exhibited several memorable character traits:

THE CRY: When all else fails, Lucy, like the great film comedian Stan Laurel, fell back on a monumental cry. Laurel's cry sounded more like a squeaky wheel, while Lucy's took on the audible characteristics of an approaching ambulance that never quite recedes as it passes by. After roughly three to five repetitions, sometimes she would follow it with a blubbering whimper—and finally one last pitiful plea for understanding.

THE SPIDER VOICE: Originated during *My Favorite Husband* commercials, when Lucille portrayed Little Miss Muffett in response to an imaginary spider terrorizing her during a pitch for Jell-O gelatin. In *I Love Lucy*, it's the high-pitched, guttural sound Lucy makes when she reacts to being caught in an embarrassing moment. Madelyn Pugh-Davis remembers: "We used to call it her spider voice. In the script we'd say she 'does the spider,' and it was this Yeeeeoooouuugh sound."

THE LANGUAGE-MANGLING COMEBACK: Whenever others became exasperated with Ricky Ricardo and he mangled his English, they would throw back at him his tendency to mangle the English tongue by repeating his mistake—especially Lucy. This became one of the most popular running gags in the series. Generally, the Lucy Ricardo character monopolized this gag, but occasionally others would

Lucy Ricardo's cry was her most prevalent characteristic and—like a siren—couldn't be ignored.

use it or at least react humorously to Ricky's language problem.

THE DRATS: A two-fisted arm drop. When something would go wrong, she would hold both her arms in front of her in a linebacker's defensive position and then drop both forearms sharply, with clenched fists. "We called that the 'Drats,'" says Madelyn.

OPEN MOUTH: This classic silent comedian/vaudeville "take" was used primarily when Lucy couldn't believe what was happening before her eyes.

THE DODGE DANCE: Whenever she was trying to avoid a threatening advance from another person, Lucy would put her arms out to the side as if for balance and proceed to launch into a dodging foot shuffle, her upper body, head and neck moving as one stiff unit as she bounces around like a moving target.

Lucy often used an "open-mouthed" silent-film reaction to display disbelief at an absurd situation.

The so-called "spider voice" originated during My Favorite Husband. This high-pitched guttural "Yeeeeooooouuugh" sound originated when Lucy reacted to the approach of an imaginary spider during a commercial as Little Miss Muffett.

Years later, Lucy would say this about her character: "She's an exaggeration of thousands of housewives. She has always done things I feel other ladies would like to do with their husbands, their children and their bosses. She goes the limit, but is always believable. She's bigger than life, but just enough to make all her wild schemes seem perfectly understandable. While I was making pictures, I always had the feeling that I was waiting for something. I never found a place of my own and I never became truly confident until—in the Lucy character—I began creating something that was really mine. The potential was there. Lucy Ricardo released it."

RICKY'S CHARACTER TRAITS

Ricky Ricardo had his own unique set of character traits:

ENGLISH LANGUAGE MANGLING: Ricky, like Desi in reality, could never completely master the complexities of the English tongue, and the creators of the show had a field day with this—to great comic effect. His pronunciations such as "dunt" (don't), "'splain" (explain) and dozens of other words in his vocabulary, all came naturally to Desi, but he had no problem making fun of his own dialect, even in real life. Many times during the initial reading or during a rehearsal when Desi would read a line that wouldn't come out right, he'd make a joke about his *español*, everybody would laugh on the set, and they'd leave the mispronunciation in.

STRING OF LATIN EPITHETS: This running gag was by no means new when it was incorporated into the Ricky Ricardo character. Hollywood had used it dozens of times for fiery

Desi Arnaz's ability to make his eyes seemingly pop out of his head is one of the most anticipated and best-loved comic traits in the Ricky Ricardo character.

Whenever Ricky became frustrated beyond words—usually by his Yankee wife—he regressed into his native tongue: "Mira-que-cosa-tiene-la-mujer-esta..."

Jess Oppenheimer created Ethel to provide Lucy with a girlfriend she could talk to, confide in, and scheme with, and to help move the plot along.

Latins, and Desi himself fell into the habit from time to time. The Spanish language in rapid fire conveys anger and frustration like no other, so careful attention was paid to make this Ricky trait work as humor, but not at the expense of denigrating Ricky's heritage. He also had to learn how to exhibit anger without carrying it over to meanness. Said Desi: "It was the most difficult problem I faced while playing Ricky. It helped to overemphasize the Latin use of hands and arms when I was excited. Most of all the rat-tat-tat-tat parade of Spanish words helped me tread that thin line between funny-mad and mad-mad. Years later kids come up to me and say 'Hey, Ricky, say *"Mira que tiene…"* how do you say it?' '*Mira-que-cosa-tiene-la-mujer-esta.*'"

BUGGED OUT EYES: No one in television had a way of making his eyes seemingly pop out of his head more effectively than Desi Arnaz. Only Jackie Gleason was on a par. A bit right out of the silent screen and burlesque, it simply worked, and nothing Desi ever did in reaction to Lucy's onscreen antics ever made as apt a statement on her outrageous escapades than this character trait. It was broad, but it never rang a false note.

CREATING THE MERTZES

Like Lucy and Desi, Vivian Vance and William Frawley provided perfect foils for each other. The idea of an older couple as a contrast to the Ricardos grew out of a plot development on *My Favorite Husband*. Jess Oppenheimer was the first to suggest the idea of an older couple, but the characters wouldn't even be close in temperament or economic status to the affluent Atterburys from *Husband*.

Fred and Ethel Mertz were less affluent than the <u>My Favorite Husband</u> *characters upon which they were based. They proved to be perfect foils for the Ricardos.*

As Oppenheimer saw it, "Lucy needed a girlfriend, someone to talk to, confide in and scheme with. A person who could help move the plot along. The same went for Ricky, who needed someone to connive with and to advise him in the battle between the sexes. So we decided to reverse roles for television, with the Ricardos to have a few more pennies than the neighbors, but not a lot more. We were very careful to make the couples different in some ways, yet very alike in others." As it turns out, the casting played a bigger role than any writer's conception in how the characters were drawn.

CASTING WILLIAM FRAWLEY

William Frawley captured the role of Fred Mertz as a result of a phone call he made to Lucy in the summer of 1951. The veteran character actor hadn't worked much in recent years and decided to take matters in his own hands. Both Desi and Jess agreed with Lucy to cast Frawley, but they received a very negative reaction when CBS and Philip Morris heard about their decision. The two companies were concerned about Frawley's alleged drinking problem. The more negative they got, however, the more determined Desi was to take a chance with him. Jess agreed, and with the back-

Fred Mertz gave Ricky an important link with a cohort in the battle between the sexes—which drove many of the I Love Lucy plots.

ing of Lucy—and a contract giving him complete creative control over the series—they forced CBS to accept Frawley. Before playing his hand, though, Desi had a real heart-to-heart discussion with Frawley, who admitted he liked to hoist a few, but assured him that he would never miss a call. He kept that promise during the entire run of the series, although his irascibility surfaced quite frequently.

Before Frawley tackled television, he had spent most of his life in front of an audience. After performing in a vaudeville song-and-dance act with his wife Louise, they divorced in 1927, and he spent the next several years playing a variety of musical comedy roles in such musicals as *Bye Bye Bonnie*, *She's My Baby* and *Here's Howe!* Then Paramount Pictures signed him to a long-term contract after he was spotted in the original 1933 Broadway production of the Ben Hecht–Charles MacArthur comedy, *Twentieth Century*. By the time he asked for the role of Fred Mertz, he had appeared in 103 movies, among them *Roxie Hart*, *Going My Way*, *Lady on a Train*, *Miracle on 34th Street*, *The Babe Ruth Story* and *The Lemon Drop Kid*.

He played the role of Fred Mertz with the same professionalism he had brought to all his other work, but though he needed the job, he did no more than was expected of him. He kept to himself, and didn't make a secret of the fact that his dialogue was all he cared about. When he got his script each week, he would tear out and keep the pages in which he appeared, and say, "I don't give a shit about the rest of that stuff!" More than once he was quoted as saying, "I'm just going to take the money and run." Frawley worked basically to support his all-consuming extracurricular activity: baseball. Though he never missed an episode, the "baseball" clause in his contract caused some major scheduling problems over the course of the show. If the New York Yankees went into the World Series, he was to be given time away

Frawley worked to support his passion for sports. Contractually he was allowed to leave whenever the Yankees were in the World Series. He owned racehorses, was a stockholder in the Pacific Coast League's Hollywood Stars and on the board of advisors for the Angels.

to attend the fall classic. Seven out of nine seasons while he played Fred, Frawley took off in October to attend the World Series. He was not only an avid baseball fan but a stockholder in the Hollywood Stars, a minor league team, and on the advisory board of the California Angels.

CASTING VIVIAN VANCE

It was director Marc Daniels who suggested Vivian Vance for the role of Ethel. Daniels had known her for ten years, and had worked with her in *Counselor at Law* with Paul Muni. A journeyman stage actress who had scant exposure in films, she was appearing at the La Jolla Playhouse in a revival of the role in the 1945 play *The Voice of the Turtle* when Daniels suggested that Desi and Jess go with him to a performance. At the end of the first act, Desi announced, "I think we found our Ethel Mertz."

Born Vivian Jones on July 26, 1912, in Cherryville, Kansas, Vance took her last name from a dramatics teacher who had been supportive during her formative years in Albuquerque, New Mexico. She pursued a musical career on Broadway during the thirties, appearing in minor roles such as Jerome Kern's and Oscar Hammerstein II's *Music in the Air* and Cole Porter's *Anything Goes*. She won her biggest accolades when, as an understudy, she

Vivian Vance's lifelong battle with emotional distress was eased by her Ethel Mertz role, providing her with an emotional stability that eluded her in her personal life during the show.

This early modeling photo was taken in the early thirties, when Vivian Vance was pursuing a nightclub career before she began landing character roles on Broadway.

had stepped into Kay Thompson's role in *Hooray for What* on opening night.

Before the role of Ethel came along, Vance had suffered an emotional breakdown, apparently brought on by a combination of career pressures, a heartbreaking set of experiences as a hospital nurse during World War II and a difficult relationship with her husband, character actor Phil Ober. Their marriage had apparently resembled the husband-and-wife relationship in the Charles Boyer–Ingrid Bergman film, *Gaslight*. Ober dominated and disciplined Vance until: "I would literally beat my head against the bedroom wall in frustration." The years she had spent in therapy since then had helped her keep a grip on life. When she accepted the role of Ethel Mertz, she would later admit that, along with her continuing analysis, it was what had provided her with the glue she needed to keep her life and her mental health intact.

Final Preparations

While Desi, Jess and others wrestled with the logistics of putting the show together, Lucy stopped work long enough to give birth to their first child at 8:15 A.M. on July 17, 1951. In addition to planning and contributing to the production of the show, Desi had personally supervised the construction of a nursery wing onto their ranch, and it was finished just in time for the birth of Lucie Desiree Arnaz. "Lucie's life changed our life," recalled Lucy. "There had been two business partners in the house, talking deals, contracts, scripts and budget. Now suddenly there was a fragile little new spark of life there, affecting everything we thought and did."

After months of frustration in trying to locate a suitable place to film the show, it was late August when production manager Al Simon learned that General Service Studios had an ideal sound stage. Desi had been focused on finding a legitimate theater to film the series in, but he, along with Ackerman and Oppenheimer, concurred when they saw the studio. It was a mere three weeks before the first episode was to go before the cameras.

In order to accommodate the four different sets that were used to

Desi and Lucy with Vivian Vance rehearse a kitchen scene in the first episode, "Lucy Thinks Ricky Is Trying to Murder Her."

tell the various stories each week, a wall between two sound stages was torn down. From left to right, the sets would include the Ricardo bedroom, living room and kitchen, while the fourth set was sometimes the Tropicana nightclub or, at various times, a TV studio, a vineyard, the Alps, the deck of an ocean liner or a chocolate factory.

In spite of the enormous technical difficulties and the nerve-wracking schedule before the show's film date in September, there were no production-stopping problems or deep personality conflicts. Editorial supervisor Dann Cahn made an astute observation about all the elements that came together to produce *I Love Lucy*: "Lucy and Desi had both been in the movies. The camera people, the editing people, we all came from film. The sound people all came from radio. And Marc Daniels and script supervisor Maury Thompson, they both came from live TV. You had a melding of radio, live TV and film all come together. That's what created the success of this show."

OPENING NIGHT

"We rehearsed the first show twelve hours a day," remembered Lucy. "Then on Saturday, September 8, 1951, the bleachers filled up by eight o'clock, and Desi explained to the audience that they would be seeing a brand new kind of television show."

Remembers Desi: "Except for some postproduction problems that cropped up when we cut the show the following week, everything went smoothly that night, mechanically and performance-wise. It all seemed effortless, which only goes to prove that it takes a lot of effort to make something look effortless. We had a wrap party onstage afterwards, and the whole atmosphere had a happy, carnival type of feeling."

Though this was the first *I Love Lucy* show ever shot, it didn't air until the fourth week of the season. There were many postproduction technical problems that had to be corrected before airing. When the footage came back from the lab, all the shots were properly exposed, but it was clear that utilizing four complete camera crews not only crowded the set, but threw off the tempo of the storyline. The fourth camera was dropped permanently, and the three-camera setup became routine thereafter.

First-year director Marc Daniels shares a light moment with Lucy, Desi and Jess Oppenheimer. It was Daniels's innovation to break the shoot into three separate acts with ten-minute intervals to allow costume changes and complicated production setups.

The crew had also attempted to shoot the entire show, from beginning to end, without a break in the action. "The tension that created on the set was intolerable at times," remembers Maury Thompson. "If there was one serious missed cue, the whole shoot would have been severely compromised." Marc Daniels suggested that it would be better to break between each ten-minute act. These breaks provided natural pauses in the action, like a three-scene, one-act play. This simple solution also gave Desi the opportunity to chat with the audience, and sometimes to lead the band in a musical interlude. It also gave the writers more creative freedom in doing last-minute rewrites on set, and allowed time for costume changes, special effects and complicated prop requirements that would provide the show with some classic moments in future episodes. From that day forward, this became the standard shooting technique for all half-hour TV sitcoms.

The first screening of the show was a nerve-wracking affair, remembers editorial supervisor Dann Cahn. When the screening room darkened and the show came on, he remembers a sinking feeling: "They're running the first show and nobody's laughing. All these guys—the agency guys, the network guys, the packaging guys. There must have been fifteen people in that room. Nobody says anything. The lights go on in the projection room. The projector stops and there's a real silence—and Lucy's sitting directly behind me. And she says 'Danny, that's damn good editing!' The silence is broken and everyone is congratulating themselves. I was a hit with Lucy."

SITCOM WRITING PIONEERS

By now Jess Oppenheimer, Bob Carroll, Jr., and Madelyn Pugh-Davis had cemented a seamless working relationship. The pressure they were used to in cranking out thirty-nine shows a year in radio would serve them well. "You did the script and pushed on," remembers Bob. "I didn't think of it as a job."

"We did thirty-nine shows in each of the first and second seasons," says Madelyn. "We didn't know any better. We used to pray

Jess Oppenheimer—watching the dress rehearsal of the first I Love Lucy episode—was an unusual combination of producing genius and comedic talent who molded the show into pioneering TV comedy.

that the president would speak or something, in order to get a break and get a week ahead." But their backlog of work on *My Favorite Husband* enabled them to craft several *I Love Lucy* episodes for the first season from old *Husband* plotlines.

Lucy always appreciated Jess's, Bob's and Madelyn's ability to think and write visually, which made the transition from radio to television even smoother than anticipated. Since they wrote the scripts eight weeks before film date, piecing together stage movement and direction was always guesswork, and they never had the luxury of examining sets or visual layouts in advance.

Working out the small bits of business and the outrageous situations, however, wasn't idle guesswork. "We'd act out or try out these props and get them from the prop department to see if they'd work," says Madelyn. "If anyone would come walking in, they'd think we'd lost our minds. We'd handcuff each other, or try to put on a coat at the same time." Adds Bob: "Plus you find out funny things when you work it out, instead of just writing it funny."

I Love Lucy director Bill Asher (1952 to 1955) remembers the importance of how well the scripts translated into physical action. "All the routines were very well written in great detail," he remembers. "They were very well structured. And most of the stuff we did was as written. The routines weren't all written the way they were filmed, but they were all worked out just as you would do a piece of music in beats. The timing is such that you have to do it that way. Nothing we did was haphazard. It was very carefully and logically worked out. Jess wouldn't introduce anything in terms of business that he hadn't worked out already with Bob and Madelyn."

Whenever the writers were out with Lucy socially, much of what she did or said would eventually wind up in the show. One time she was talking about the chickens they had at their Chatsworth ranch, and she said they had the oldest chickens in the world because they couldn't bear to kill them. "We worked that into a show," says Bob. "When we learned she played the saxophone as a child, we used that. When she went back to her high school reunion—also used. Anything was fair game."

"We'd get an idea," Madelyn remembers, "and we'd call up Lucy at home and say, 'If we did this, would you mind doing that?' Or we'd walk down the hall and ask Desi, 'Would it be OK to do this?' We had total access and freedom. Desilu was small enough that it was easy to go down and look at the props in the prop room and get an idea. We'd ask the prop master to have a particular prop brought to our office to see if it would work."

FIRST-SEASON MILESTONES

When *I Love Lucy* premiered on October 15, 1951, the critics were unanimous in their praise of the show. Within two months it ranked sixteenth in the nation, and by the end of the season it was number three behind *Arthur Godfrey's Talent Scouts* and the *Texaco Star Theater*, starring Milton Berle. *Variety* reported that an average of twenty-nine million viewers were watching the show every week, that it was the first TV show in history to reach over ten million homes.

All the innovative technical achievements had been laid down, and dozens of other production companies throughout Hollywood were following the trend. Desilu was providing a fertile training ground for those who would learn the process and move on to other studios to repeat it elsewhere. And Desilu was fast becoming not only one of the most influential production companies in Hollywood, but one of the most powerful in the industry. Desi had already struck an agreement with CBS to produce *Our Miss Brooks* for the network, and other shows would soon follow.

When Red Skelton was accepting his award for excellence in comedy at the 1952 Emmy Award ceremony, he said graciously, "Ladies and gentlemen, you've given this to the wrong redhead. I don't deserve this. It should go to Lucille Ball." The audience was so overcome they leapt to their feet and cheered for over two minutes. Lucy and Desi were so overwhelmed that they openly wept in response to the accolade.

A Week with "Lucy"

By the time the show ended its first year, it was running like the proverbial Swiss watch. How did it work? How was the production structured from week to week? How were all production elements coordinated from department to department? Who did what? What was a typical work week like?

MONDAY:

Writers: Monday morning was "plot day" for Jess, Bob and Madelyn, who would gather in Jess's office and start tossing around ideas for the script, which would be finished by the end of the week and filmed eight weeks later. By noon, the three would have nailed down a plot idea described in one or two sentences: "Lucy goes to work in a chocolate factory," or "Lucy falls in a vat of starch," or "Lucy gets locked in a freezer." After lunch they would go through all the various scene possibilities, and then work their way backward scene by scene to the beginning of the show. Then they would draft an outline for every scene and the key dialogue in each scene. By the end of the day, they had the show plotted out—how it pro-

This was the well-known four-headed "monster," a pioneer multitrack movieola developed exclusively for I Love Lucy. Editorial supervisor Dann Cahn (left) and film editor Bud Molin assemble the rough cut for "Lucy Learns to Drive."

gressed, scene by scene, from beginning to end, and what the payoff was, and the major lines—written in the form of a story treatment.

PRODUCTION CREW: Editors Dann Cahn and Bud Molin would get the dailies from the previous week's shoot in the morning, and spend all day Monday and part of Tuesday assembling a rough cut. The grip crew would get an early morning call to strike last week's sets and to prepare for the new sets that had been constructed the previous week. Various production meetings would be held between the craft departments to discuss any special handling of props, sets, animals or any other unusual items used in Friday's filming.

TUESDAY:

CAST: The principal players would assemble at ten o'clock around a table on a dubbing stage for the first read-through of the script that was written eight weeks before. It would be a nerve-wracking moment for the writers, because no one, except for Bob, Madelyn and Jess, and sometimes Desi, would have read one word of the script or even knew what the plot would be. The reading

On Tuesdays the cast assembled in a backstage area to block out the scenes. Here director Marc Daniels (seated, center) works out blocking while Desi and Lucy wait their turn.

would last until lunch, with frequent stops along the way to assess, adjust, edit and revise the story. The balance of the day would be spent delving into the rehearsal process. It was anything-goes during this phase of rehearsal, and everyone who had ideas to contribute was seriously considered. Bob and Madelyn would return to their office after lunch, and begin writing the first draft of the Monday's new story idea in script form.

PRODUCTION CREW: During the previous eight weeks, the art department had designed and the carpentry department had built the various sets needed for that week's show. Under the direction of the production manager and the set designer, the grip crew would begin assembling those sets so that the actors could begin working on them by Wednesday morning. The stage usually consisted of three to six separate locales, two of which were almost always the Ricardo's bedroom, living room or kitchen area.

WEDNESDAY:

CAST/CAMERA/LIGHTING: At the 10:00 A.M. call, the cast would see the finished sets that the crew had assembled by the previous day. They would try to rehearse "without book" (sans script) on the newly completed set to give a more accurate feel to the rhythm of the story. Jess Oppenheimer considered this the most important rehearsal time, with all major stage direction "locked." Jess would watch what they were doing, and analyze the basic business. Said Jess: "This would give me a good idea as to what was working and what wasn't. Then we had a 'note session' where we'd discuss everything that I made notes about. I'd give my suggestions about line readings, or whatever wasn't working." They would usually manage to go through the script at least twice before 4:30 P.M., when Karl Freund would scrutinize the sets, the actors' blocking and any special lighting problems. Freund would also discuss camera movement with the camera coordinator, and work around whatever limitations the script placed on the action. They would have a long discussion about all acting business when they ran the note sessions after the Wednesday's dress rehearsal. Lucy never overruled Oppenheimer's decisions, nor did she ever say, "No, I won't do that" once Desi or Jess gave it his blessing.

Lucy discusses costume designs with designer Elois Jenssen while wearing one of her creations. Jenssen, one of the most well-known designing talents in Hollywood, gave Lucy a look that has stood the test of time.

WRITERS: Bob and Madelyn would deliver their final first draft script to Jess, who would then analyze it for dialogue, pace, credibility, logic and humor. "Sometimes I didn't touch a word of their script," remembered Jess. "Other times I changed a great deal. I might be wrong when I changed it, but I had to do what I think was right. I dictated the entire script into a Dictaphone so I could give it the consistency and constancy every show needs. That way it sounds the same each time it funnels through me. I know the mood and the feel of our other shows; I can bring it all into line, so that nothing sounds too different or out of character. That's one of the things that made the show stay on top."

Jess would hand over the Dictaphone recording to his secretary,

Mercedes Manzanares, who was also in charge of casting. "I would get to something and reread it," recalls Mercedes, "and I would go into Jess and say, 'This stinks.' And he'd say, 'Okay, it stinks, but tell me why.' He'd say, 'If you can prove to me why it stinks, then we'll make the change. It's better than having it get down on the set and find out it stinks.'" Said Jess: "The best reason *I Love Lucy* clicked, aside from the fact that Lucy was a great girl, is that our show was tailored to get the greatest identification. We never started off from an unbelievable premise. If the audience can accept the beginning of our show, and know it's real, then they will go along no matter how extreme the show gets."

PRODUCTION CREW: By the end of the day, with a first rough cut finished by the editing department, the prop department had usually raided its storehouse and laid the props on carts which would be rolled down to the stage for the Thursday evening dress rehearsal.

THURSDAY:

LIGHTING: At 8:00 A.M. cinematographer Freund would work with the gaffer crew to electronically "paint" the set with lights. By noon he was finished, with all light cues solidified and chalk lines laid down and numbered for dolly movement and positioning. Then, at 4:30 P.M., a complete run-through with the camera crews, gaffers, soundmen and prop crew. It was the first time the near full complement of cast and crew had been assembled.

ENTIRE CREW: Finally, just like a stage play, a full dress rehearsal would commence at 7:30 P.M., without cameras, to minimize distraction and to allow everyone to focus more carefully on story and character alone. It also allowed the camera crew to gain some perspective on the action. Everyone then broke for dinner, which was served adjacent to the set. Afterwards, a final polish session was conducted, during which last-minute script cuts were wrapped up, and every bit of business and all camera directions ironed out. Generally this was conducted on the set, and usually present were Desi, Lucy, Vivian, Bill, Jess, Bob, Madelyn, the director, Karl Freund, assistant directors Jim Paisley, Jerry Thorpe or

Jack Aldworth, and key personnel in the costume, prop and special effects departments. The script was reviewed page by page. "They were wonderful sessions," remembered Oppenheimer. "We'd even get into the philosophy of the script. We really dug into the characters, because we took these people very seriously, and tried to make everything logical." After notes, Jess, Desi and Lucy would go to the screening room to look at a rough cut of last week's show, followed by another note session. Intensive blocking rehearsals and running lines comprised the order of the day, many times to the point of exhaustion.

FRIDAY:

WRITERS: During the course of the day, Jess returned Bob's and Madelyn's script to them, with his comments and suggestions for rewrite and revision, and they would deliver a final polished draft to him the following Monday, just in time to start all over again. So each week they concerned themselves with three scripts—the one they had just finished, the one they were writing, and the

Camera movement and logistics were plotted and coordinated with the actors' blocking on Wednesday and were finalized by Thursday's dress rehearsal.

Desi used the "warm-up" to introduce the cast and crew to the audience, including the most important reason why the show existed—Lucille Ball.

The actual filming of I Love Lucy would take place on Friday (later Thursday) with Desi doing the audience "warm-up," inaugurating a TV tradition.

one that was in production that week. In addition to the new storyline, they would also go to the various rehearsals from time to time for the show that was filming that week. Jess, Bob and Madelyn always attended the first run-through, rehearsals, dress rehearsals and the show, and would provide the cast with any changes necessary to make the script work after it was put on its feet.

CAST AND CREW: There was 1:00 P.M. call for the entire cast and crew to incorporate any changes made the night before, then a final dress rehearsal at 4:30 P.M. with a full contingent of camera crews and cameras. Freund would make final lighting adjustments before the dinner break. Dinner would be served in a family picnic environment, with the entire company joining in, and then everyone would assemble on the set to take their positions. By now the

CBS ushers had given the bleachers one last going-over and were busy taping off the VIP seats, where the network brass, the sponsors, family members and important guests would sit. The audience was brought in and was seated by 7:30, when Desi would come out and do the warm-up. Finally, at 8:00 P.M., the band would strike up the familiar *I Love Lucy* theme, the director would call "Action!" and the filming would begin. For the next sixty minutes, the audience would roar at the antics of the Ricardos and the Mertzes. With only five- to ten-minute breaks for film reloads between scenes, the show was shot chronologically to retain the proper dramatic form for audience understanding.

And so it went. And even though in the third year the entire production schedule was brought up one day, with filming wrapped up by Thursday, this production method has stood the test of time for over forty years since then, and was all laid down into a smooth working operation within a few short weeks after the start of production.

Lucille Ball's Genius

By the end of the first season, the world had fallen in love with the series, and critics were acknowledging the comic genius of Lucille Ball's work. What well of talent she drew from, one can only guess. It started with a prodigious natural talent that was seasoned by years of journeyman's work as a contract player at both MGM and RKO. Then she put in years learning her craft at the feet of some of the greatest motion picture performers who ever lived.

In the twilight of her years at MGM, Lucy used to hang out with director Eddie Sedgwick and Buster Keaton. The MGM brass had dismissed them as "has-beens on salary," dubbing Sedgwick as "incurably old-fashioned" and Lucy as "washed up." During many hours of idleness in Sedgwick's MGM office, she would join the pair and help build little machines invented by Keaton, who was employed at that time as a gag writer. Fellow writer Lewis Jacobs called these inventions "whole logical continuities of mad activity.

The engineers from the nearby Consolidated Aircraft actually came over to MGM to see them. They called them 'mechanical wizardry.' *Popular Mechanics* ran articles about them."

Remembering these hours of comic apprenticeship years later, Lucy said: "I rarely had the opportunity in my life to experience such liberating creative expression except when I'm onstage and everything's working. Buster and Eddie were the first people to really teach me all about slapstick comedy and the importance of props. They were masters, and they taught me attention to detail. If I had to work with grapes, a loaf of bread or whatever, I had to test them first to know what I was eating or drinking, how hot or cold it was, how it got there, how it would ride on the tray. I learned much from those two men, and I'll be forever grateful."

But it wasn't until *I Love Lucy* that Lucille Ball found herself in the perfect environment to bring her talent to full flower. With her gifted ensemble of players and writers on *I Love Lucy*, she was able to create moments of pure joy and inspiration that only a few comic geniuses have ever reached. Few would dispute that Lucille Ball deserves a place on the same stage with Charlie Chaplin, Buster Keaton and Stan Laurel.

Maury Thompson, who spent the better part of twenty-five years watching Lucy, first as a script supervisor, then as a camera coordinator and finally as director, has this to say about her: "You could hold a camera just on her for the whole show. Her reactions to other people's lines were brilliant. It was a sense that she was completely aware of everything around her, the actors, the lights, the camera positions—everything."

Lucy had an astonishing knack for picking up skills. "If, for instance, the script called for her to walk on stilts or play a musical instrument," recalls Madelyn Pugh-Davis, "she had gotten so good during rehearsals that sometimes we had

Lucy director Maury Thompson: "You could hold a camera on her for the whole show. Her reactions to other people's lines were brilliant."

to tell her not to be so good. She was almost too good. It was amazing." Adds Bob Carroll: "Without a lot of practice."

"We'd tell her, 'It's not funny anymore,'" says Madelyn. "And she had to kind of pull back. And that happened almost every time."

"Her perfectionism at learning skills sometimes conflicted with her sense of comedy," adds Bob. "It was a teeter-totter process that led to wonderful moments on film."

The one quality Lucy seemed to lack was a well-developed sense of story. She relied completely on the talents and instincts of Desi, Jess, Bob and Madelyn. "She just wanted to read the script and perform it," says Madelyn. "So we never talked story with Lucy," says Bob. "She didn't want to hear it. She wouldn't know what to do about it. Desi would know, though. You'd show him a script and he'd say 'there's something wrong on page twelve,' and he was always right. Or he would say, 'I think it's a little long in the middle.' He had a great comic sense. Lucy would read a script and say 'this is not going to work,' and he'd say, 'Honey, please try it. Jess, Bob and Madelyn wrote it to work.' And she would try—and she'd love it."

"Lucy was so visual that it made it easy to think of things for her to do," recalls Madelyn. "As we went along in that first year, we realized how great she was, and that she'd do almost anything we'd ask her. You didn't have any limitation with her, so we really could let go."

Jess Oppenheimer wrote not only one of the best observations about Lucille Ball's almost preternatural ability to create character, but one of the most cogent statements ever written about any per-

Lucy writer Madelyn Pugh-Davis: "*Her physical dexterity was astonishing. Sometimes we had to tell her to hold back or it wasn't funny anymore.*"

Jess Oppenheimer: "*I Love Lucy was a 'star' piece. The entire project rode on the radiant talent of one woman. In every sense she was a star.*"

former anywhere. What follows is his entire essay: "In taking a backward look at *I Love Lucy*, I acknowledge the importance of every element in the series, but I want to especially emphasize that it was a 'star' piece. The entire project rode on the radiant talent of one woman. The Lucille Ball of the 1950s was a simply incredible, stunning performer. In every sense, she was a star. Remove any other actor from the project and it would be diminished. Take away Lucille Ball and it would be demolished. As good as the supporting cast was, to my mind, no combination of them could sustain interest on the screen without Lucy, unless they were talking about her.

"Most comedy writers feel it is exceptional if a star realizes sixty percent of the values they've written into a script. Lucy, somehow, returned about 125 percent. Unexpected qualities appeared out of nowhere. Little, human, ordinary, recognizable values. Inflections that were exactly the way your sister or your mother or the lady bus driver used to sound. She was everywoman. Ask her to be a tough showgirl and you got back a broad who simply could not look and move like that unless she'd been pumping out bumps and grinds in

Jess Oppenheimer: "After Lucy took the script to the mat and fought with it, examined it and internalized it, she owned it when it reappeared....She was Lucy Ricardo."

a burlesque house for twenty years. Ask her for royalty and she became a queen. And she kept astounding us that way every week.

"Curiously, if any one of you had been asked to sit in on a first reading of *I Love Lucy*, and then asked for your assessment, you probably would have said, the story is fine, the dialogue is excellent, most of the cast is great, but get rid of the redhead, she doesn't know what the hell she is doing. And you would have been right. She didn't know what the hell she was doing—at the first reading. Deliver me from actors who sound exactly the same after the fifteenth time around. No depth, no improvement, no nothing. But Lucy stumbled through the first reading and then took the material to the mat. She fought with it, examined it,

Jess Oppenheimer: "Most comedy writers feel it is exceptional if a star realizes sixty percent of what they've written into the script. Lucy returned 125 percent."

internalized it, and when it reappeared, she owned it. There was no feeling that the audience was watching her act. She simply was Lucy Ricardo. And if you looked carefully, you would marvel that every fiber in the woman's body was contributing to the illusion.

"Did Ricky catch her in a lie? She wouldn't be just a voice denying it. Her stance would be a liar's stance. Defensive. There would be a tell-tale picking at a cuticle, or a slight, nervous jerking of an elbow, or a finger brushed against an upper lip, which is the first place you feel the perspiration of anxiety. Her hands, her feet, her knees, every cell would be doing the right thing. This was an exceptionally talented young lady, and I don't know enough superlatives to do her justice. Just remember that in any discussion about *I Love Lucy*, her presence must be acknowledged in every sentence."

CHAPTER THREE

THE SECOND SEASON

1952 to 1953

"We're Having a Baby"

An event would dominate the second season of *I Love Lucy* that would change the course of broadcasting. The birth of both Lucille Ball's and Lucy Ricardo's real and fictional babies broke more barriers than any other single airing of its kind in television history. Never had any major TV program dealt with the subject of pregnancy or childbirth, and it created a national sensation during the 1952 to 1953 season.

But it began with what Lucille Ball and Desi Arnaz perceived as a disaster for the life of the show. They were about to wrap up the last few episodes of the season before the summer hiatus when Lucy and Desi walked into Jess Oppenheimer's office and closed the door. He was startled at their behavior. "I could see that whatever the news," he remembered, "it could only be bad." Desi broke the ice: "Well, *amigo*, we've just heard from the doctor. Lucy's having another baby in January. We'll have to cancel everything. That's the end of the show."

"Why should it be?" Jess shot back. "This is wonderful!" He paused and leaned forward, looking deeply into Lucy's eyes: "I wouldn't suggest this to any other actress in the world, but we can continue the show. You'll have your baby and Lucy Ricardo can have a baby, too. It's just what we need to give us some excitement in our second season."

Lucy and Desi were ecstatic. "Do you think we could? What about the network and the sponsors?" asked Desi. They decided to call for a reaction.

When the Ricardos and the Arnazes announced Lucy's pregnancy, the news changed the way television dealt with matters regarding pregnancy and birth.

Six months pregnant with Desi, Jr., Lucy shares a warm autumn evening on the Chatsworth ranch with Desi, Lucie and their cocker spaniel.

Predictably, CBS was concerned about what they called "good taste." The ad agency told Desi, "You cannot show a pregnant woman on television" and suggested that they hide Lucy behind furniture. Insulted, Desi hit the roof and immediately wrote a letter to Philip Morris chairman, Alfred E. Lyons. At the time the letter hit Lyons's office, he was in England. His cabled reply minced no words: "Don't f*** around with the Cuban!" Case closed.

This response set the production of the series on an accelerated course. Rather than take the usual three-month hiatus, they geared up to shoot as many shows as possible into the new season before the birth. Everyone's personal summer plans had to be rescheduled in order to film the pregnancy episodes before Lucy would have to stop in her final months.

Matters of taste had to be considered to head off any censorship problems, and three religious advisors—a Catholic priest, a Protestant minister and a Jewish rabbi—were commissioned to approve the scripts for the episodes. At their insistence, CBS refused to allow use of the word "pregnant," and insisted on substituting the word "expectant."

Of the sixteen shows filmed before Lucy would start her six-month leave of absence in November, seven would chronicle Lucy Ricardo's pregnancy, and nine "nonpregnant" shows would go in the can, giving her time to recover before the next season's shooting would begin.

Despite the burden of such a rigorous schedule, Lucy thrived on it, and enjoyed herself during this entire period. Everyone pitched in to make her job easier, including new director William Asher, whose ability to manage Lucille Ball's tendency to direct herself and those around her would set the tone for their entire professional relationship. Says Asher: "She stopped the rehearsal and said 'No, no, no. I'm not going over there, I'm going over here and Viv, you stand over there.' And I said, 'Wait, hold it. Whoa! You don't need me here!' I walked off the set, and she apparently went over to Desi and broke down, crying. Desi charged in to confront me and I said, 'Wait a minute. Let me tell you what's going on here…' I told him and he said, 'You're right. Go and talk to Lucy. She's in tears.' And I went to her dressing room and wound up crying with her. After that she was well behaved.

"It was a great relief to her when I was staging the shows without her during the pregnancy. In rehearsal, I used to play her part and do all the staging. After we had it all staged, she would come in and watch the scene and step in and do it herself. So there was very little input from her at that point, and she felt secure with that.

"She was a professional, total concentration on getting the thing down. She was a good worker on the very tough physical routines which would be awkward to work. A lot of the stuff was pretty silly and was very hard to get into—crawling around, barking like a dog. It's gotta make you feel like a fool. So we would stay after rehearsals and request that there would be nobody on the stage when she ran through the difficult or unusual scenes. First, it doesn't take up valuable production time for others, but more importantly she wouldn't have to feel like a fool."

Lucy's physical stamina was legendary, and during the first five years of the show she was never sick, but during her pregnancy with Desi, Jr., she often napped on the set while waiting for her call.

FILMING "LUCY IS ENCEINTE"

The birth announcement episode, "Lucy Is Enceinte," was so named because the French word for "expecting" sounded more romantic than others that were considered. The script had been intensely scrutinized not only by the network but by the three religious leaders, who attended the dress rehearsal. After the performance, they gave unanimous praise of the show, and when asked if they found anything objectionable, their reaction was, "What's wrong with having a baby?"

When the show was actually filmed, in the much discussed final scene when Lucy Ricardo breaks the news of her pregnancy to Ricky, it was very apparent that the couple was swept up in the emotion of the moment. As originally written, Ricky's reaction was to be a joyful roar, and apparently during rehearsals, nothing special happened. The performers went through their paces, hit their marks, and were more than ready for the filming. But then the electricity of the moment took over; Jess Oppenheimer's reflections best describe the scenario: "Lucy and Desi got to this point in acting out the script, and then this strange thing happened. Suddenly they remembered their own real emotions when they discovered that they were going to be parents and both of them began crying, and Desi couldn't finish the song he was performing at the end of the show. It was one of the most moving things I've ever seen."

Years later Lucy reflected on the moment: "When we did this scene before an audience, Desi suddenly recalled our emotions when we discovered our pregnancy with Lucie almost two years before, after ten childless years of

Lucille Ball on the final scene in "Lucy Is Enceinte": "Desi recalled our emotions when I was pregnant with Lucie, after our ten childless years. His eyes filled up and he couldn't finish the song, then I started to cry, too."

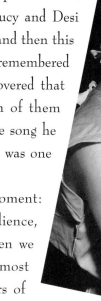

This official first photo of Desi Arnaz, Jr., was shot on the day of his birth, January 19, 1953.

marriage. His eyes filled up and he couldn't finish the song, I started to cry, too. Then Vivian started to sniffle and even the hardened stagehands wiped their eyes with the back of their hands."

THE MILLION-DOLLAR BABY

The birth of Lucy's second child was a national obsession during the 1952 to 1953 television season. Never before had the birth of a baby generated as much public interest. It had been decided that both the fictional and the real-life condition of Lucy be kept a secret until the "enceinte" show was to air on December 8, 1952. A publicity campaign had to be carefully orchestrated in order to maximize the impact of the Ricardo baby.

After the "enceinte" episode aired, the promotional push went into high gear. The public relations departments at Desilu, CBS and Philip Morris inundated the nation's media machine with hundreds of features, announcements and blurbs, most of it speculation about the sex of the baby.

By the time the date of birth arrived, the public was whipped into such a frenzy that practically every other news story of the day was ignored. On the Sunday night before her caesarean, Desi drove Lucy the almost thirty miles from Chatsworth to Cedars of Lebanon Hospital, which had been Lucie's birthplace. With the world's media poised and Desi on the edge of his waiting room seat, Lucy was taken into the operating room at six o'clock and given a spinal anesthetic so that she could remain conscious during the operation. And on January 19, 1953, at 8:15 A.M., their doctor announced the birth of an eight-pound, nine-ounce boy—Desi, Jr.

Desi went wild, yelling "It's a boy!" He turned to

Lucille Ball gives daughter Lucie a chance to share in the joy on the day of Desi, Jr.'s baptism.

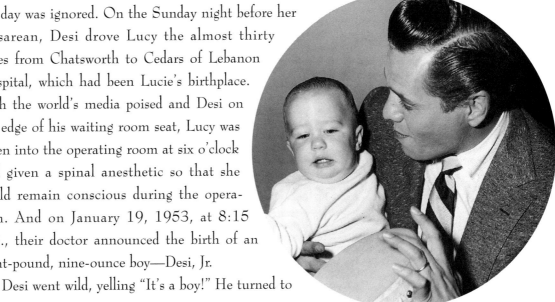

Desi introduces his son to the instrument that made him famous—the conga drum.

Desi photographed this warm moment in the Arnaz nursery.

Desi shoots home movies after his son's baptism on the steps of Our Lady of the Valley Church.

columnist James Bacon—the only newsman he had allowed in the waiting room—and said, "That's Lucy for you. Always does her best to cooperate. Now we have everythin'!" Desi called Jess Oppenheimer with the news, shouting, "Lucy followed your script! Ain't she somethin'?" Bacon informed the battalion of press standing by and the birth was worldwide news within minutes. Never before had the birth of a baby generated such worldwide interest.

"That afternoon I awoke to find Desi sitting on my bed sobbing," remembered Lucy. "There were seven thousand letters and a thousand telegrams waiting for me. But that was only the beginning. Counting the telegrams, letters, phone calls, baby booties, cards and other

Lucy and Desi celebrate Desi Jr.'s christening with their mothers, Dolores and DeDe.

gifts, one million people sent some expression of their good wishes for the new baby." Four temps would be hired to process the mail, and every one of the letters was replied to with a note of thanks. Desi would give Lucille a Hammond organ as a gift, along with a Tree of Life medallion with the inscription "Lucy and Thumper," the nickname they gave the restless fetus.

Later that evening, when "Lucy Goes to the Hospital" aired, a record forty-four million people

The Arnazes await the verdict at their first Emmy Awards presentation. They won three: Lucy for Best Comedienne, Vivian Vance for Best Supporting Actress, and the show picked up a statue for Best Situation Comedy.

Lucy accepts her first Emmy on February 5, 1953, as emcee Art Linkletter (left) and Ralph Edwards look on.

tuned in to witness the birth of "Little Ricky," garnering a record 71.7 percent of the viewing audience—topping even the 67.7 rating for Dwight Eisenhower's inauguration coverage the following morning. As if all this weren't enough, the couple walked onto the dais at the downtown Statler Hilton Hotel eighteen days later to accept their first Emmy Awards for "Best Comedienne" and "Best Situation Comedy."

It was a banner year in every way for television's first couple: the nation's number one television program, a new son, two key awards from the television academy, and a new eight-million-dollar sponsorship deal with Philip Morris that made them television's highest paid stars. In March, two months after Desi, Jr.'s birth, they would begin production on MGM's *The Long, Long Trailer.*

They were also looking at a plethora of merchandising contracts for pajamas, dolls, games, nursery attire and supplies, clothing, costume jewelry and dozens of other items. In April they appeared on the cover of *Life,* and a week later on the covers of *Look* and the first issue of a brand-new magazine called *TV Guide.*

CREATIVE DIFFERENCES

When the episode "Ricky and Fred Are TV Fans" was filmed on May 22, 1953, just over two months had passed since Lucille Ball had returned to work after the birth of Desi, Jr. This was the second-to-last episode of their phenomenal second season. But there were signs that not everything was going well within the Desilu creative team.

Desi Arnaz was a brilliant negotiator and a strategist when it came to solving problems and maneuvering the company into more and more lucrative enterprises, and in the coming years he would spend an increasing amount of time working on numerous projects that would continue to elevate the studio's financial and artistic position in the entertainment business. But at this point in time, he felt he needed to enhance his credibility as an executive in the Hollywood community. At his 1952 birthday party, he approached Jess Oppenheimer, and asked if it would be all right for him to take "executive producer" credit on the show in order to help solidify his growing reputation as a producer. Jess agreed, and without changing anything except the addition of Desi's new title on the show's credits, not a line was changed on any

*D*esi and *J*ess Oppenheimer had intense after-rehearsal note sessions, and though they fought for control, everyone acknowledged that their rivalry sharpened the quality of the show.

contract. Oppenheimer had already established himself as a producer, and he had a contract with Desilu that gave him total creative control over the show

At first Oppenheimer saw no harm in letting Desi contribute more to the show. After all, Desi had proved himself one tough *hombre* in dealing with the network, the sponsors and the power brokers. He would not be the final authority on creative decisions, and the lion's share of producing would continue to fall largely on Oppenheimer's shoulders, but as president of Desilu, Desi was already making significant business decisions on the direction of the company, and Lucy had complete faith in his ability to run the company.

At his birthday party, Desi approached Jess Oppenheimer to ask him if he would mind letting him use the title "Executive Producer" on the show. That change in show credits led to an on-again, off-again feud between the two.

The rift that materialized between Jess Oppenheimer and Desi Arnaz began with difficulties over Oppenheimer's percentage ownership of the show. Both Desi and Jess were gracious men who liked each other personally, but when Harry Ackerman gave Oppenheimer that twenty percent ownership—without informing Desi—it set into motion a dispute between the two men that began to affect the production of the show and their working relationship.

Lucy, Desi and Jess were all very concerned about the problem, and eager to find a solution. "We're fighting onstage," said Desi, "and that's no good." But when Martin Leeds, a new Desilu executive, was hired in February 1953, he was able to arbitrate their differences. "What I had to do," says Leeds, "was simply to define what their needs and functions were." According to director William Asher, each man had a role to play, and did it with tremendous energy and creativity. "Both were indispensable factions in the success of the show. Jess was responsible for getting the show on the air. He was involved with the scripts, the costuming, the lighting, the cameras, every aspect of production. He was the guy who nailed the whole thing together. But Desi was ultimately responsible for the show—to the network, the industry and the public at large and all of the business involved with *I Love Lucy* and Desilu. He had this innate sense of what worked on screen and what didn't work, and he knew how to handle Lucy. He would tell Lucy to do things that nobody else would ever give to her. I can remember times even when they weren't getting along that she could be pissed off—big-time— but when it came to the show, she never lost her faith in him."

TV's Funniest Straight Man

It's well known that Desi had an incredible memory and could memorize a script after one reading, and his performance of the Ricky Ricardo character was almost perfect from Tuesday's first reading through the final, filmed performance in front of a studio audience on Friday. This was an anchor that Lucille could depend on. But with the brilliance of Lucille Ball driving the show, it's easy to understand how any performer—no matter how exceptional—might be overlooked in terms of creativity and craftsmanship. Bill Asher felt that Desi's contribution as an actor in the series was one of the most underrated and forgotten elements of the show. "Desi made the Ricky character a wonderful partner to Lucy," he observed. "He was gold in that show." In any other situation, Desi might have been more recognized for his contribution as a performer, but like everyone else around Lucy—a performer of genius level at the height of her creative powers—he was in the position of second banana. It was in this role that he provided such a perfect foil for Lucy Ricardo's antics.

Desi publicly downplayed his acting and performing ability, but it didn't help that he never received the acknowledgment of an Emmy for

Desi was a consistent performer and provided Lucy with the stability she needed to let loose with Lucy Ricardo's antics.

his work on the show. He even joked about it once: "I'm waiting for them to put in a category of bongo drummer—and if they have one and don't nominate me, then I'll squawk."

But as valuable as Desi was to the show as a performer, his greatest asset to Desilu was as a producer, and when rehearsals dragged on too long, he'd get impatient to return to the office and take care of company business. "Desi was a great problem-solver," Asher says. "He would make more contributions at the initial note sessions. Desi was also a substantial contributor and really had a tremendous instinct. And he was right most of the time. I didn't have a problem with that. Where I might be conducting the notes, Desi was really the person in charge, and very effectively, with Jess."

Desi's ability in handling people and business persisted even during the toughest days. The show and studio chores also provided a discipline and a structure that meshed well with his management style, and when he got involved with the production of the many pilots and other television programs, he thrived and gained strength from the whole production process.

"He never felt that there was a closed door in any situation," remembers Desi's longtime personal assistant, Johny Aitchison. "He would always find some kind of workable solution to almost every problem, and never respected anyone who wouldn't try to work through solutions themselves. A lot of people would say, 'You can't do this or you can't do that,' and he would prove that you could. His thinking was never linear—he would pick apart a problem and think the unthinkable solution. He was a genius at handling people. He was a real 'people' person who could charm anybody."

SECOND-SEASON MILESTONES

By the close of the 1952 to 1953 season of *I Love Lucy*, the show had blasted the competition out of first place, and finished

In his new office—and his new role as a major television producer—Desi discusses new non-"Lucy" shows with Desilu's most important asset.

After Desilu Productions moved to Motion Picture Center in 1953, for the next six years thousands of <u>I Love Lucy</u> fans passed through these doors to watch the Ricardos and the Mertzes. <u>Our Miss Brooks</u> was filmed next door.

off in the number one spot, with a 67.3 rating of more than forty-five million viewers. General Service Studios had outgrown the company's explosive growth, and with a slew of other television productions on the horizon, plus a million dollars in cash from CBS, Desilu Productions signed a lease on Motion Picture Center, a seven-acre facility with nine sound stages. Desilu's best years lay just around the corner. With the production of *The Long, Long Trailer* behind them, and a year filled with so many extraordinary highs, the Arnaz family settled down to a well-deserved rest in their beloved Del Mar retreat before the beginning of the third season. But before their summer was over, an obstacle lay directly in their path that threatened the entire *I Love Lucy* phenomenon.

CHAPTER FOUR

The Third Season

1953 to 1954

"THE RED SCARE"

In the early 1950s, a senator from Wisconsin—Joseph McCarthy—took up the banner of destroying communism in the United States, and as the power of the House Un-American Activities Committee (HUAC) grew, citizens accused of being communists were dragged through excruciating public testimony to prove their innocence. It was an ugly chapter in American history, and the shadow of this "witch-hunt" reached out to touch Lucille Ball.

The entire episode had its roots in Lucille's childhood. Her beloved grandfather Hunt was a man deeply committed to social causes. Even after Lucy had achieved some measure of success as an RKO contract player in 1936, grandfather Hunt was still involved in leftist political activities, holding rallies in the garage of the West Hollywood house the entire family shared. He had a friend running for a city council seat on the communist ticket and insisted that DeDe, Fred and Lucy register to vote as communists.

In the late 1940s, she and William Holden had gone before HUAC in Washington, D.C., to support actor Larry Parks and MGM producer Dore Schary when they were subpoenaed to testify about their political background. "We did that at the request of the Screen Writers' Guild," said Lucy. "Then when my own union told me my support was needed, I didn't ask questions." After she testified, a scandal-sheet reporter went through all her voting records and discovered her registration

On September 11, 1953, the night of the so-called "Red Scare," Lucy and Desi's performances in "The Girls Go into Business" belied the anguish they went through that week after the groundless accusation that Lucy was a communist.

card as a member of the Communist Party.

In 1952, the FBI called to question her about that affiliation, and Desilu business director Andrew Hickox, in the spirit of cooperation, set up a hush-hush meeting at the Chatsworth ranch at which agents questioned Lucy for several hours. "I did it to please Daddy," she told them, and she was completely cleared, with the FBI calling her actions "politically immature." She thought the matter was closed. But almost seventeen months later, she was summoned to appear once again before HUAC in a "closed-door" meeting, to review statements she had made to the FBI. The committee completely cleared her—but two days later, her appearance wound up as a closing item in a Walter Winchell broadcast: "The top television comedienne has been confronted with her membership in the Communist Party!"

"We didn't know whether or not we should do the show that next week," recalls director Bill Asher. "But Desi stepped up as the leader on Monday morning. He said, 'We have nothing to be ashamed of. Whatever's being said, let 'em say it. We should do our job—we should do the show.'" Desi eventually reached CBS president, Dr. Frank Stanton, and Philip Morris chairman, Alfred

Lucy reflected on the "Red Scare" incident years later: "My years of rigid self-discipline paid off. I lost myself in Lucy and clowned without a sign of strain."

Lyons, who were both supportive. Desi then contacted FBI Director J. Edgar Hoover to confirm their original findings when they had met with his agents almost a year and a half before. Hoover reportedly said, "She's one hundred percent clear as far as we're concerned," and Desi finally persuaded a reluctant spokesman for HUAC to hold a press conference to publicly clear Lucy of all the accusations that were being leveled at her. If it went off as planned, it would provide an important psychological boost before the show went before the cameras a scant two hours later.

Without the usual musical fanfare, Desi walked out center stage before three hundred people, and said, "Welcome to the first *I Love Lucy* show of the season. We are glad to have you back, and we are glad to be back ourselves. But before we go on, I want to talk to you about something serious. Something very serious. You all know what it is. The papers have been full of it all day." With his lip visibly quivering and his voice cracking, he paused, then continued: "Lucille is no communist. Lucy has never been a communist—not now and never will be. We both despise the communists and everything they stand for! I was kicked out of Cuba because of communism."

His eyes quickly welled with tears, but just as quickly his legendary anger replaced the tears, and exploded in a passionate finish. "Lucille is one hundred percent an American! Tomorrow morning the complete transcript of Lucille's testimony will be released to the papers and you can read it for yourself. Then you will know this is all a pack of lies!"

If there was ever any doubt about the public's reaction, it was all washed away when the audience leapt to its feet, thundering their unanimous approval. One man shouted, "We're with you, boy!" Limp with emotion,

Lucy shows director Bill Asher how much she appreciates his support during the "Red Scare."

Desi said a humble "Thank you" and promptly introduced William Frawley and Vivian Vance. Then, wiping away the tears, he said, "And now I want you to meet my favorite wife—my favorite red-head—in fact, that's the only thing red about her, and even that's not legitimate—Lucille Ball!"

"Feeling stiff as a fireplace poker," reflected Lucy, "I walked out into the limelight. I couldn't speak and my face was working with emotion."

Hollywood Reporter TV columnist Dan Jenkins was in the audience; he recalls her entrance: "Lucy stepped quietly out from behind a door at the rear of the set. The heavy makeup for the show concealed the lines of worry and strain. She was smiling, but it was a set smile. She got her answer in short order—an ovation. Still smiling, she punched the air lightly, with both hands, as though to say, 'We'll fight this thing out.'"

To the strains of the *I Love Lucy* theme, she hugged Desi, Vivian and Bill, then went to the bleachers, kissed her mother and other friends in the audience. "Still speechless, with tears in my eyes," said Lucy, "I turned and walked back through the curtains."

Show number 68, "The Girls Go into Business," began filming.

"So Desi was the man of the hour," says Asher. "The emotional impact of that show and the love that those three hundred people showed for Lucy is something that gives me goose bumps to this day. When she came back on for the first time during the filming, the first applause that hit her as she walked in the door was enough to drive her back through. So we started again."

"How the hell she ever got a hold of herself and went on to do one of the finest performances of her life after all this," said Desi, "only proves what a tremendous actress this girl is."

"My years of rigid self-discipline paid off that night," Lucille revealed. "I lost myself in *Lucy*, and clowned and cavorted without a sign of strain. At the end of the show, the cast came out as usual for a farewell bow. My 'Lucy Ricardo' voice—that high, bubbly, childlike voice—dropped to my normal, low tones. 'God bless you for being so kind,' I told them."

Arm in arm with Desi, they took a long walk across the length of the soundstage, with the audience applauding her every step.

"After the show, they (the audience) just wouldn't leave," says Asher. "They just stood there and screamed. Emotionally I think that night and that week was the most memorable in my life. How they did the show under those circumstances was a tribute to both of them."

"Finally, in my dressing room, I could give way to the tears I had been holding in since early in the morning," reflected Lucy later.

THIRD-SEASON MILESTONES

Having weathered the "Red Scare" incident, Lucy and Desi shifted into high gear, and no outside force would ever threaten Desilu again. Its success would continue to confound the naysayers, as one of the most rapid rises to power in the history of Hollywood entertainment continued. In just three short years, with a hit show and plans on the table for dozens of television projects, *I Love Lucy* would begin its fourth season.

To add to the triumph, the show won its second consecutive Emmy for Best Situation Comedy, and Vivian Vance walked home

It's Emmy night at the Hollywood Palladium on February 11, 1954, where I Love Lucy picked up two awards: Best Situation Comedy and Vivian Vance won for Best Supporting Actress. Lucy was nominated but best friend Eve Arden nabbed the prize.

with Best Supporting Actress in a Comedy, although Lucy lost the Best Comedienne award to her friend Eve Arden. Again, the show finished as the number one rated show on television, with an overall rating of 58.8. Some of the novelty of the series had worn off, since this rating position was 8.5 points less than the previous year, but the show and its phenomenal success showed no signs of abating.

In the summer between the third and fourth season, big things were happening at Desilu. The company was renting nine sound stages at Motion Picture Center, and Desi offered to buy the eleven-soundstage studio from owner Joseph Justman. In order to swing

The Arnazes had a lot to be happy about on New Year's Eve, 1953. They had had quite a year—Emmy Awards, the number one rated show, the birth of Desi, Jr., the completion of their first motion picture, and weathering the communism controversy.

the deal, Desi had to give up twenty-four percent of Desilu to CBS to obtain funding from the network. Justman would retain twenty percent while Desilu split the remaining eighty percent with CBS.

The box-office success of *The Long, Long Trailer* had prompted heavy bidding by MGM, Warner Bros. and Universal International to film the next Arnaz-Ball motion picture. Even though no properties had been chosen, Metro would finally prevail, signing a multiple-picture contract that not only gave Desilu profit participation but allowed it to film these productions at Desilu's own studio. This unprecedented deal was the harbinger of many more similar pacts to come. Desilu's contracts with the unions were not mired in the huge overhead commitments that MGM had been saddled with for years. Besides, the unions were happy with the Desilu machine, because it kept a lot of their employees working all year round.

As if all this weren't enough, during that same summer, Desi was putting the squeeze on the network to renegotiate his own contract. Desi was holding firm on forty separate points, and when he refused to budge on any of them, no less than CBS chairman William S. Paley flew out to see if he could make Desi yield. He couldn't.

CHAPTER FIVE

THE FOURTH TO

1954 to 1957

SIXTH SEASONS

THE FOURTH SEASON: 1954 TO 1955

It was in the middle of the third season of *I Love Lucy* that Jess Oppenheimer came up with the idea of taking the Ricardos and the Mertzes to Hollywood. *Time* magazine reported at the time: "As chief writer, Oppenheimer had a problem last week. He told [Bob] Carroll and [Madelyn] Pugh [-Davis]: 'We've got to do something new. When we started out, Desi is in show business and Lucy tries to get into the act. Later we did more about the husband-and-wife angle, and when that got heavy we were lucky and Lucy had her baby. Now we've got to think of something else. Let's take them from New York to Hollywood. Desi could get a studio offer.'

"Carroll put in: 'Let Desi take a screen test. That would give us a couple of funny scenes with Lucy.' Madelyn Pugh-Davis added: 'Suppose Hollywood was shooting *Don Juan* and they thought Ricky would be perfect for the part. This opens up all kinds of scenes. Lucy trying to play femmes fatales, Lucy getting jealous of the women Ricky has to make love to in the show…'"

So it was a symbolic milestone when the Ricardos left New York on their trip to Hollywood, and the song they sang en route, "California, Here I Come!" had a prophetic ring both in fiction and in real life. Only three years before, Hollywood's powerful motion picture studios were still ignoring television and dismissing Lucy's and Desi's success in

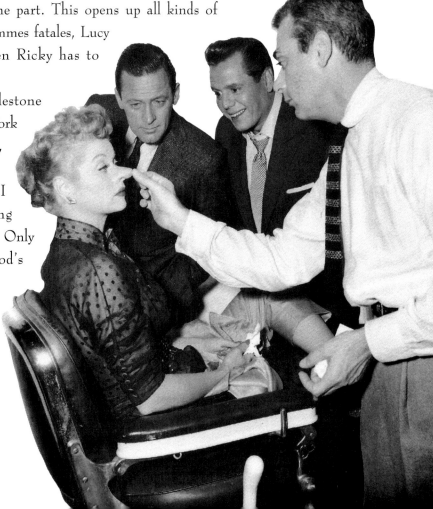

William Holden and Desi oversee makeup artist Hal King applying the famous "flaming nose" for "L.A. at Last!" It was a carefully planned prop with a wick strategically placed within the putty.

Lucy, Desi and Vivian discuss the final scene in "Lucy and John Wayne." Though they were political opposites, Lucy and Wayne's paths crossed many times, and they respected each other's talent.

this upstart medium. But by now it was clear that television, not motion pictures, would drive the entertainment business. And major movie stars began lining up for guest appearances on *I Love Lucy*: William Holden, Richard Widmark, Cornel Wilde, Rock Hudson, Harpo Marx, Van Johnson and John Wayne, with others soon to follow.

The Hollywood shows were extremely popular, successfully blending the show's characters with a supporting cast of motion picture personalities. It was never the intention to arbitrarily graft the guest star concept into a storyline, but it came out of the natural plot device of Ricky Ricardo aspiring to film stardom because he had gained notoriety as a New York–based nightclub entertainer. And with

Lucy, Desi and William Frawley monkeyshine for the camera behind a prop cabinet with Harpo Marx.

his Latin good looks, it was entirely plausible that he would be an ideal candidate to portray the legendary Don Juan. It would also serve to ignite renewed viewer interest in the program and rev up the show's slightly declined ratings.

When the final Nielsens were tabulated for the end of the year, *I Love Lucy* was again at the top of the heap, with a 7.1 rating distance separating it from *The Jackie Gleason Show*. The creative team looked forward with anticipation to the 1955 Emmy Awards ceremony in March—they were nominated in a record five categories—but the show did not capture a single award. The disappointment of the evening had barely worn off when sponsor Philip Morris announced the following morning that it was dropping its sponsorship of the show, but General Foods jumped at the opportunity to take it on. Since *I Love Lucy* was a family show, the demographics for food company sponsorship could not have been more appropriate.

While these negotiations were going on, the team

Lucie and Desi, Jr., accompany Mom backstage to watch their parents shoot "Ethel's Birthday" on October 7, 1954.

The Arnazes celebrate their thirteenth wedding anniversary on the floor of their den. Behind Desi on the chair is a Lucy Ricardo doll.

Lucy and Desi celebrate their fourteenth wedding anniversary backstage at a party thrown after the filming of "L.A. at Last!"

paused to weigh how much longer they were willing to go on with the show and the studio. Both Lucy and Desi had accomplished what they had set out to do, and then some. Though they had set the industry standard for live-on-film sitcom production, it was still a commitment that took away from their personal lives together and with their children. Standing at a crossroads in their personal and professional lives, Desi recalled offering Lucy two alternatives: "We can sell four years of *I Love Lucy* shows for at least three million dollars, and if we invest it safely and conservatively, it should bring us at least $150,000 a year income. We could spend more time with the children and you wouldn't have to do anything else. I would still run Desilu, continue to produce our other shows and supervise the ones we'd film for others, but without spending fifty hours a week on *I Love Lucy*. The other alternative is to go on and get as big as any of the other studios. That means more people—rent or buy a bigger studio to compete on an equal footing."

"I don't want to quit," she said.

It was this decision that led to the exponential growth of the Desilu empire, but it was also the moment when the couple traded their marriage for their careers. The symbolism of that moment became clear when the couple reluctantly sold their Chatsworth ranch to live closer to the studio. The unforeseen success of the series made the commute from Chatsworth a real effort so, with much sadness, they moved out, in May 1955, to a house on Roxbury Drive in Beverly Hills.

At a family get-together for Lucy's forty-third birthday, Desi plays "gaucho" for his son while Desi's father, Desiderio, supervises.

The Fifth Season: 1955 to 1956

Far more important to the show than the change in sponsors was the addition of two new members of the *I Love Lucy* writing team in the summer between the fourth and fifth season: Bob Schiller and Bob Weiskopf. Like Bob Carroll, Jr., and Madelyn Pugh-Davis, they had cut their comedic teeth on radio sitcoms. Weiskopf had written for almost a decade for the legendary Fred Allen, Schiller for a variety of programs, including *Duffy's Tavern* with Larry Gelbart, future creator and cowriter of *M*A*S*H*.

Lucy lets the kids sample Desi, Jr.'s birthday cake on his first birthday, January 19, 1954.

They couldn't have come along at a better time. By 1955, the show had been on the air for four years and Jess, Bob and Madelyn needed a respite from the grind of cranking out thirty-eight to thirty-nine half-hour scripts per season. On a typical half-hour sitcom today, an average of five to eight writers produce a maximum of twenty-four scripts in a given year, and they also have all the advantages of working in a medium whose guidelines have been established for over forty years.

The fifth season would see the Ricardos and the

In April 1955, the Arnaz family take a ride on the fairway in Palm Springs while Desi looks at land to develop for his Indian Wells Country Club.

Mertzes travel to Europe, with storylines culled from the experiences of Bob Carroll and Madelyn Pugh-Davis, who were dedicated worldwide travelers.

During that first year with Schiller and Weiskopf, Oppenheimer continued in his role as head writer and as the final word, Lucy and Desi aside, on anything involving script and story. The five followed the same procedure that had been established from the beginning. Every Monday the writing crew was locked up in Jess's small office while the idea bank was raided to come up with a situation to build a story around. "There was very little rewriting because of the emphasis on preparation, because we didn't leave the room until a story was right," says Schiller.

The resignation of Jess Oppenheimer to take a five-year contract with NBC was by far the most significant staff departure from the show. Oppenheimer had been a key element in the success of Lucille Ball for seven of her most prolific years, but he felt it was time for him to leave. With almost 130 shows in the can, it seemed to him that they had done practically everything that there was to do. Quite simply, he felt it was getting old. "Let's go off as a champion," he said. "Let's not be one of those shows that gets tired." But everybody disagreed with him.

A deeper reason for his discontent was that he had been unable to fully reconcile his differences with Desi. "Jess and Lucy got along fine," said Bob Schiller, "but Jess continued to feel aggravated by his ongoing dispute with Desi over who was producing the show.

"With Desi it was always a struggle to validate his stature as studio head," says Schiller. "And Jess didn't get the credit that he deserved either. There was enough for both of them, but there's no such thing as stars without egos. Desi found it hard to reconcile that, without Jess, the show wouldn't have been a success. But without Desi, it wouldn't have been a success either; and of course

During the filming of "Bon Voyage," Lucy was suspended more than a hundred feet above the stage, with no net. Though she put a smile on, she was petrified during the scene.

there wouldn't have been a show without Lucy."

The announcement of Oppenheimer's departure, however, seemed to diffuse the situation to a large extent, and the two men reached a new understanding during their last year together as creative heads of the show. Says Schiller: "They had a meeting. Desi proposed, 'Look, we'll do it democratically, because if you and Lucy feel something's right, you and Lucy win.' He said, 'If Lucy and I think something's right, we'll do it democratically; we win.' Jess said, 'Good deal.' But as he's walking out the room, Jess says, 'Wait a minute. Suppose Lucy wants something, and you and I want it another way?' Desi said, 'We'll do it democratically; Lucy wins.'"

Despite Desi's increasing production responsibilities, his self-doubt about not being given enough credit as a producer and the fact that Lucy was the star of the show continued to plague his sense of self-worth. Desilu was on an unprecedented growth curve, but Desi was beginning to drink earlier and earlier each day. Add to this the fact that Lucy's and Desi's day-to-day relationship was relegated more to business than personal or family matters, and it's no surprise that deepening estrangement began to creep in to the marriage.

In the face of all these personal adversities, Desi was still able to

When Charles Boyer came to film "Lucy Meets Charles Boyer," he wore his own clothes and refused to let a squirting pen damage his shirt. The prop department had to demonstrate how disappearing ink worked before he consented to the gag.

direct his young, aggressive staff in developing a slate of television shows like no other production company in town. The studio produced its first motion picture, *Forever Darling*, starring Lucy, Desi and James Mason, and while this would ultimately prove an unsuccessful attempt to enter into motion picture production, the TV side of the studio was growing exponentially. Desilu was producing 295 half-hour television programs, and was paying the salaries of over eight hundred employees during the peak of the season. Said executive Martin Leeds: "We were very lucky—everything we touched did well—we could do no wrong. We were the right people at the right time in the right spot for something that the public wanted."

On March 17, 1956, Lucille Ball accepted her second Emmy for Best Actress, but William Frawley again lost to Art Carney for the third consecutive year, and Vivian Vance wasn't nominated at all. And for the first time *I Love Lucy* didn't finish as the number one show. *The $64,000 Question* edged it out by 1.4 points.

Five reasons why Lucy has endured were locked in a room each week. Left to right: Oppenheimer, Weiskopf, Pugh-Davis, Schiller and Carroll. Schiller: "Lucy scripts were the least rewritten in TV history. We wouldn't leave the room until all the rules of logic applied to the story."

The new writing team, affectionately known as "Three Bobs and a Babe," assembles for a formal photo with their bosses. Left to right: Bob Schiller, Bob Carroll, Jr., Lucy, Desi, Madelyn Pugh-Davis and Bob Weiskopf.

THE SIXTH SEASON: 1956 TO 1957

The major shift in the storyline during the show's sixth season was the Ricardos' move to Connecticut, as well as casting young Richard Keith (Keith Thibodeaux) in the role of Little Ricky at the end of the last season. He had been hired for the part when Desi took one look at him and heard about the youngster's talent on the drums: he had rightly been billed as "The World's Tiniest Professional Drummer" on the Horace Heidt program, *Show Wagon*.

Lucy bids Jess Oppenheimer goodbye after presenting him with her own "Oppie" award at a farewell party.

The Connecticut move was a timely one, because the writers felt they had exhausted every conceivable New York storyline, and a move to the suburbs could supply additional story possibilities without straining credibility. Two new supporting roles were added with the characters of Mr. and Mrs. Ramsey, their new Westport neighbors, portrayed by veteran character actors Frank Nelson and Mary Jane Croft. One additional change was that Ricky Ricardo's success as a bandleader had allowed him to finally buy the Tropicana Club and rename it Club Babalu.

As the studio operation continued to mushroom,

Lucy and Desi prepare to cut their fifteenth wedding anniversary cake before the entire cast and crew after filming "Bon Voyage."

Desilu kept finding itself short of cash, until finally Leeds, along with Lucy's attorney Art Manella, suggested the possible sale of the company's most important asset to CBS: *I Love Lucy*, the complete half-hour package of 179 episodes. CBS agreed to the terms, which proved to be one of the best deals CBS ever signed. For Desilu, it was a landmark capital-gains deal, which the U.S. Treasury Department would never allow to happen again. The net gain for Desilu was four and a half million dollars in cash from CBS. Leeds and Manella calculated that they would net more money from a sale than if Desilu itself tried to syndicate it. Leeds says, "We were growing and we were feeding on ourselves and we needed the money to keep growing. We were the biggest television operation in the world."

Discovered on Horace Heidt's Show Wagon *and billed as "The World's Tiniest Professional Drummer," Richard Keith was cast as Little Ricky because of his astonishing resemblance to Desi.*

At the end of that season, Desi would take on hosting chores at the 1957 Emmy Awards, but it was a ceremony that didn't even acknowledge *I Love Lucy* as a series. Lucy would lose to Nanette Fabray for Best Continuing Performance by a Comedienne in a Series, and both William Frawley and Vivian Vance would lose in their respective Supporting categories.

Despite the fact that *I Love Lucy* was still the top program, with a 43.7 rating, Desi wanted no part of a weekly half-hour *Lucy* series after the close of the season. He felt the half-hour format had become a terrible grind, and he decided to film future shows with the same characters in a series of hour-long programs airing once a month as *The Lucille Ball–Desi Arnaz Show*. As a result of this dramatic programming

Lucy takes time out for her favorite afternoon snack—a peanut butter and jelly sandwich with milk.

change, General Foods decided to drop out as sponsor, citing the price tag of $350,000 per hour as too high and their need to get exposure for their commercials weekly rather than once a month. The network affiliates were equally unenthusiastic about the loss of *I Love Lucy* as a weekly series, and after the public heard the news, Desilu was deluged with calls, telegrams and letters pleading with the couple to change their minds. Of course, they did not.

THE "I LOVE LUCY" HEART "BREAKS"

Lucy had enough to worry about, without having to continue turning out a weekly show. Her marriage was in trouble. "Desi and I didn't seem to enjoy the same kind of leisure activities any more," she recalled later.

"He stopped discussing personal problems, and I'd have to dig to find out what caused his rages," said Lucille. Her attention to the minutae of stage business began to annoy him, and his preoccupation with studio business would lead to clashes on the set.

By now Desi's drinking problem was beginning to affect studio operations in subtle and not so subtle ways. Even Desi was aware of the problem; he sought the advice of longtime friend and physician Dr. Marcus Rabwin, who put him on a schedule designed to help him cut down on his drinking and the workload. Desi's executives managed to keep the studio on a firm course, and despite everything, he still had that spark of genius, that special touch for making the whole enterprise work. Incredible as it may seem, he was still able—in spite of his alcoholic memory lapses—to

Desi Arnaz, Jr., and Richard Keith conga jam with the band during the filming of "The Ricardos Visit Cuba." The two boys grew up together and became surrogate brothers until the early sixties.

The Mertzes arrive at the Ricardos with a Christmas tree. While Fred tries to "shape" the tree, they reminisce about Lucy revealing her pregnancy to Ricky, her barbershop quartet rendition of "Sweet Adeline," and finally the chaotic time when Little Ricky was born. Note: This episode, the "I Love Lucy Christmas Show" (December 24, 1956), is not part of the I Love Lucy syndication package and is only broadcast on "special" Chrismas time slots.

retain almost everything he read and heard, and could recall contract items and entire conversations when he was sober.

Says Martin Leeds: "Psychologically he felt she was the star, and he couldn't handle that. I thought he was a remarkable human being, but he had that hangup. And yet all the way through, she never gave up loving him. He may have loved her, but he couldn't deal with it. What was amazing was that during the later years of the show, it never showed on film. Never."

It wasn't his extramarital behavior that led to his downfall. It was alcohol. During the fifth season, Desi's drinking habits gathered steam, and would, in the final analysis, be the weak link that broke the chain of his career.

"If you wanted to talk to Desi," says Martin Leeds, "you had to talk with him between 8:30 and 10:30 in the morning, because he usually had his first daiquiri by eleven o'clock and wouldn't remember things after that. But you couldn't always bring the subject of drinking up to Desi all the time. We had a great deal of respect for him, so you just had to go along with it and work around it."

The problem was compounded by his need for validation. "He really had gained the respect that he felt he didn't have," says Leeds. "The problem was that he didn't feel it inside." This was also complicated by the fact that when he wasn't being referred to as Lucille Ball's husband, he was often called Ricky Ricardo.

The pressure grew and grew from the fifth season on, and at one point Aitchison remembers asking Desi why he wouldn't slow down. "The more we get, the more money there is," said Desi. "What do you want more money for?" asked Aitchison. "Oh, it's for the kids—the children," said Desi. It wasn't enough.

CHAPTER SIX

THE HOUR SPECIALS

1957 to 1960

THE LUCILLE BALL–DESI ARNAZ SHOW: TAKE ONE

With a June start date, production on *The Lucille Ball–Desi Arnaz Show* (also called the *Lucy-Desi Comedy Hour*) began shortly after the last half-hour episode of *I Love Lucy* wrapped on April 4, 1957. The show found a new sponsor with Ford, which agreed to underwrite the two-and-a-half-million-dollar budget for five specials throughout the coming season.

Five one-hour specials were filmed that season, and while the basic cast remained the same, the character of the show changed in many ways. Though the specials produced many classic moments of television comedy, they lacked the tight-knit quality of the half-hour episodes. And with the new hour format and the emphasis on guest stars, the roles of Ethel and Fred Mertz grew increasingly limited. This caused no problem for Frawley, who welcomed the lighter work load, but Vivian Vance viewed the change with animosity. In an effort to placate her, Desi first proposed a Fred and Ethel Mertz spin-off, but she wanted no part of it.

It has become part of the *I Love Lucy* lore that Vivian Vance and William Frawley disliked each other offstage. Frawley limited his conversations with Vance to the logistics of stage direction, and little else. They never talked backstage, and he would refer to Vance in a variety of colorful epithets and off-color remarks. Vance was up to the challenge, and returned many of his volleys—most of them equally bawdy. She used to thumb through the script before the first reading to find

The screen time for Fred and Ethel's characters was reduced during the Lucy-Desi Comedy Hours. Frawley liked the lighter work load, but Vance resented the change.

out how many scenes she would have alone with him. "I used to pray," she once admitted, "that I wouldn't have to climb in bed with that square-headed little Irishman."

The first hour-long show, "Lucy Takes a Cruise to Havana," was a flashback story that detailed how Lucille McGillicuddy—her maiden name— met Ricky Ricardo on a cruise to Cuba. The second special teamed Lucy and Ricky with the unpredictable Tallulah Bankhead, who stirred up the staff with her erratic rehearsal style. The backstage escapades during the remaining episodes—"Lucy Hunts Uranium," with Fred MacMurray and wife June Haver, "Lucy Wins a Racehorse," featuring Betty Grable and husband Harry James, and "Lucy Goes to Sun Valley," with Fernando Lamas—were not nearly so eventful.

After the Sun Valley episode wrapped, Bob Carroll and Madelyn Pugh-Davis decided to call it quits on generating further stories for the Lucy and Ricky characters. They felt they were creatively played out and needed a break, so despite a three-year contract that had another full year to go, Desi generously granted them the time away, while Schiller and Weiskopf took over the creative reins on the show.

Lucy cuddles Desi, Jr., just before a scene in the 1958 Lucy-Desi Comedy Hour special, "Lucy Wins a Racehorse."

Desilu Buys RKO

With all the production space that Desilu was now using, it needed more, and an opportunity came along in September of 1957 that would make the company a very big major studio. Desi had already turned down a twelve-million-dollar bid to sell Desilu Productions, but he needed more capital to expand further into production. The company had already racked up an incredible 534 hours of filmed television product, and projected an average yearly output of 222 hours of film, roughly the equivalent of 148 full-length motion picture features. Desilu also owned a controlling interest in Motion Picture Center and a highly profitable commercial production unit churning out advertisements for forty national brand-name products.

With four and a half million dollars in his pocket from the sale of *I Love Lucy* to CBS the previous year, and his Motion Picture Center bursting at the seams, the next natural move for Desi was for more room to operate. In September of 1957, Desilu executive Martin Leeds received a call from a senior executive at RKO who told him he had heard Desilu was looking for more space. He said RKO was willing to sell their facility for six and a half million dollars—and he needed an answer the next day to offset a capital gains tax crisis.

Desi offered 6.1 million dollars, and the deal closed within the twenty-four-hour deadline. While the deal didn't include the valuable RKO film library, it gave Desilu the right to call itself the largest owner of Hollywood film production real estate in the world: thirty-five sound stages at three separate locations, eleven more than Fox and four more than MGM—a total of over sixty-five acres.

Lucy-Desi Comedy Hour: Take Two

"Lucy Goes to Mexico" kicked off the eighth season, with Maurice Chevalier as the guest star and Desi as the host of their

Lucy and Desi complete the paperwork to acquire the RKO Studios from General Tire & Rubber Company. RKO's Dan O'Shea (pictured) completed the deal for Chairman Thomas O'Neil.

Life had come full circle for Lucy as she toured the backlot of Desilu Studios in 1957: after starting out as a seventy-five-dollar-a-week RKO contract player in the thirties, she now owned the studio— Hollywood's largest chunk of real estate.

first show under a new title: *Westinghouse Desilu Playhouse*. A pet project of Desi's, based on the prestigious *Studio One* concept, it would include serious hour-long dramas in addition to the *Lucy-Desi Comedy Hours*.

Four more *Comedy Hours* would round out the 1958 to 1959 season. "Lucy Makes Room for Danny" was a clever blending of the Danny Thomas television family with the Ricardo family in a domestic squabble plot. "Lucy Goes to Alaska" was highlighted by a wonderful Lucille Ball–Red Skelton pantomime sketch with Skelton's Freddie the Freeloader character, reminiscent of Lucy's classic pairing with Harpo Marx during the half-hour series. "Lucy Wants a Career" paired Lucy with character actor Paul Douglas, and "Lucy's Summer Vacation" featured Howard Duff and wife Ida Lupino in another domestic romp set in a Vermont lodge. The five *Lucy-Desi Comedy Hours* all ranked in the top five of the seventy specials the three networks aired during the season. But the other shows under the *Desilu Playhouse* banner, though critical successes, were ratings disappointments, and the series ended up twenty-fourth in the Nielsens.

Despite the ratings failure of *Playhouse*, Desi had reason to celebrate when Desilu went public in December of 1958. The official reason was to acquire more capital for further expansion, and although this was true, the real reason was to satisfy Desilu's debt to Bank of America, which had lent Desi 1.6 million dollars and was pressuring him to pay it back. So on November 11, 1958, the company announced it had filed with the Securities and Exchange Commission for a public offering of 525,000 shares of common stock. They were all snatched up on opening day—December 3—and rose quickly from ten dollars a share to fifteen dollars. It was an extremely successful offering.

THE FINAL CURTAIN

The public offering was an extremely difficult undertaking, and after the last *Lucy-Desi Comedy Hour* wrapped, Lucille Ball and Desi Arnaz needed a rest. On May 13, 1959, they sailed for Europe on the liner *Liberté* with Lucie, Desi, Jr., Lucy's cousin Cleo and her husband Ken Morgan. "It was just a nightmare," Cleo recalled. "Desi was falling down drunk everywhere, and in France Desi became 'Mister Ball' and 'the Cuban.' He did not draw a sober breath. He chased everything in heels."

Lucy had looked forward to London, but she was so incensed at the way Desi was acting and the rude way she was treated by the tabloid press at her first conference, that it set the tone for the remainder of the trip. "That same day, I decided to divorce Desi," she recalled. "He disapproved of my moderation and my conservatism. I disapproved of the way he worked too hard, played too hard and was never moderate in anything."

After returning from Europe, Lucy took solace in the one thing that had given her so much satisfaction: her work. They had to film three more *Lucy-Desi Comedy Hour*s, and she started looking for a possible Broadway vehicle. Desi, meanwhile, was spending less and less time in their Roxbury house and began taking residence at the Chateau Marmont, a well-known hideaway for the rich and famous.

The first *Lucy-Desi* special for the new season, "Milton Berle Hides Out at the Ricardos," was filmed without a studio audience, in an effort to limit already heightened tensions on the set. For the first time, Desi also stepped in as director, and he wasn't easy on himself or others during the shoot. When he wasn't on the set, working himself into a veritable frenzy, he would go to his office and conduct Desilu business with a vengeance, allowing himself no downtime at all.

By the time Desi took over directing chores again on the twelfth of their thirteen *Lucy-Desi*

Lucie Arnaz manages to get some time with her parents as Maurice Chevalier looks on during filming of "Lucy Goes to Mexico."

specials, "The Ricardos Go to Japan," with guest star Robert Cummings, it was increasingly difficult for the couple to continue working together. Though it wasn't officially over, their marriage was in essence finished, and Lucille was overwrought with anguish. Close friend Carole Cook remembers: "She was playing a geisha with the white, white makeup, and she had been crying a lot. The eyes were extremely red. It gave her what I thought was a grotesque, sad look."

The thirteenth episode, filmed in March of 1960, would mark the last time Lucille Ball and Desi Arnaz would appear professionally together in front of a camera. "Lucy Meets the Moustache" was the final *Lucy-Desi Comedy Hour*, starring another husband-and-wife combination, the legendary Ernie Kovacs and his wife, Edie Adams. It was a difficult shoot. Although there were none of the shouting matches that took place at previous rehearsals, an undertone of uneasiness and tension pervaded the set, and again there were moments when Lucille broke down and cried.

In his autobiography, Desi recalled the moment: "Doing that last *Lucy-Desi Comedy Hour* was not easy. We knew it was the last time we would be Lucy and Ricky. As fate would have it, the very last scene in that story called for a long clinch and a kiss-and-make-up ending. As we got to it, we looked at each other, embraced and kissed. This was not just an ordinary kiss for a scene in a show. It was a kiss that would wrap up twenty years of love and friendship, triumphs and failures, ecstasy and sex, jealousy and regrets, heartbreaks and laughter—and tears."

"In the final scene," remembered

By the time "The Ricardos Go to Japan" was shot, her marriage to Desi was ending. Friend Carole Cook remembers: "She was playing a geisha with white makeup, and her eyes were red from crying."

An intense presence on the set, Desi Arnaz finally took over as director in 1959 in the final season of the <u>Lucy-Desi Comedy Hour</u>.

Lucy, "Desi was supposed to pull me into his embrace and kiss me while saying tenderly, 'After this, Lucy, remember you can help me most by not helping me.' When the cameras closed in for that final embrace and curtain line, I started to cry. We shot it over and over until everyone was misty-eyed. It marked the end of so many things."

"After the kiss," wrote Desi, "we just stood there looking at each other and licking the salt. Then Lucy said, 'You're supposed to say "Cut."' 'I know. Cut, goddamn it!'"

The next morning, March 3, 1960, Lucille filed for divorce on the grounds of mental cruelty in Santa Monica Superior Court. Though the divorce hit the nation's media like a bombshell, the couple had long since reconciled themselves to the situation, and were nearly amicable about the separation. There was virtually no bickering about property or business matters, and Desi was given unrestricted visitation rights to the children. "It was an easy divorce to litigate," recalled attorney Art Manella. "It was not rancorous or adversarial. They had already agreed on many of the key issues by the time it had reached the legal system."

Thirty-three years later, when Lucie Arnaz reflected on her parents' final day together as a professional team as husband and wife, she was stunned to realize that this last day in front of the cameras was not only Desi's forty-third birthday, but also nine years to the day after the *I Love Lucy* pilot had been produced. It had all come full circle, though not the way everyone had wished so long ago.

The dreams that began so brightly had all been realized, but now they were over. Lucy and Desi had achieved their dream of working together. They had been successful far beyond their wildest hopes. But they had paid the price. The heart that framed the words *I Love Lucy* was finally breaking.

Ernie Kovacs's humorous presence on the set of "Lucy Meets the Moustache," the final TV appearance of the Ricardos, was appreciated by the Arnazes. Although the couple had already agreed to a divorce and had worked out an amicable settlement, the final days in front of the camera were emotionally draining.

CHAPTER SEVEN

LIFE AFTER LUCY

The laughter had died and the smiles were gone. Ricky and Lucy Ricardo and Fred and Ethel Mertz had had their last adventure. Their real-life counterparts, though, moved on.

Though he was divorced from Lucy, Desi continued in his role as president of Desilu. He and his team had built it into a corporate giant producing dozens of popular television programs that continued well into the sixties. Among them were *The Ann Sothern Show*, *The Danny Thomas Show*, *December Bride*, *The Dick Van Dyke Show*, *Harrigan and Son*, *The Life and Times of Wyatt Earp*, *My Three Sons*, *Our Miss Brooks*, *The Real McCoys*, *The Texan*, *Those Whiting Girls*, *The Untouchables* and *Whirlybirds*, and later, *Mannix*, *Mission: Impossible* and the landmark *Star Trek*. Desi continued as chief executive until 1962, when Lucy bought out his twenty-five percent ownership for an estimated three million dollars, invoking a buyout clause because it was increasingly difficult to run the studio effectively with Desi's escalating alcohol-related problems. By default, she became the first and—to date—the only woman ever to own a major motion picture studio.

On the day Desi finally left the studio for the last time, he walked into his office and the only thing that he took with him, observed Johny Aitchison, was a little photo cube on the desk with pictures of his children in it.

Except for 1963, when the company lost over a half-million dollars, Desilu continued to show a profit until the stu-

In order to get as far away as possible from her life in Los Angeles, Lucy went to New York in 1960 to star in the Broadway musical Wildcat! It was a hit, but ill health forced her to drop out, which shut down the show permanently.

In 1966 Lucy won her second Emmy. It had been thirteen years since she won her first Emmy. The win caught her completely off guard and, when accepting, she confessed that she hadn't prepared any acceptance speech. She would win another one—her last one—the following year.

Lucy and Vivian Vance were reunited in The Lucy Show, *which ran from 1962 to 1968.*

In 1968 Here's Lucy *premiered on CBS with Lucy's real-life daughter, Lucie Arnaz, and son, Desi Arnaz, Jr., portraying her fictional offspring. The show ran for six years.*

dio and all its properties were sold to Gulf + Western industries on February 15, 1967, and became part of the Paramount Pictures studio lot. Desilu passed into history.

Still under contract after the last *Lucy-Desi* show, William Frawley landed the role of Bub on *My Three Sons* with Fred MacMurray. The show was extremely successful and provided him with continued work, until ill health forced him to retire after five years with the show. On March 3, 1966, he collapsed on Hollywood Boulevard after leaving a movie theater and was pronounced dead from heart failure.

Vivian Vance rejoined Lucille Ball in 1962 on *The Lucy Show*, which remained on the air for six years. After that, she limited her acting to annual guest appearances with Lucy on *Here's Lucy* and the final hour special, "Lucy Calls the President," in 1977. She divorced Phil Ober in 1959, and her subsequent marriage to literary agent John Dodds provided her with stability and happiness for the rest of her life. She died on August 17, 1979, after a long battle with cancer.

After leaving Desilu, Desi Arnaz divided his time between his Corona horse-breeding ranch and his Del Mar retreat. On his birthday in 1963, he married the ex-wife of millionaire sportsman Clement Hirsch, Edith Mack Hirsch,

with whom he spent the rest of his life. Several years later, he formed Desi Arnaz Productions and bankrolled several television pilots. Only one sold, in 1967: *The Mothers-In-Law*, starring Eve Arden and Kaye Ballard, and written by Bob Carroll and Madelyn Pugh-Davis during its two-year run on NBC. In 1974 Desi wrote his autobiography, *A Book*, which surfaced on the best-seller charts and was subsequently successful in paperback. Plans for another book, entitled *Another Book*, never materialized. After a three-year battle with cancer, Edith passed away in 1985. Desi spent his remaining time struggling with alcohol and, with the help of his son, who had conquered his own chemical dependency problems, he finally stopped drinking entirely. Though this gave him some quality time, the years of abuse had taken their toll. The last time he talked to Lucy was on November 30, 1986, forty-six years after they first exchanged vows. He died at the age of sixty-nine on December 2, 1986, with his daughter, Lucie, cradling him in her arms.

Mame received mixed reviews, and although box office sales were so-so, it would have been far less successful without Lucy.

After a stint on Broadway with the mildly successful musical *Wildcat!* Lucille Ball returned to television in two hit television series—first *The Lucy Show* with Vivian Vance, and then *Here's Lucy*, costarring her old chum, character actor Gale Gordon and her children Lucie Arnaz and Desi Arnaz, Jr. After *Here's Lucy*, she also made several hour-long specials with such guest stars as Jackie Gleason, Dean Martin and Art Carney, and in 1976 a CBS retrospective, *Lucy: The First 25 Years*. In 1986, she attempted to make a sitcom comeback in *Life With Lucy*, but the ratings that came so easily in years past eluded her on this outing. She would also make four more motion pictures, *Critic's Choice* (1963) with Bob Hope, *A Guide for the Married Man* (1967) with Walter Matthau, *Yours, Mine and Ours* (1968) with Henry Fonda and the film version of the Broadway musical *Mame* (1974), in which she played the title role. She also made one highly acclaimed movie for television, *The Stone Pillow* (1985), in which she portrayed a feisty bag lady. With a total of thirteen Emmy nominations, she won four, and in 1984 was among the first seven stars inducted into the Television Hall of Fame. Two years later she received the Kennedy Center Honors, the nation's highest honor for performing arts.

On April 26, 1989, while recovering from surgery to correct cardiopulmonary problems, Lucy died unexpectedly at Cedars-Sinai Hospital of a ruptured aorta. The news of her death generated a media tempest that rivaled the death of a head of state. Headlines distilled the message to two words: LUCY DIES. It was the lead story in every news broadcast, and regular programming was preempted with extended news reports on her life and career. The world hadn't experienced such grief over the death of an entertainer since the assassination of John Lennon. Special memorial masses were held in Los Angeles, New York and Chicago, and with pews filled to capacity, special loudspeakers were set up for those outside to hear the ceremony.

For days and weeks afterward, eulogistic prose inundated the media. President George Bush issued a statement: "Lucille Ball possessed the gift of laughter. But she also embodied an even greater treasure—the gift of love. She appealed to the gentler impulses of the human spirit. She was not merely an actress or a comedian. She was 'Lucy' and she was loved." *Los Angeles Times* arts editor Charles Champlin wrote: "The cameras have X-ray properties, and the millions who saw and loved her were not wrong to think they perceived a generous and loving woman, as well as a glorious clown who knew the world was better off laughing."

But a *New York Post* editorial summed it up best: "*I Love Lucy* ran for only six years and Lucille Ball starred in a lot of good TV shows, in films and on Broadway. But if she had ended her career when *I Love Lucy* ended its run, she'd have died famous. One reason has to do with timing: Lucille Ball helped inaugurate the age of television just as surely as Charlie Chaplin helped inaugurate the age of movies. A second reason has to do with timelessness: Nowhere is *I Love Lucy* more honored than in its enduringly popular reruns. The shenanigans of Lucy, Ricky and their best friends, Fred and Ethel, are as fresh and funny today to their third generation of viewers as they were to their first."

To this day, *I Love Lucy* remains not only the most popular situation comedy of all time, but also the most well-conceived and well-executed sitcom ever created for the small screen. When *I Love Lucy* debuted, the public was used to the outrageous tomfoolery of Milton Berle and Red Skelton, but Lucille's antics were packaged in a skillfully plotted story with characters the audience came to care about. It was a melting pot of popular entertainment forms—in addition to situation comedy, there were vaudeville shticks and entertaining musical numbers, created by people from every segment of the entertainment business: theater, motion pictures, live television, radio, vaudeville and burlesque. But most of all, it had the core relationship of an American couple from dissimilar backgrounds who loved each other dearly. Everyone believed that no matter what Lucy did, no matter how crazy her schemes, Desi would keep loving her.

The Desilu publicity offices would routinely get letters from husbands and wives who would write in to say that the show had saved their marriages. The incredible irony here is that, in giving the public that kind of gift, they lost their own marriage in the process.

Desi was philosophical about the loss of the marriage and the success of the show. At the end of his book, he said: "If we hadn't done anything else but bring that half-hour of fun, pleasure, and relaxation to most of the world, a world in such dire need of even that short time-out from its problems and sorrows, we should be content."

The linchpin of the whole phenomenon, though, was the luminous presence of Lucille Ball.

A striking study of the beautiful, wistful clown who made the whole world laugh.

4

Chorus, Brightly

I LOVE LU - CY and she loves me,____

We're as hap-py as two can be,____ Some - times we

quar-rel but then____ How we love mak-ing

up a - gain.____ Lu - cy kiss - es like no one can,____

960-3

Song continues on page 270

PART TWO

Thirty-five Classic Episodes

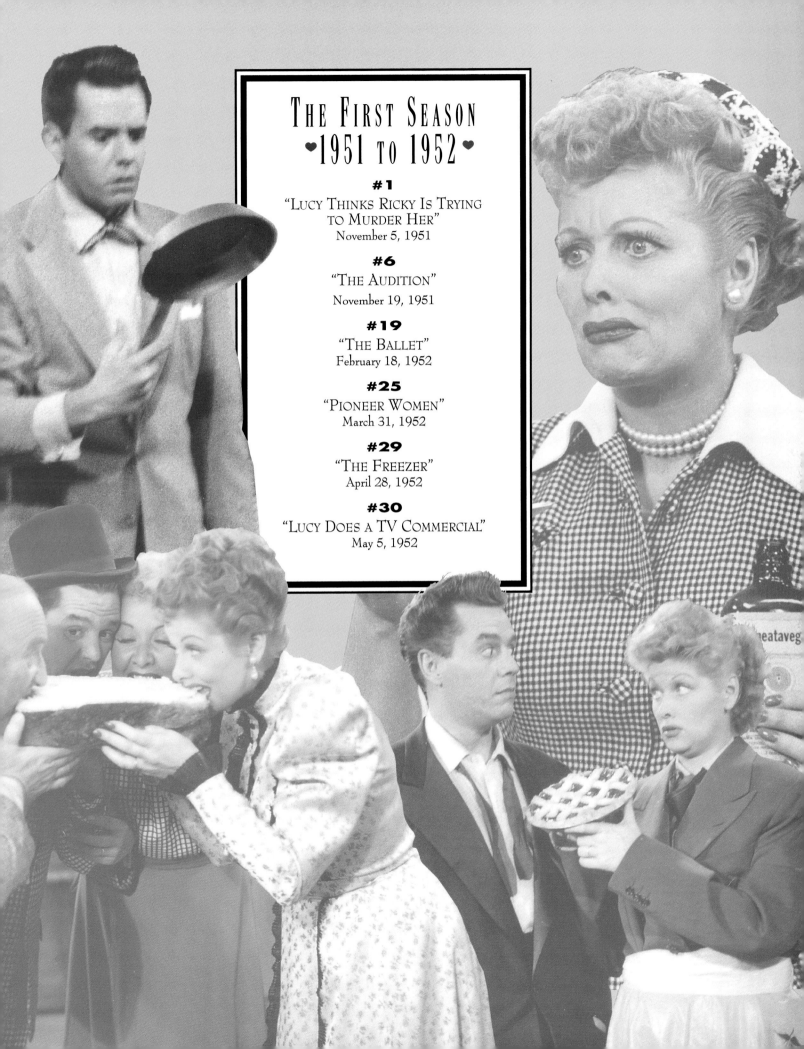

THE FIRST SEASON
♥ 1951 TO 1952 ♥

#1
"LUCY THINKS RICKY IS TRYING
TO MURDER HER"
November 5, 1951

#6
"THE AUDITION"
November 19, 1951

#19
"THE BALLET"
February 18, 1952

#25
"PIONEER WOMEN"
March 31, 1952

#29
"THE FREEZER"
April 28, 1952

#30
"LUCY DOES A TV COMMERCIAL"
May 5, 1952

"LUCY THINKS RICKY IS TRYING TO MURDER HER"

*L*ucy's obsession with the plot of a murder thriller, *The Mockingbird Murder Mystery*, convinces her that Ricky is about to bump her off.

THE MOCKING-BIRD MURDER MYSTERY

One evening just before bedtime, Lucy has her head buried in a mystery, oblivious to the world around her. Ricky startles her, causing Lucy to throw the book out of the window. He mocks her jumpiness by acting out the imaginary murder of a wife by her husband. Lucy almost forgets the incident until Ethel reveals her newest pastime—fortune-telling. Armed with her deck of cards, she tells Lucy's fortune, and finds death in the future.

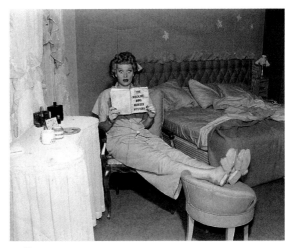

Lucy's imagination starts working overtime as she scares herself silly reading The Mockingbird Murder Mystery.

Later, when she overhears Ricky talking on the phone, Lucy's apprehension escalates into full-blown hysteria when she hears such phrases as "I'm going to get rid of her," "She's been with me a long time—too long," "I'll get another one in the next couple of weeks," and finally, "The gun? I've got it right here in my desk drawer…"

He reaches into the drawer where the "gun" is, grabs something and slams it shut. Hearing the slam, Lucy thinks it's a gunshot, and drops onto the couch. Ricky leaves, and Lucy checks herself for wounds. The entire conversation, of course, was nothing more than Ricky telling his agent about replacing a singer at the club, booking a dog act and getting a novelty gun for a Western skit.

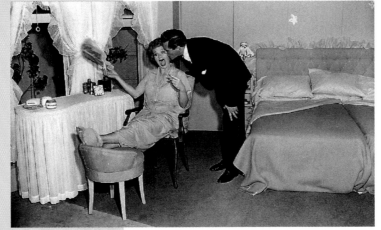

Buried deep in her thriller, Lucy doesn't notice Ricky's arrival, and she's so startled when he kisses her that she throws the book out of the window.

Panic-stricken, Lucy screams for Ethel, and picks up the pad Ricky was writing on to find out what he has in store for her. She reads the names of the dogs: "Ann, Mary…oh, I'm not even cold and Ricky's lining up girls to take my place," she surmises. Continuing: "Helen, Cynthia, Alice and…Theodore. Theodore! Who's Theodore?"

Later, just before Ricky comes home, Lucy shows Ethel the pots and pans she has draped over her for protection. Ethel ducks out of the back door as Ricky walks in. Lucy goes into a "dodge dance" so that he can't get a bead on her, then runs into the bedroom and locks the door. "Lucy seems to have some idea that I'm going to kill her," Ricky tells Fred. "Sooner or later, every wife decides that her husband

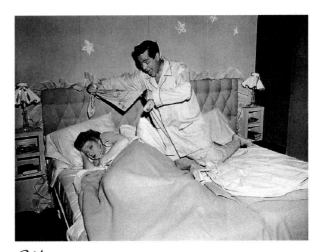

When she tries to prevail on a tired Ricky to go outside and get the book, he playacts a husband's "murder" of his wife because she wouldn't let him sleep.

The next morning, Ethel reveals her newest pastime: fortune-telling with a deck of cards. Dealing Lucy a hand, she finds "death" in her future.

Ricky tells his agent what he plans to do with a girl singer at the club: "I'm going to get rid of her." Overhearing, Lucy thinks he's going to murder her.

Lucy falls to a chair, convinced that Ricky's tried to shoot her, but the "shot" was a drawer slamming after he pulls out the prop gun he's using for an act.

After Ricky leaves, Lucy and Ethel look for bullet holes, but the fact that they don't find any doesn't dissuade Lucy from believing her life is in danger.

Distraught, Lucy reads a note Ricky left behind with what she believes is a list of women to replace her. But she's puzzled at the name "Theodore."

In a feeble attempt to protect herself from Ricky's "murder" plot, Lucy shows Ethel how she plans to safeguard her vital parts from a frontal assault . . . or a rear attack.

With Ricky coming in the front door, Lucy pleads with Ethel to stay with her to keep him from killing her.

Running to hide, Lucy leaves a trail of pots and pans—and a puzzled Ricky—behind in the living room.

wants to kill her," says Fred. "She's usually right."

Fred gives Ricky a sedative for Lucy, but she sees him put the pill in her drink and assumes it's poison. Offering to dance with Ricky, she switches the cups while his head is turned. While *her* head is turned, he switches them back. When he starts to drink, she stops him—she can't bear to see him die. He tells her he saw what she did and switched them back again. Realizing she has drunk the "poison," she plays out an elaborate "death" scene. Convinced the sedative has taken effect, Ricky leaves for work.

Assuming Lucy has expired, Ethel is scared into the middle of next week when her friend wakes up and announces, "I got a Mickey from Ricky." Finally she can't stand it anymore—she picks up the gun from the drawer and marches down to the Tropicana to confront him. There she sees the dogs—Ann, Mary, Helen, Cynthia, Alice and Theodore—and finds out the "gun" is one of those prop models that shoots out a flag reading "Bang." The case is solved and Lucy is guilty—of an overactive imagination.

Ricky puts a sedative in Lucy's drink, and she thinks it's poison. After a game of "switcheroo," she's afraid he's about to drink it and tries to stop him.

With the prop "gun" in hand, Lucy goes to confront Ricky at the club, only to find him with Ann, Mary, Helen, Cynthia, Alice and Theodore—the dog act!

"THE AUDITION"

*I*n a desperate ploy to get into show business, Lucy finds out that a TV talent scout will be at Ricky's club, so she takes the place of Boffo the Clown in a burlesque skit.

Lucy tries to sell herself as a model to pitch a sponsor's product, but Ricky says he just wants a wife who'll clean house, bring his slippers, cook and be the "mama of my children." But she won't give up, and continues to extol her talents as a showgirl, a singer, a dancer and a jokester.

Ricky leaves her to answer the door, where Fred hands him a telegram informing him that a network television talent scout will be at the club that evening. To keep Lucy from finding out, he hatches a plan: he needs his will to be taken down to the attorney's office, and if he can persuade Lucy to do it, that errand will keep her out of the way.

After Fred leaves, Lucy comes in wearing a lampshade, and with her usual tone-deaf delivery, warbles "A Pretty Girl Is Like a Melody," ending her showgirl stroll with a pelvic bump, causing Ricky's cigarettes to literally jump out of their container. He stops her with a firm and final "No!"

He tells her about the will that needs to be signed, and she finally agrees to make the trek.

Down at the Tropicana, Ricky is having nothing but trouble. While rehearsing a burlesque skit, Boffo the Clown flies off his bicycle and, since he's a bit shaken up, Ricky sends him to rest at the Ricardo apartment before the show. When Lucy comes home to find Boffo, he tells her about the TV talent scout. When he's trying out his bicycle again, and vaults headfirst into the kitchen door, he becomes so addled that he suggests Lucy take his place on the show. Reaching into Boffo's bag of trick props, Lucy schemes her own brand of revenge on her husband.

After a scorching rendition of "Babalu," Ricky is about to wind up the show when Lucy enters in Boffo's baggy pants and an old hat. He recognizes her beneath the clothes, of course, as

Lucy begins to pester Ricky about being part of the act while he's trying to get ready for his show.

To enhance his chances at getting a break on television, Ricky hires Boffo, a vaudeville clown, to add comedy to the show, but Boffo's injured in rehearsal.

Ricky sends Boffo to his apartment, but Boffo takes a header into the Ricardo kitchen door trying to reprise a difficult skit on a bicycle.

As Ricky performs a searing rendition of "Babalu," he's unaware that Boffo's out of the show and is beside himself that the clown hasn't shown up.

*T*hen Lucy arrives carrying a cello, dressed up in an ill-fitting suit, asking to see "Risky Riskerdough." "I want to be in the band," she says.

*F*rom the cello she's been carrying, she pulls out a small chair, then starts to remove her gloves, pulling and pulling and pulling . . .

*U*sing a toilet plunger to hold up the cello, Lucy "plays" the instrument, but the band mercifully drowns her out.

*R*icky tells her he doesn't need a cellist, but she's got a job if she can play a new instrument they've added to the band: a "saxo-vibro-trumpa-phonavich."

*L*ucy plops down on her knees, shuffles over to the instrument like a seal and proceeds to play "How Dry I Am" with her nose.

*A*fterward, as she claps her hands and barks at him, Ricky offers her a fish to coax her off the stage.

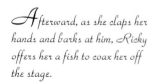

she strolls over to him and asks if he knows a bandleader named "Risky Riskerdough." She's looking for a job with the band, and to prove it pulls out a preposterous-looking cello that appears to have come from the Rube Goldberg school of music. Planting the instrument on the floor with a toilet plunger, she draws the bow across the strings and watches it fly like an arrow across the stage, barely missing the seat of Ricky's pants.

When Ricky returns home later, he's annoyed that she was offered a TV contract.

Before she can do any more damage, he stops her and says he has an instrument she *can* play: a "saxo-vibro-trumpa-phonavich." As the instrument is whisked out onstage—it resembles a row of horns used in a seal act—Lucy drops to her knees, waddles over to it like a seal and plays "How Dry I Am."

The audience roars with enthusiasm, and when Ricky comes home after the show, he's miffed that the contract was offered to Lucy, not to him. But she tells him she's turning it down, and joyfully says she'll stick to her wifely duties.

"The Audition" was a television version of Lucy's and Desi's famous nightclub/vaudeville routine, and became their pilot episode for *I Love Lucy*, as well as the sixth episode in the series after it went on the air.

Lucy brings out a fresh pie from the oven and says she's sorry she caused trouble.

Massaging his feet, she says she turned down the offer and just wants to be his wife.

"THE BALLET"

Determined to wangle her way onto the roster of performers at Ricky's club, Lucy puts herself through a punishing session of ballet and an even more punishing rehearsal with a rowdy burlesque comic.

Lucy is at it again: she wants to break into show business, and Ricky is trying to keep a lid on it. But he needs a ballet dancer—so Lucy declares her expertise in ballet. He also needs a burlesque comic to balance out a program of music and dance.

To win a spot in a ballet number at the club, Lucy signs up for lessons.

Lucy signs up for a ballet class under the stern eye of Madame Lamonde, who happens to be staging Ricky's ballet number. Armed with her formidable baton, the madame cuts an imposing figure as Lucy tries her best to keep up with the exercises, but her legs seem to have a mind of their own as they wobble and wiggle all over the floor. At one point Lucy's legs kick into a Charleston that turns into a high-step shuffle, cheapening the entire exercise.

Although Lucy claims she's been classically trained, she has trouble keeping up.

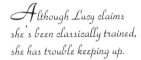

With haughty indignation, Madame Lamonde dismisses the class except for Lucy, and suggests that they "go to the barre." "Oh good, 'cause I'm awful thirsty," says Lucy, brightening up. Says the madame, pointing to the exercise barre, "*This* barre." She points the dreaded baton at Lucy and announces: "Your posture is atrocious. Now—shoulders back, hips under, stomach in, chest out, chin out, knees straight. Now, remembering all these things, raise your right leg even with the barre."

Breaking into a hoe-down high-step . . .

Lucy manages to do it in one motion, but she finds her leg stuck in the barre. "Leg down slowly—À bas!" she commands. Lucy repeats the litany louder and louder, commanding her foot to obey, like a recalcitrant pet. In utter frustration, she finally hits her leg, grabs at her toes—and her leg falls through between the wall and the barre. Now she is really stuck. In one final move, she tries to extricate herself, only to slip completely through, causing her to turn completely upside down and dangle like a monkey from the barre while Madame looks on in consternation. Finally Madame orders her to perform five hundred *pliés*, performed to the rhythm of her baton.

Exhausted, Lucy decides that a burlesque act might be easier, so she hires a clown comic to teach her the old "Slowly I Turn" routine. They rehearse, Lucy feeding him lines, and every time Lucy mentions

. . . she twirls out of control and . . . stops the class in its tracks.

The formidable Madame Lamonde steps in to bring Lucy in line with the class . . .

. . . but our bowlegged ballerina's posture prompts ridicule.

Lucy finds her leg has a mind of its own . . .

. . . as it snakes through the barre and makes a monkey out of her.

Her ballet career in a shambles, Lucy decides to become a clown and hires a professional to teach her the old "Slowly I turn, step by step . . ." routine.

Unfortunately, she winds up on the receiving end of his shtick. Every time she utters the name "Martha," he lets her have it. First a rubber bag on the head, then a shot of seltzer . . .

. . . and finally a custard pie she's had cooling on the table finds its mark.

the name of a long-lost wife, Martha, the comic goes into a well-rehearsed frenzy. "Slowly I turn," he says, "step by step, inch by inch, I crept up on the beast that had ruined my life. I looked around for a rock and let him have it." He proceeds to clobber Lucy with his rubber-bag prop. Every time thereafter, when Lucy mentions the name Martha, she gets it again, first a seltzer bottle squirt and finally a pie in the face.

Ethel calls Lucy to tell her that Ricky just hired a couple of burlesque comics. Discouraged, she decides to stay home while Fred and Ethel join Ricky at his opening. But when Ethel phones to tell her that Ricky is having a problem with one of his performers —a ballet dancer—Lucy mistakenly believes that he needs a burlesque comic.

She arrives to find Ricky singing the song "Martha" with the ballet dancers. Thinking she's the comic relief, she makes herself part of the number, hitting the dancers with the rubber bag, squirting them with seltzer and finally, at the conclusion, when she's picked up by the dancers and carried across the stage, she grabs the pie she brought along, and lets Ricky have it in the kisser.

He's waiting for Lucy when she comes home: as she walks in the door, a bucket of water falls on her while Ricky looks on with satisfaction.

"The Ballet" demonstrates Lucille Ball's range in performing distinctly different aspects of comedy. Lucy's leg slipping through the barre space during the ballet wasn't planned, but that little accident created a clever bit of physical improvisation that came off very well. She had an uncanny knack for a variety of physical skills that allowed her to practice the routines of many trades. Desi was always in awe of Lucy's talent and frequently, during a particularly outlandish bit of tomfoolery, his distinctive laugh could be heard over the audience laugh track—listen carefully after Lucy gets the pie in the face, and you can hear it.

With ballet and burlesque confused, Lucy breaks into a classic dance number at the club and . . .

. . . she wreaks havoc while performing to the song "Martha."

Finally, at the end of the number, Ricky utters the name "Martha" one more time and Lucy lets him have it right in the kisser.

But he has the last laugh: when Lucy returns home later, the bucket of water he's rigged over the door cascades over his burlesque bride.

"PIONEER WOMEN"

The girls corner their spouses into a wager that takes the two couples back before the turn of the century, steering clear of modern appliances—except for an oven that produces a colossal loaf of bread.

Lucy and Ethel march into the living room and declare "We're revolting." "No more than usual," is Ricky's predictable reply. Their complaint about kitchen chores all leads up to a request for an automatic dishwasher. After his usual negative response, Ricky reminds Lucy that their grandmothers were able to do all the household work without any modern conveniences. This prompts a bet between the boys and the girls: the first one who resorts to using an appliance made after 1900—a utensil, a piece of clothing or anything else—loses the bet.

Lucy is fixing breakfast for Ricky, nineteenth-century style—an ungodly mixture of coffee grounds and eggshells—when Fred tells Ethel that they're out of butter. As Ethel heads for the door to go to the store, Lucy tells her to pick up a loaf of bread. Ricky and Fred remind their wives that—under the rules of the bet—the butter needs to be churned and the bread needs to be homebaked.

Later in the kitchen, Lucy is knee-deep in bread dough, and Ethel points out that she used ten times the yeast needed in her bread recipe. They shrug it off, set the bowl down near the oven to let the dough rise and leave to work with Ethel's butter churn. When they come back, the dough has risen to three or four times its original size. They wrestle it into a baking tin, put it in the oven, leave the kitchen and start a round of canasta to pass the time.

During one canasta hand, a telegram arrives informing the girls that they're going to be "scrutinized" at a tea the next day for possible entry into the Society Matrons' League. The girls are thrilled.

Lucy's nose detects that the bread might be ready. Entering the kitchen, she sees the oven door is ajar. She opens the door. And out it comes. Bread. More bread. Eighteen feet of it. Lucy backs up before the advancing loaf. She winds up trapped between the end of the bread and the kitchen cabinet on the opposite side of the room.

The bread affair behind them, Lucy plans to declare herself a

Lucy: "We're revolting." With that defiant declaration, Lucy demands an automatic dishwasher, but it's met with the predictable response.

After discussing their reliance on modern wares, the four agree on a husband vs. wife wager: The first party who uses anything made after 1900 loses $50.

The first casualty of the bet is Ricky's face after shaving with a straight razor. With apprehension he watches Lucy concoct coffee—nineteenth-century style.

The rules also require the girls to make homemade bread, but soon they're wrestling with rising dough . . .

. . . and Ethel has to use her head to bring it under control.

A telegram from the Society Matrons' League informs the girls that they're being considered for entry, but they'll have to be "scrutinized" first.

Back in the kitchen, Lucy gets more bread than she bargained for: Grown to gargantuan proportions, the loaf comes out of the oven like a freight train and chases our vintage baker across the kitchen.

winner if Ricky comes home by any modern means of transportation. She figures she's got him—but he rides in on a horse! The next morning, as Ricky takes a bath in a vintage bathtub, Lucy, in a turn-of-the-century dress, insists that Ricky must wear old clothes, too. He protests, but she ignores him as she pours hot water down his back.

Later, two surprise inspectors from the Society Matrons' League drop in on the two couples while they're all dressed up in their old-fashioned clothes. Covering for Lucy, Ricky explains that their outfits are part of an act they perform. But when the women find out they're "show people," their attitude turns to condescension. Annoyed, Ricky tells them he does this for a living because "We like to eat." Lorgnettes in hand, the women say they would be willing to make "allowances" because the league needs the money. That's the last straw for Lucy, who tells them that "the Ricardo-Mertz investigating committee has looked you over and we have no desire to join your phony baloney club."

Everyone gathers around Lucy with pride and Ricky declares Lucy the winner of the bet. Ricky proposes going out to dinner, but Lucy says she has plenty to eat—she reaches for a huge slice of her baked bread, and everybody dives in for a bite.

The "Pioneer Woman" episode features another recurring theme: the couples' switching roles or instigating a bet in order to prove the other wrong. This episode also features one of the most remembered scenes in the entire series. That loaf of bread the size of a rolled carpet coming out of the oven is one of the funniest sight gags ever devised for the small screen. Most Lucyphiles are aware that the loaf was no prop, but an actual loaf of rye bread baked at the Union Made Bakery in Los Angeles. Not only did it have the look and the texture of real bread, it had the weight, which required the construction of a special rolling device that the propman pushed out through the back of the stove.

Lucy figures she'll be able to win the bet if she catches Ricky coming home on the subway, but he's one step ahead when he arrives on a horse.

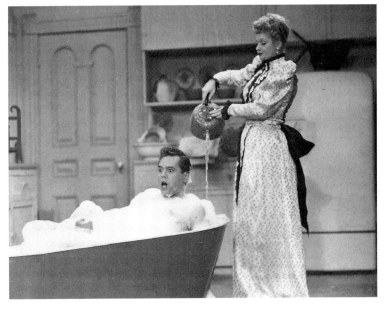

Lucy insists Ricky take an old-time bath, which he heartily enjoys . . .

. . . until Lucy heats up the suds with boiling water from a tea kettle.

When the Society Matrons' League reveals its snobbish ways, Lucy gives the ladies a piece of her mind and declines their "phony baloney" offer.

The Ricardos and the Mertzes enjoy a slice of Lucy's lengthy loaf.

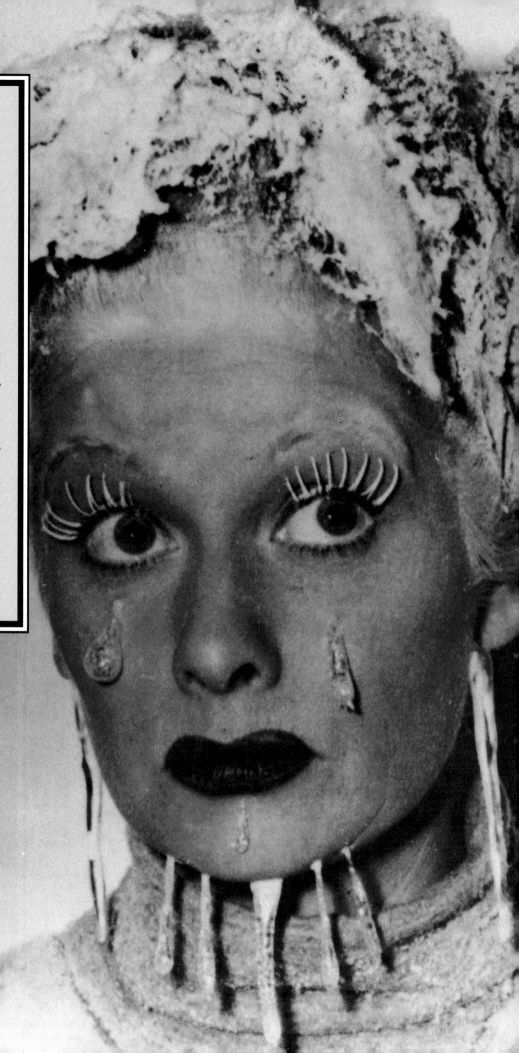

"THE FREEZER"

Lucy and Ethel get a freezer to save money on meat, but the idea backfires, and they wind up with more beef on their hands than a Texas cattle drive.

Ethel buys a walk-in freezer from her Uncle Oscar and has it installed in the basement. Lucy calls Johnson's Meat Packing Company to stock up. She finds out that meat bought this way only costs sixty-nine cents a pound and goes into a buying frenzy, ordering two sides of beef. When the delivery man arrives, he sets a sizable bundle on the kitchen counter and Lucy exclaims, "Gee, that sure is a lot!" "Oh, there's more," he assures her. Then a second bundle of equal size is dropped on the counter. After eight bundles, the foreman announces "Well, that's one side. Now let's go down and get the other." They're handed the bill: $483 for seven hundred pounds of meat. Flabbergasted, Lucy tries to get them to take back the order, but they can't once the meat has been cut.

In a panic, Lucy and Ethel hatch a plan to unload their meat in the waiting area of a local butcher shop. Using a baby carriage for their inventory, Lucy saunters near the counter, pulls a housewife over to the corner she's staked out, and begins her spiel in shifty-eyed, nasal, New York fashion: "Psssssst. C'mere. Are you tired of payin' high prices? Are you interested in a little high-class beef?" Slapping her hands together and jerking the hapless woman by the lapel, she continues, "Tell you what I'm gonna do. Now you look like a smart dame, what'll it be? I got sirloin, tenderloin, T-bone, rump, pot roast, chuck roast, oxtail, stump." Pretty soon a crowd gathers around, including the butcher, who moves toward them ominously. They quickly shut down operations and scurry out of the back door.

Back in the basement, Lucy and Ethel unload the rest of the beef into their newly delivered freezer room. Exhausted, they sit down in front of the locker and ponder how they're

After Ethel gets a discount on a walk-in freezer, the girls decide to stock it with wholesale meat. They hadn't bargained on 700 pounds of it.

To unload the meat, they open their own mini meat market at the butcher shop. Lucy: "Psssssst! Are you interested in a little high-class beef?"

Business is booming with Lucy collecting customers and Ethel collecting the money on an inventory that's tucked away in a baby buggy.

When the butcher moves in to investigate, they shut down and move out.

The girls ponder how to tell their husbands about the meat. Says Lucy: "You don't suppose they'd believe a cow wandered in there and fell apart, do you?"

The boys return home, and while Ethel keeps them occupied, Lucy frantically unloads the meat from the freezer . . .

. . . and stashes it in the nearest hiding place: the idle furnace.

On her final trip to the meat locker, Lucy inadvertently locks herself inside.

While she's downstairs freezing, Ethel is stalling by asking Ricky to sing for her—and he's only happy to oblige. Fred endures the serenade with long-suffering enthusiasm.

going to explain it to Ricky and Fred. "You don't suppose they'd believe a cow wandered in there and fell apart, do you?" At that moment, through the furnace vent, they hear Ricky and Fred come home.

The boys are eager to take a look at the freezer, but Lucy tells Ethel to stall them while she takes the meat out of it. "Ask Ricky to sing some of his favorite songs," she tells Ethel. It works.

Lucy rushes downstairs and unloads the meat into the idle furnace. On one of her last passes, she bumps into the freezer door, which slams shut, locking her in. By the time they get her out, she's as stiff as a popsicle, her face covered with icicles.

While Lucy thaws out, bundled in an electric blanket, Ricky notices a pleasant smell permeating the atmosphere. Ethel pipes up: "It smells like someone's cooking a roast." After Fred tells her he lit the furnace, Lucy wails "Unplug me...unplug me...unplug me!" and, still shrouded in the blanket, rushes to the door and—holding back tears—blurts: "Don't ask questions, just get a knife, a fork and a bottle of catsup and follow me to the biggest barbecue in the whole world."

By the time they arrive at the freezer, Lucy's as stiff as a popsicle. After they discover she has the key, Fred goes to fetch a crowbar. Afraid Lucy's tears might freeze up, Ricky shouts: "Don't cry!"

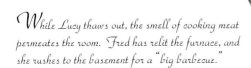

While Lucy thaws out, the smell of cooking meat permeates the room. Fred has relit the furnace, and she rushes to the basement for a "big barbecue."

"LUCY DOES A TV COMMERCIAL"

*L*ucy enlists Fred's help to persuade Ricky to use her in a television commercial. She gets her way, but the alcohol in the product gets Lucy into a heap of trouble.

Lucy's attempt to demonstrate her thespian abilities backfires when she takes out the insides of the television set and crawls into the TV cabinet to perform. But Ricky refuses to budge about giving her the commercial spot—he has already hired another girl.

The next morning, after he leaves for work, the girl for the commercial calls, and Lucy tells her they filled the spot with someone else. We know exactly who that is.

At the TV station, as the director and the stage manager prepare for the commercial, the manager notes that the product— "Vitameatavegamin"—contains twenty-three percent alcohol.

Lucy tries a run-through: "Hello, friends. I'm your Vitameatavegamin Girl. Are you tired, run down and listless? Do you poop out at parties? Are you unpopular? The answer to all your problems is in this little bottle: Vitameatavegamin, containing vitamins, meat, vegetables and minerals. Yes, with Vitameatavegamin you can spoon your way to health. All you do is take a tablespoonful after every meal." She takes off the top and pours a tablespoon. "It's so tasty, too."

Swallowing the spoonful with a big smile, she makes an awful face as the liquid hits her stomach. "Just like candy. So why don't you join the thousands of happy, peppy people and get a great big bottle of Vitameatavegamin tomorrow?"

Ricky is anything but pleased when he discovers Lucy's ruse, but the director says that she's actually doing very well. He tells her to run through it again, and she does, almost letter perfect. Ricky admits she's good, and agrees to let her do it.

The director prompts her to run through it once again, but this time, after another sample of the product, she reads her lines with a silly smirk and a giggle. "Tastes just like candy. Honest," she says, laughing at her words. By the time she ends her spiel—pronouncing the name of the product "Migavatameatamat"—her eyes have begun to glaze over.

Concerned, the director asks her if she's all right. "It's *hot* in

When Lucy finds out there's a commercial spot available on a TV show, she tries to impress Ricky with her ability to be a pitchman.

She took out the innards of the TV set to accomplish the illusion, and it's going to cost a hefty service charge to put it back together.

Lucy sulks as Ricky informs her that he's already hired another girl for the commercial . . .

. . . and as he leaves, she expresses her opinion about his decision.

When the girl calls about the commercial, Lucy says the part has been filled.

"*Hello, friends. Are you tired, run-down and listless? Do you poop out at parties? Are you unpopular? The answer to all your problems is in this little bottle: Vitameatavegamin . . .*"

"*It's so tasty, too!*"

Ricky's not happy when he finds out about Lucy's charade, but she convinces him and the director that she's up to the challenge.

"*So why don't you join the thousands of happy, peppy people and get a great big bottle of Vitameatavegamin tomorrow?*"

The alcohol in the product begins to take effect: "*Well, I'm your Vita-veeda-vigee-vat Girl. Do you pop out at parties—are you unpoopular? The answer to allllll your problems is in this li'l ole bottle . . .*"

So why don't you join the thousands of happy, peppy people . . ."

"*. . . and get a big bottle of Vita-meedy-mega-mee-nee-minie-moe-a-min.*" *By now, Lucy's completely crocked and has to be escorted off the stage.*

here!" she says. But in the next run-through, she falls completely apart, leaning on the podium with drunken self-assurance as she begins: "Well, I'm your Vita-veeda-vigee-vat Girl. Are you tired, run-down, listless?" Then, taunting the audience: "Well, are you? Do you pop out at parties—are you unpoopular? The answer to ALLLLLL your problems is in this li'l ole bottle. Vita-meeta-vegamin." Looking at the name on the bottle, she says, "That's it!" pleased with herself for actually getting it right.

She has difficulty getting her spoon under the neck of the bottle, so she puts the spoon down on the table and tries to pour the stuff into it. But it pours out onto the table, too. Looking down at the mess, she gives it up and takes a big swig directly from the bottle. "It tastes like candy," she says. "So why don't you join the thousands of happy, peppy people and get a big bottle of Vita-meedy-mega-mee-nee-minie-moe-a-min." By now the director sees she's in no condition to go on, and advises her to lie down.

Ricky has no idea of Lucy's condition as the live show hits the airwaves. Not realizing she's on TV, she staggers out on the stage and, with a sappy, adoring smile on her face, wanders in behind him. He makes a desperate attempt to get away from her, but she moves between him and the camera with a "Hi Ethel, hi Fred," then starts to sing, sounding like a rooster having its tail yanked.

She goes into her Vitameatavegamin patter when Ricky grabs her around her knees and carries her through the center curtain, still spieling.

The "Vitameatavegamin" routine is acclaimed as one of the all-time classic moments in television. Lucille Ball's portrayal of progressive intoxication is on a par with anything ever performed by the great silent comedians, including Stan Laurel, with whom she has often been compared. The late director George Marshall, who directed Laurel and Hardy in their heyday as well as Lucille Ball on *Here's Lucy*, once remarked that "Lucy and Viv could remake most of the Laurel and Hardy films without changing a line."

Back onstage in a drunken stupor, Lucy admires her husband from the sidelines as he begins to sing.

She joins Ricky in a duet, but the resulting cacophony stops him cold.

The Second Season
♥ 1952 to 1953 ♥

#37
"The Handcuffs"
October 6, 1952

#38
"The Operetta"
October 13, 1952

#39
"Job Switching"
September 15, 1952

#50
"Lucy Is Enceinte"
December 8, 1952

#56
"Lucy Goes to the Hospital"
January 19, 1953

"THE HANDCUFFS"

Tired of being neglected, Lucy handcuffs herself to Ricky while he dozes. The trouble begins when she finds out there's no key.

Fred is trying to get Ricky, Lucy and Ethel interested in his old magic act. Realizing he's getting nowhere, he finally pulls out an old pair of trick handcuffs, vowing to mystify everyone by escaping from them. But when Lucy unceremoniously slips them off with no trouble, Fred walks out in a huff with Ethel in tow.

Lucy is ready to enjoy their usual "free" Monday night out with dinner and a movie, but Ricky tells her he has too much to do with his act for a TV broadcast the next day. Apologizing, he sits down to study his lines, and a pouting Lucy goes down to see Ethel. A couple of hours later, she comes back and handcuffs herself to a dozing Ricky. He's startled when he wakes up, but Lucy vows she's going to do this to him every Monday so that he can't get away from her.

But when they try removing the cuffs, they don't come off as easily as when she took them off Fred, who comes barreling in at that moment and warns Lucy not to put the handcuffs on. They're not his trick cuffs. The ones she picked up were an old set from the Civil War that had been given to Fred at a police benefit, and there is no key.

As Ricky's temper escalates, Lucy reminds him of his marriage vow. He says: "As I recall it was 'till death do us part.' That event is about to take place right now." They can't find a locksmith at 8:30 P.M., so Ricky has to cancel his rehearsal. They both decide to turn in for the night, but the handcuffs prove to be worse than a case of insomnia. Locked at the wrists, they try to take their clothes off and it's all but impossible. When they finally get in bed, they find themselves entangled in all kinds of contortions in search of a comfortable position.

The next morning, Ethel ushers in a locksmith who proceeds to babble endlessly about his wife, who's a real Ricky Ricardo fan,

One evening, Fred tries to mystify everyone with feats of legerdemain, but his trick handcuffs don't fool Lucy, who slips them off with ease.

Later, Ricky's preparations for a TV appearance put a damper on their evening, and Lucy slips Fred's cuffs on him so he can't ignore her.

Lucy's attempt to get Ricky's attention falls flat when Fred tells them that the handcuffs were a real pair from the Civil War that has no key.

Ricky calls a locksmith after Lucy reminds him of their vows in an effort to calm him down. "Till death do us part," he says, "is about to take place right now."

With no locksmith available until morning, the couple is joined at the wrists for the night. Removing their clothes is all but impossible . . .

. . . so they try to go to their respective sides of the bed, but it's a futile effort.

In a tangle of hands and feet, they try removing each other's shoes, then . . .

. . . they try to switch sides, but it doesn't work. So . . .

. . . Lucy thinks a new position might be the answer, but first . . .

. . . to get the right position a wrestling maneuver . . .

and about his own "hankerin' to get into showbiz." Ricky and Lucy suffer through this harangue as he keeps trying an assortment of keys tethered to an enormous ring. After a while he finally gives up, and says he'll have to go back home where he has an old set of keys that will probably work. But he lives in Yonkers—about a two-hour round trip. Ricky has to be on television by then.

At showtime he's introduced and walks out in front of the curtain, but he and Lucy are still locked at the wrist, and her left hand is attached to his right hand. While he talks to the hostess of the show, his "right" hand (Lucy's) takes on a life of its own as he talks to her about his latest projects and then sings "Santiago, Chile."

When the locksmith finally shows up and walks out onstage, Lucy's hand grabs him by the scruff of his neck and yanks him out of sight behind the curtains. Ricky's shackled hand suddenly springs free, and when Lucy pops out in a final hammy grin, he uses his freed hand to push her face back behind the curtain.

The basic plot gag for "The Handcuffs" came out of a personal experience of Jess Oppenheimer's father as an actor at the Jewish Community Player's Theater in San Francisco. The elder Oppenheimer was portraying a detective in a murder mystery, and in one of the performances, he had handcuffed himself to a suspect and was supposed to turn him over to the police, but somehow the handcuffs got hooked in his belt. The police were supposed to take the actor offstage, but couldn't. The next scene was a love scene, and while Jess's dad was passionately romancing the actress, the actor portraying the murder suspect was still attached to his wrist and whistling nonchalantly as he tried to ignore the situation on the couch next to him.

. . . only manages to drop her—and himself—on the floor.

*B*eat beyond belief, the Ricardos settle down for the night.

*T*he locksmith says he's going to have to go home for the right key—but he's not going to make it back in time to unlock Ricky before the show.

*T*here's only one solution: take Lucy along and let her hand double for Ricky's. The problem: that hand seems to have a life of its own . . .

*W*hen the hostess asks Ricky about his latest engagements, he says, "Let me think . . ."

*F*inally the locksmith removes the handcuffs, and Ricky's hand springs free just in time for the finale.

*A*s he sings "Santiago, Chile," Lucy's hand keeps time to another tune.

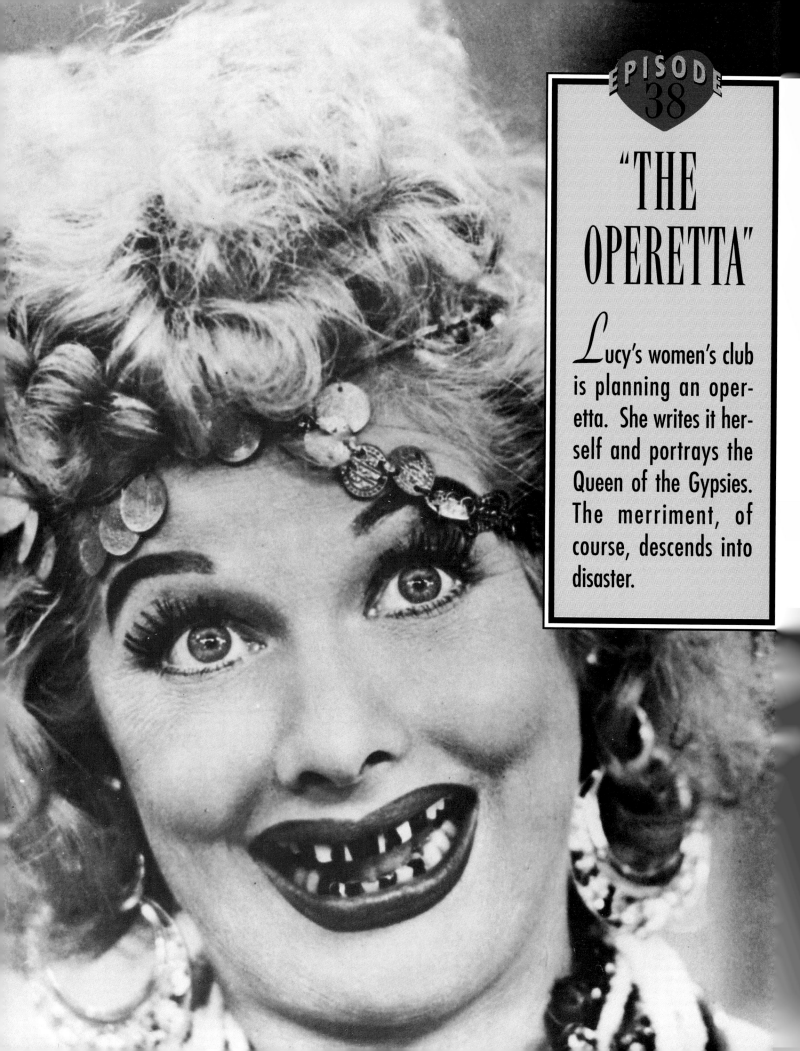

"THE OPERETTA"

Lucy's women's club is planning an operetta. She writes it herself and portrays the Queen of the Gypsies. The merriment, of course, descends into disaster.

In her role as treasurer of the women's club, Lucy has used the funds to make up a series of shortfalls in her household allowance. After transferring money back and forth, she's wound up short in both places, but she's got a plan. If she can put on a show for the women's club, she'll be able to make it up with the take at the door, and write a postdated check to the theatrical supply company.

Ensconced behind the piano and the typewriter, she begins composing an operetta entitled "The Pleasant Peasant." She's staked out the lead part for herself as the comely maiden, Lilly of the Valley, and for Ethel a role as Camille, Queen of the Gypsies, a snaggletoothed old crone. Ethel thinks they should switch roles. "Give me one good reason why you should do the female lead instead of me?" challenges Lucy. "Because you can't carry a tune," says Ethel, who executes a melodious operatic trill to prove her own claim on the role. Lucy tries to do the same, but it sounds more like a cry of pain. Giving up, she asks, "Where do I go to get my teeth snaggled?"

On the night of the performance, the operetta begins with a couple of pleasant little ditties, sung by the female chorus, about Quinn (Fred), the Innkeeper. Ethel enters, her hands clasped sweetly, and sings a delicate song about unrequited love.

As the heartbroken Lilly is about to leave, Lucy as the Queen of the Gypsies bursts forth in a puff of smoke. As she struggles to find a note, the chorus drowns out her caterwauling. Then Prince Lancelot (Ricky) arrives with a trumpet fanfare and serenades Lilly in Jeanette MacDonald/Nelson Eddy fashion. Camille is busy spouting dire prophecies when one of the peasant ladies sings to her in operetta style: "There's a man backstage taking away the costumes and the sce-e-e-e-e-nery."

"I gave him a che-e-e-e-e-e-e-ck," Lucy sings.

In an operatic trill, the woman sings, "It bounced.

As the treasurer of the women's club, Lucy's mixed her own funds with the club's, and there's a shortfall. The club's annual show is in jeopardy.

So Lucy decides to write the show herself—an operetta—and plans to pay the rental company for props and scenery with proceeds from the box office.

An argument ensues about who'll play Lilly—the ingenue—and Camille, an old gypsy. Ethel proves she's right for Lilly by performing an operatic trill.

Lucy tries to do the same, but can only screech out an off-key nonoperatic shrill: she'll be playing the crone.

Ricky's concerned about the damage Lucy will inflict on the audience's eardrums, but Ethel says she's instructed the chorus to drown her out.

Ethel's Lilly delivers a melodic aria while waiting for her paramour.

With tambourine in hand, Lucy's Camille, Queen of the Gypsies, bursts from the village well in a puff of smoke.

The chorus does its best to camouflage Camille's caterwauling.

Ricky's Prince Lancelot enters, dismissing Camille's gloomy predictions.

Bounced...bounced...bou...ou...ou...ou...ou...ou... ounced." Deadpan, and completely out of her operatic character, Lucy says, "It came back?"

"Post-dat-ed," sings the peasant.

"Tell him to wait a mi-i-i-i-i-nute."

"Don't take all da-a-a-a-a-y."

"Well, take a stab at it," squawks Lucy, pushing her offstage.

It doesn't work. Men in coveralls enter and start carting off the props and the scenery. Complete chaos ensues as people chase each other around the set and costumes are taken off the performers. In desperation, Lucy begins singing her big number, "Camille, Queen of the Gypsies," as the rental company carts her offstage on a bench.

As Lilly and Lancelot sing a duet, a chorus lady tells Lucy the rental firm has arrived to repossess the props. Lucy: "I gave him a che-ε-ε-ε-ε-ε-ε-ck!"

The rental company carts off their furniture while Lucy continues warbling.

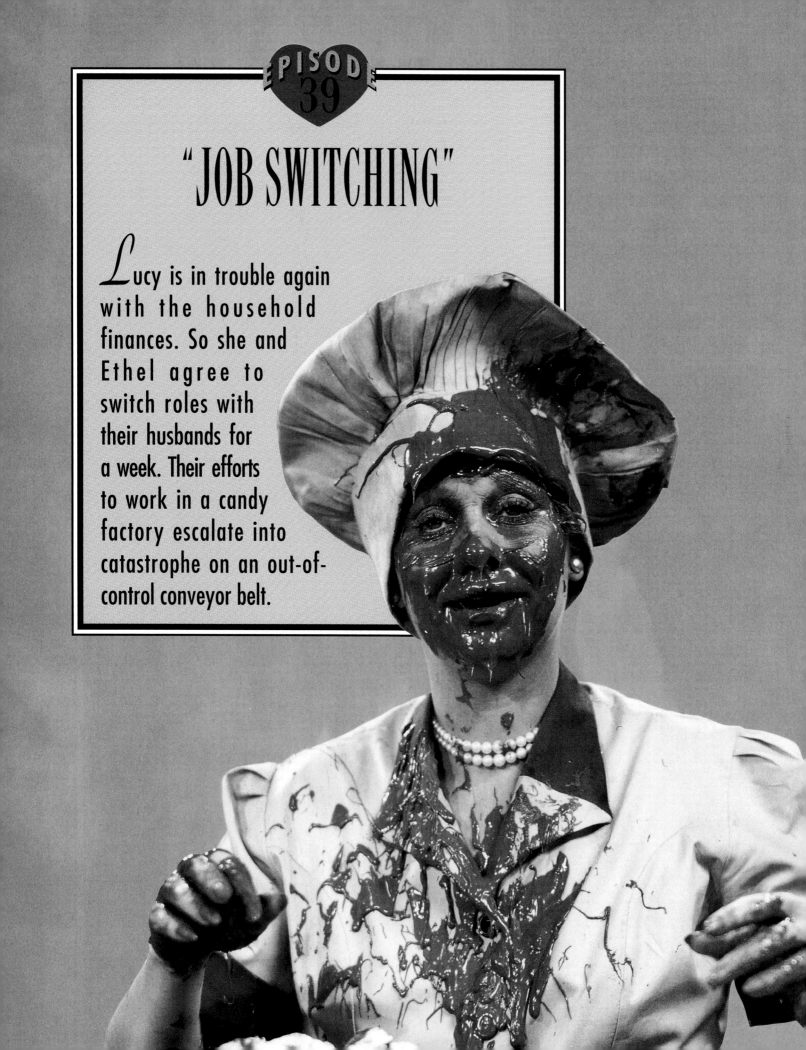

"JOB SWITCHING"

*L*ucy is in trouble again with the household finances. So she and Ethel agree to switch roles with their husbands for a week. Their efforts to work in a candy factory escalate into catastrophe on an out-of-control conveyor belt.

Ricky learns about some of Lucy's bounced checks, and blows his stack. The girls minimize the problem while the boys chide them for "lying around the house" and "playing canasta." Both think the others have it easy, so Lucy challenges Ricky and Fred to swap roles with her and Ethel for a week. The bet is on.

In his role as househusband, Ricky serves an almost perfect breakfast the next morning—eggs, ham, potatoes, orange juice and exquisitely brewed coffee. But Lucy's amazement quickly turns to disdain when she answers the phone and tells Ricky to pick up his hat, which he left at the corner drugstore lunch counter after picking up the two breakfast orders.

Ethel walks in, and the two march out the door to go job hunting. At the Acme Employment Agency, Mr. Snodgrass grills Lucy and Ethel about their qualifications, and finally settles on candy-making.

At home, Ricky and Fred aren't coping very well with the household chores. Fred has dropped the dishes on the floor, both of them have left iron-shaped burn marks on all the clothing, and Ricky starches Lucy's nylons into a piece of cardboard.

At the candy factory, the forewoman sternly instructs Lucy in the candy-dipping department. Lucy watches the woman next to her as she deftly picks up a cream center, drops it into a puddle of chocolate, rolls it, covers it with chocolate and sets it aside, making a swirl design on top. With a big smile, Lucy tries to imitate the woman and smears her fingers in the chocolate on the slab of marble with the abandon of a child making mud pies. She finally manages to complete one, and drops it into the finishing tray with a flourish. It's a misshapen mess. "Hey, this is fun!" she says.

A fly lands on the other woman's face and Lucy, her hand covered with chocolate, takes a swipe at it, leaving a brown splat on the woman's face. Her coworker promptly smacks Lucy back, leaving her face completely covered with chocolate. They exchange more and more swats until they're both dripping.

The boys, meanwhile, have completely ruined dinner. Fred

Ricky's furious with Lucy's overdrawn account. When she says the problem is that he doesn't give her enough money, he goes into orbit.

The Mertzes walk in and Ricky asks Fred if Ethel overdraws her account. "She spends money like I was printing it in the basement," he says.

The husbands tell the wives that they don't know the value of a buck. Ricky: "If you had to earn money, you would think twice about spending it so fast."

A challenge is thrown out among the four as husbands and wives agree to reverse roles for a week. The men will be househusbands and the women will get jobs.

At the Acme Employment Agency, Lucy and Ethel listen to the list of jobs but none of them seem to fit until candy-making is mentioned.

At the candy factory, the forewoman explains Lucy's duties as a dipper. Lucy says she's "a big dipper from 'way back,'" but the joke falls flat.

After Ethel and the forewoman leave, Lucy carefully watches the professional dipper work with finesse and speed, and soon Lucy thinks she can do it.

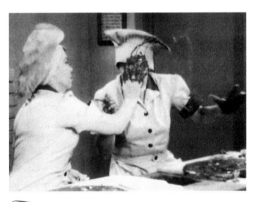

After mooshing a cream center around the chocolate, she dumps it with a flourish in front of her. It's not even close to the neat little row of chocolates that the woman has lined up.

Soon a fly begins to buzz around the room, landing finally on the woman's face. Lucy reaches over and swats her cheek.

The woman returns the slap, covering Lucy right in the mug with a faceful of chocolate.

Ricky and Fred turn the kitchen into a real mess, with chickens exploding from the pressure cooker and rice cascading out of the stove.

Demoted to the wrapping department, the girls are warned that if one piece of candy gets past them, they'll be fired. At first, the candy comes through slowly.

As the belt picks up speed, the girls start shoving candy in their mouths, and when they hear the forewoman approach, they hide the rest in their caps.

makes a "seven-layered chocolate cake" that is flatter than a pancake, while Ricky's chicken-and-rice concoction sends several poultry carcasses onto the ceiling.

Back at the candy factory, Lucy and Ethel have been demoted to the wrapping department. As the candy enters the room by way of the conveyor belt, their job is to wrap each piece in paper and return it to the belt. "If one piece gets past you and into the packing room unwrapped, you're fired," warns the forewoman. "Let 'er roll," she yells.

At first the candy comes through at an easy pace, but the belt speeds up, and the pieces double in volume. To keep up, Lucy starts to put some of them next to her, and she gulps down others. Mercifully the belt stops, but the two hear the forewoman coming— they frantically gather up all the loose pieces, dropping them in their cook's caps.

Scrutinizing their progress, she says, "Fine, you're doing splendid. Speed it up!" she shouts.

The speed and quantity of chocolate on the conveyor have become preposterous as Lucy and Ethel each gather up all the pieces and stuff them down their blouses.

Holding their aching stomachs as they walk through the front door at home, Lucy finds a note: "Please do not go into the kitchen until we explain. We'll be back in a few minutes." Lucy can't resist going in, and a primal scream comes from the kitchen as she runs back out, describing the mess on the floor, the walls and the ceiling.

When Ricky and Fred return, they admit that they're lousy housewives and want to call the whole thing off. When the girls agree, Fred and Ricky show their appreciation by presenting each of the girls with…a five-pound box of chocolates.

Pleased with the progress Lucy and Ethel are making, the forewoman yells: "Speed it up!"

The girls get home with stomachaches, and Lucy heads for the kitchen for a remedy. Instead, she finds the mess the boys left behind.

The boys get home and soon they all agree to call the whole thing off—whereupon the husbands each produce a box of chocolate to show their appreciation.

EPISODE 50

"LUCY IS ENCEINTE"

Lucy discovers she's pregnant but can't bring herself to tell Ricky. So she heads down to the club, and reveals her condition in a touching way.

Lucy tells Ethel that she's feeling "dauncey," a term her grandmother used for feeling lousy. So she's decided to go to the doctor to find out what's wrong.

ucy tells Ethel one morning that she is on her way to the doctor. She's feeling "dauncey." "Dauncey?" asks Ethel. "That's a word my grandmother made up for when you're not really sick but feel lousy." She continues describing her symptoms to Ethel, but when she mentions that she's been putting on a lot of weight, a red flag goes up, and Ethel suggests that she might have a baby in the works. "A baby!?" exclaims Lucy. "Yeah. Baby," says Ethel. "That's a word my grandma made up for tiny little people."

As Lucy describes some of her symptoms, Ethel thinks she might be having a baby: "That's the word my grandma made up for tiny little people."

Lucy returns from the doctor, and walks around the room with a dreamy-eyed look on her face, confirming Ethel's prediction. "We're going to have a baby!"

"We are?" says Ethel. "Isn't that wonderful! I've never had a baby before!" As she rushes out the door to tell Fred, Lucy stops her. She doesn't want anyone else to know until she's told Ricky herself. She enacts the scenario for Ethel: "Ricky, darling, our dream has come true. You and I are going to be blessed with something that means more to us than anything in the whole world," followed by a tender, romantic kiss.

Ricky comes home for lunch preoccupied with club problems. Lucy tries to calm him down by serving him a special lunch. Between mouthfuls of food, she does her best to cozy up to him for the big moment, but the phone rings with more problems from the club.

"You think you know how tough my job is, but believe me, if you traded places with me, you'd be surprised," he says to Lucy.

"Believe me, if I traded places with you, *you'd* be surprised," she says knowingly.

Another call from the club takes him rushing out of the door before she has a chance to break the news. In frustration, she comes down to the club, where Ricky is in the midst of instructing the band and the club's staff about the opening number. There are more interruptions, until Lucy finally blurts

Lucy's back from the doctor: "We're going to have a baby!"

She's rehearsing how she'll announce the baby when Ricky comes home for lunch.

Fred brings Lucy a ball and a bat. He's already got plans for the little tyke.

Lucy tries to tell Ricky after lunch, but they're interrupted by a call from the club, and he races out of the door without hearing the news.

Lucy finally rushes down to the club to get Ricky's attention, but she can't make a private announcement so publicly and runs out without another word.

out that she came to tell Ricky something very important. He finally brings everything to a screeching halt and yells: "I don't want anyone to make a move. My wife came down here to tell me something very important. I don't want to hear a pin drop. All right, honey, what is it?"

People have stopped in mid-stride, waiting breathlessly and staring at Lucy. She lets out a big cry, and darts out of the door. Ricky is perplexed.

Later, in performance, after finishing "The Lady in Red," Ricky reads a note he has just received from a member of the audience: "Dear Mr. Ricardo, my husband and I are going to have a blessed event. I just found out about it today and I haven't told him yet. I heard you sing a song—'We're Having a Baby, My Baby and Me.' If you would sing it for us now, it would be my way of breaking the news to him." Ricky tries to get the couple onstage and begins to sing "Rock-A-Bye Baby" as he walks between the tables. He passes Lucy seated at one of them and smiles at her: "Hi, honey." She nods at him as he walks on, continuing the song. Finally, it hits him like a thunderbolt, and when he looks back at her, she nods vigorously. He rushes over on bended knee. After she confirms it, he pops up and shouts to the audience "It's me! I'm going to be a father!" Then, in confusion, he introduces Lucy as his mother.

He ends by singing "We're Having a Baby," as he holds her tenderly and gives her a loving kiss, a kiss made even more poignant by the fact that Lucille Ball and Desi Arnaz really were having a baby, and everybody knew it.

Ricky gets a note from an expectant mother requesting him to sing "We're Having a Baby, My Baby and Me," so he obliges with a sentimental rendition. . . . But before he does, he begins to sing "Rock-A-Bye Baby" as he walks through the audience to find out who gave him the note.

When he sees Lucy sitting in the audience, he stops in the middle of his song after a big nod from her.

Rushing over to her table, he confirms her condition and yells the news to the audience. With Lucy on his arm, Ricky strolls across the stage singing "We're Having a Baby, My Baby and Me." And as the song continues, Lucy's true emotions well up about her real-life pregnancy.

The final, tender moment.

"LUCY GOES TO THE HOSPITAL"

*I*t's almost zero hour on the Ricardos' maternity time clock, and everyone is on watch. Ricky's new act at the club has him gussied up in one of the most preposterous makeup jobs ever concocted, and the result is chaos at the hospital.

With Lucy in the last month of pregnancy, her harried husband assumes the baby is on its way at any moment. The Mertzes also fall prey to Ricky's malaise, and start viewing Lucy as a ticking bomb. While she's lying down to get away from everyone's anxiety, Ricky suggests that they rehearse their part in getting her to the hospital on time. Everyone completes the drill perfectly and, with smug satisfaction, they sit down and reflect on the blessed event. Moments later, Lucy pads quietly into the living room and says softly, "This is it."

They all vault out of their chairs and clash into each other. "Call the doctor!" someone yells, and while they're all descending on the phone at once, the word "suitcase" erupts from the melee. Fred and Ricky play tug-o-war over the valise until it comes apart, its contents falling all over the floor. Desperate hands scoop up clothing and jam it in with frenzied abandon. Lucy makes a forlorn request for a cab and they all drop what they're doing and run out of the door, leaving her behind.

"Hey, wait for me," she whimpers.

As she walks toward the door, it flies open, almost squashing her into the wall. Just as everyone manages to get out of the door with Lucy, she chokes out, "My suitcase!" Ricky runs back into the room, stuffs the clothes back into her suitcase—along with the telephone—and leaps toward the door. Like a fish at the end of a line, he flops helplessly in the hallway after the cord runs out of length.

At the hospital, a dizzy Ricky is the one in the wheelchair and Lucy is trailing behind with her suitcase. And he's not much help checking Lucy in—he forgets not only the name of the doctor but his own name and address.

In the waiting room, he begins pacing. Mr. Stanley, another waiting father, is completely relaxed. Ricky finds out why: he already

With the baby on its way and everyone safely in the taxi for the trip to the hospital, Ricky runs back to get Lucy's valise.

After Lucy goes into the maternity ward, Ricky's so stressed he can't remember the name of the doctor, his address or even his own name.

As he paces around the waiting room, Ricky strikes up a conversation with a Mr. Stanley, who's been through this already with six daughters.

*R*icky is due on stage at the club, so he picks up the phone to call Fred and have him bring a makeup kit for his voodoo number.

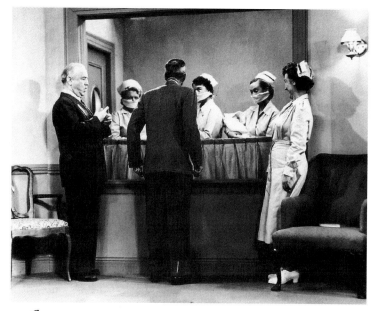

*A*s Ricky leaves to put on his makeup in the men's room, the nurse tells Stanley he's got a surprise: triplets—all girls.

*I*n full makeup, Ricky's about to leave for the club, but the sight of him scares a nurse, who runs out of the door.

*W*ith his gun drawn, a policeman comes in moments later with the frightened nurse in tow. "If he's in the hospital," says the cop, "we'll find him."

*A*t the club, Ricky's in the midst of his voodoo number when Fred calls.

has six girls.

Ricky calls Fred to have him bring his makeup kit for the "voodoo" number he has to perform at the club in a few hours. After Fred arrives with it, Ricky goes into the rest room to change. While he is there, a nurse walks into the waiting room and tells Stanley that his wife just gave birth to triplets—all girls. As he shuffles dejectedly out the door, Fred tells him jokingly: "Well, you can always plan on a girl's softball team." Stanley glowers at Fred.

When Ricky comes back into the waiting room, Fred nearly jumps out of his skin. The voodoo make-up is a grotesque amalgam of whitened eye sockets, darkened skin, painted-on fangs and a fright wig of black hair. Just then, a nurse walks into the viewing area behind the plate glass, sees Ricky, and screams, throwing the towels she's carrying into the air and running out of the door. After he leaves for the club, a policeman enters the waiting room, called by the frightened nurse. "If he's in the hospital, we'll find him," he promises.

In the middle of his voodoo number at the club, the maître d' hands Ricky the phone: It's Fred, telling him the baby has arrived. Ricky runs out of the door in full witch doctor regalia. When he enters the waiting room this time, Fred passes out in a state of shock. Just as Ricky is trying to revive him with a good shake, the policeman and a hospital orderly rush in to stop him from "attacking" Fred. Ethel arrives, and everyone calms down just as a nurse comes into the waiting room to tell Ricky that they're bringing his boy to the viewing window. Holding on to Fred and Ethel for support, he goes over to the window, takes a long look—and falls backwards in a dead faint.

When he rushes back to the hospital, the policeman and an attendant try to apprehend Ricky, but Fred and Ethel come to the rescue.

Everyone relaxes except Ricky, who goes into shock when he finds out he's got a brand new baby boy.

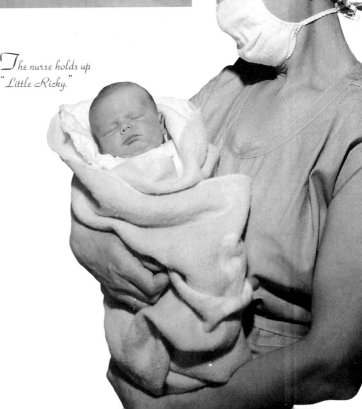

The nurse holds up "Little Ricky."

THE THIRD SEASON
❤ 1953 to 1954 ❤

#79
"THE MILLION-DOLLAR IDEA"
January 11, 1954

#87
"BONUS BUCKS"
March 8, 1954

#94
"TENNESSEE ERNIE VISITS"
May 3, 1954

"THE MILLION-DOLLAR IDEA"

Criticized for their spending habits, Lucy and Ethel go into the salad dressing business, but the road to riches proves more troublesome than anticipated.

As Lucy talks to Ethel about her latest budget battle with Ricky, she comes up with an idea she thinks is worth a million dollars. They'll sell Lucy's salad dressing, calling it "Aunt Martha's Old-Fashioned Salad Dressing," and they decide to promote the idea on television.

"You'll be a cooking expert and I'll be one of those women they get up from the audience," says Lucy. *The Dickie Davis Show* is a perfect place to promote their product, and their friend Carolyn Appleby's husband manages the TV station that runs it.

Ethel is introduced on camera as home economist "Mary Margaret McMertz," who hypes the dressing and introduces Lucy as "an average housewife." Dressed up in a black straw hat and Harold Lloyd–type glasses, Lucy introduces herself as "Isabella Klump" and stands there dazed and daffy, watching herself on the monitor throughout the entire commercial spot.

Ethel hands Lucy the bottle of dressing and tells her to pour it into the salad bowl. When she starts to eat the salad while she's tossing it, Ethel asks what she thinks of it. Lucy shovels it in her mouth, dressing oozing over her lips, and says finally, "This is the best salad dressing I've ever eaten." With that, Ethel wraps it up and tries to take away the bowl, but Lucy tries to horde the contents, stuffing her bulging cheeks with increasing fury. Finally, she picks up the open bottle and drinks directly from it. By the end of the show, they already have twenty-three orders by phone.

When Ricky comes home, Lucy explains their new business enterprise. Wary, he does some profit-margin calculations and figures that based on their forty-cents-a-quart price, they are going to lose money on the deal. Ricky tells Lucy to fill the twenty-three orders and promptly get out of business before they blow any more money.

At that moment, Fred walks in lugging a sackful of orders, and says there are two more sacks downstairs. Lucy rationalizes that if they can sell this well, they should be able to "unsell" just as well.

The next day on the program, she comes on as another average housewife, "Lucille McGillicuddy," decked out like a hillbilly. When

Ethel tries to console Lucy while she fights the budget blues.

Lucy comes up with a million-dollar idea: She thinks her salad dressing will go over big if she can just get a little television airtime.

So she calls Carolyn Appleby, whose husband runs a local TV station. Carolyn will arrange for them to pitch the dressing on The Dickie Davis Show.

As "Isabella Klump," average housewife, Lucy tosses the salad while homemaking expert "Mary Margaret McMertz" looks on.

Isabella taste tests Aunt Martha's Old-Fashioned Salad Dressing . . .

. . . and likes it so much that she takes a swig directly from the bottle.

Dickie Davis shows Lucy and Ethel the orders from TV viewers.

Back in the kitchen, they go to work fulfilling orders while onion fumes tear up their eyes.

Ricky and Fred tell them they're losing money on every jar they sell, so Lucy plans to go back on TV to "unsell" the dressing.

"Lucille McGillicuddy" gives Aunt Martha's dressing a try . . .

. . . and comes up reeling from the taste.

Aghast, Mary Margaret warns viewers not to buy the dressing.

Ethel offers her the open jar of dressing, she takes a sniff, and reacts as if it were filled with week-old body parts, as she looks for a place to dump it.

Opening a new jar, Ethel suggests, "Try this."

Lucy drinks from the jar, drops to the floor and blurts out, "What's Aunt Martha trying to do, poison me?" Ethel says she can no longer endorse this product and the viewers should cancel their orders immediately.

The next day Fred lugs in another sackful of mail, and joy quickly turns to panic as the girls discover that their efforts have resulted in only more orders—with everybody complimenting them on a funny commercial that poked fun at the dressing.

The next scene opens with Lucy walking through stacks and stacks of salad dressing jars, lined up throughout their apartment. "One thousand, one hundred and fifty-three jars," says Lucy, jotting it down in a notebook. When Ricky comes in the door, he's amazed at the roomfuls of inventory. He can't believe his ears when Ethel tells how they did it: they went to the store, bought salad dressing already made, and relabeled the bottles. It has cost them ten cents more to do it this way, but at least they can fill the orders.

"That's okay," says Ricky, "but what are you going to do about mailing them?"

"We've got that all figured out," says Lucy, grabbing Ethel and leaving the room.

They glide back in on roller skates, bedecked with newspaper carrier sacks and pushing shopping carts filled to the brim with Aunt Martha's Old-Fashioned Salad Dressing.

"You take the East Side and I'll take the West Side and I'll be in Jersey before you," says Lucy, skating out of the door with Ethel behind her.

It doesn't work. The viewers were bowled over by their comic kidding of the product, and they've sent in more orders. What to do?

The solution: Lucy and Ethel buy pre-made dressing, slap on their own labels, then set out to deliver their orders on skates.

"BONUS BUCKS"

*R*icky gets a winning number in a "Bonus Bucks" contest, but the lucky bill winds up in the pocket of one of his pajamas, bound for the laundry truck.

icky is poring over his winning numbers—worth about three hundred dollars—posted in the newspaper's Bonus Bucks Contest. He's ecstatic, but he tells Fred he'd feel better if Lucy felt that she had won it herself, so he tells Fred he'll slip his winning bill in her purse to give her the thrill of winning. Later that evening, when he comes home from the club, he does just that while she's sleeping.

The next morning, the grocery boy comes to the back door and, in making change, Lucy inadvertently gives him the winning dollar. A short time later, Ethel bursts into the Ricardos' apartment, squealing with delight over the the bonus buck she has just got in change from the grocery boy.

Lucy shares Ethel's joy, until Ricky comes into the room and tells her he slipped a winning bonus buck in her purse last night. Lucy's and Ricky's eyes move in Ethel's direction. "Wait a minute, I gave our bonus buck to the grocery boy. He said he was going over to your apartment, so that must be ours," exclaims Lucy, grabbing the dollar out of Ethel's hand.

Fred sides with Ethel, declaring, "Possession is nine points of the law." What follows is a childish game of "keep away" in which the dollar gets torn in half. They reach a compromise and decide to split the money. Each couple will keep half of the winning dollar, which has to be turned in by three o'clock that day in order to collect on it.

Ricky puts their half of the bonus buck in his pajama pocket. While he's showering, though, Lucy grabs his pajamas and gives them to the laundryman. Later, as the Ricardos and the Mertzes prepare to go downtown to pick up their winnings, Lucy realizes what she's done, and the others unleash their wrath on her. Ricky suggests that Ethel

Everyone's got "Bonus Bucks" fever, a lotto contest run by the newspaper. Lucy checks out serial numbers to find out if they've won. They haven't.

Later, when Ricky finds out he won $300, he tells Fred he's going to slip the winning bill in Lucy's purse so that she can get the thrill of the prize herself.

*W*hen *R*icky tells *L*ucy about the bonus buck he slipped in her purse, she exclaims, "*O*h, no! *I* gave all the money in my purse to the grocery boy!"

*L*ucy and *R*icky realize that the grocery boy gave *L*ucy's bonus buck to *E*thel.

*E*veryone explains to *F*red how the bonus buck wound up with *E*thel and the four decide to split the winnings—but a three o'clock cash-in deadline looms.

*A*fter *R*icky smuggles *L*ucy into the laundry processing room in a sack, a worker sees it come to life and reaches for a stick . . .

*H*alf of the winning buck went to the laundry, and it's all *L*ucy's fault. *F*red and *E*thel will go to the newspaper office while *L*ucy and *R*icky head for the laundry.

. . . *B*ut *L*ucy escapes from the bag just in time to avoid getting clobbered.

and Fred should go down to the newspaper office with their half of the dollar, while he and Lucy track down their half at the laundry.

At Speedy Laundry, the Ricardos try to persuade the foreman to let them in the processing room, but he's worried about losing his job. They leave and, in a desperate move, Ricky comes back in dressed in laundry employee coveralls.

Pushing a handcart filled with laundry sacks, he runs past the foreman, leaves the handcart in the processing room, and runs through another door with the foreman in hot pursuit. With the coast clear, the bundle in the handcart takes on a life of its own, and waddles across the room. A woman working nearby looks aghast and picks up a stick for protection. Bursting back into the room, Ricky grabs the woman around the waist, and the foreman grabs Ricky— who yells at Lucy to make her move.

Lucy emerges from the bundle, finds Ricky's pajamas and extracts the bonus buck just as other workers join in and chase her up a conveyor belt that carries her through a trapdoor leading to the starching vat.

Ricky runs into the newspaper office in the nick of time and makes the deadline. Unfortunately, the damage they incurred at the laundry cost them all the bonus bucks winnings— except one dollar. That's Lucy's cue to shuffle into the room with her clothes, her hair and her face as stiff as an ironing board.

After rummaging through laundry sacks, Lucy finds the bonus buck and gets chased onto a conveyor belt that takes her to a vat of starch.

Ricky makes the prize deadline, but their winnings are just enough to cover damages at the laundry. That's Lucy's cue to walk in, starched from head to toe. But everyone gets stiffed in this Lucy lunacy.

"TENNESSEE ERNIE VISITS"

*L*ucy's mother writes to announce the imminent arrival of Lucy's hick cousin Ernie, who walks into the Ricardos' life for an unforgettable stay.

After Ernie (Tennessee Ernie Ford) arrives, he relates his experience in trying to find them, after an eight-hour stint riding "that train in the hole in the ground." When the Mertzes drop in and introductions are over, Ernie says "Where do I sleep? I can sleep hangin' on a nail."

The last thing Ricky wants is to put up with one of Lucy's relatives, especially one with Ernie's unsophisticated ways, so he tries to convince him that there is no place for him to bunk, but Ernie says he can "be as comfy as a wet dog behind the kitchen stove." The Ricardos resign themselves to being overnight innkeepers, and Fred helps bring out a roll-away bed. Later, since Ricky can't get to sleep, Lucy tells him to check on Ernie, who has bundled himself up like a slab of meat between two slices of bread within the still-unfolded rollaway bed.

Come the dawn, he's up at first light, plucking away on Ricky's guitar in a full-throated version of "Wabash Cannonball." When he simulates a train whistle, Lucy and Ricky both jump out of their beds in unison, sleep shattered.

Later in the kitchen, Ethel and Lucy are discussing Ernie's voluminous food intake when Ricky storms in, brandishing his maracas. One in each hand, he flails at the air, but they make no sound. Lucy explains that Ernie "fixed" them because they rattled inside. Ricky reverts to Spanish, then finishes with "Out he goes! Out!" He walks out of the door to give him the bad news.

Later in the day Ernie walks in and asks Lucy to correct the "bloopers" in his letter to his mother. Lucy sends him down to the mailbox to check the time of the last pick-up, and while he's gone, she reads the letter aloud to Ricky: "Dear Mom: How is my hound dog and how are you? My, you was all wrong about New York. I ain't seen hide nor hair of no wicked city woman like you warned me agin'.

Ricky's not happy: a letter from Lucy's mother foretells the arrival of "Cousin Ernest," her "mother's friend's roommate's cousin's middle boy."

As the Ricardos prepare for an evening of cards with the Mertzes, the argument over Lucy's mother is still simmering when the doorbell rings.

It's Cousin Ernie, who recounts his eight-hour trip around New York and Long Island on a subway in search of the "Ricker-doughs."

"I went down some steps in a hole and found some people staring in a ditch," observes Ernie about the subway. "That driver never got that thing out of that hole."

But i'fn I do, I'll hightail it right back to Bent Fork. The Ricker-doughs is two of the finest critters on this earth. I git down on my knees and ask the good Lord to bless cousin Lucy and cousin Ricky."

Ricky admits he can't throw him out after hearing the letter. The only thing that would make Ernie leave is a real, live, painted-up, wicked, city woman, and Lucy knows where she can find one.

Later, while Ernie is sitting in the living room and strumming the guitar, the doorbell rings, and he beholds Lucy, dressed to the hilt in a black sequined dress and wearing a black wig. As she slinks in with an exaggerated stride, Ernie says, "You got quite a hitch in your geta-long!"

"I'm a wicked city woman," says Lucy, purring.

"Oh, Lord have mercy!!" He retreats from her.

"I'm gonna vamp you!" She promptly starts rubbing the top of his head, and after a few rubs, he says; "Are you vampin' me?"

"Uh-huh."

"You know what? I like it!"

Lucy stops, stunned.

With his head bowed, he begs her, "Vamp me some more!"

She backs away from Ernie and reminds him what his mother said about wicked women.

"She couldn't have meant you," he swears.

Lucy runs out the door and into Ricky, explaining what happened.

"Well, I'll be ding donged!" he says.

The appearance of Tennessee Ernie Ford marked an important milestone in the *I Love Lucy* series, beginning a tradition that stayed with the Ricardos until the Lucy saga ended with the *Lucy-Desi Comedy Hour* in 1960—the use of guest stars. Though it was used strictly as a device to boost ratings, the shows with famous guest stars not only accomplished exactly that, but are considered among the finest in the entire series.

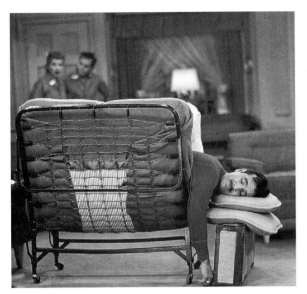

Stuck with him, the "Ricker-doughs" have to put him up for the night, but he's not up on citified "contraptions," so Ernie uses a fold-away bed Tennessee style.

At dawn, Ernie's regimen includes a wake-up-the-dead version of "The Wabash Cannonball," jarring Lucy and Ricky from a sound sleep.

After Ernie "fixes" the rattle in Ricky's prized maracas—and other well-intentioned but annoying self-appointed duties—Ricky's had it with their houseguest.

Lucy reads Ernie's pitiful letter to his mother—complimenting Cousin Lucy and Cousin Ricky on their hospitality—and Ricky's campaign to evict him withers.

Lucy then tries confronting Ernie with a "wicked city woman," but it backfires. When she "vamps" him, he likes it and he chases her around the room. Ernie's still staying at "Hotel Ricker-dough."

THE FOURTH SEASON
♥ 1954 TO 1955 ♥

#98
"LUCY CRIES WOLF"
October 18, 1954

#110
"CALIFORNIA, HERE WE COME"
January 10, 1955

#111
"FIRST STOP"
January 17, 1955

#114
"L.A. AT LAST!"
February 7, 1955

#116
"LUCY GETS IN PICTURES"
Februay 21, 1955

#124
"HARPO MARX"
May 9, 1955

#127
"THE TOUR"
May 30, 1955

"LUCY CRIES WOLF"

*A*fter reading a newspaper item about a husband who didn't come to his wife's aid during a robbery, Lucy wonders whether Ricky might do the same, and stages several bogus, life-threatening incidents to test him.

In one of those typical spouse-doubting moments, Lucy asks Ricky if he would come running if she was in danger. He proclaims that he would "come flying from the ends of the earth."

Later that morning, she phones him at the club, and describes a man on the fire escape who "had big bulgy eyes, a long black droopy moustache and long snaggly teeth, and was seven feet tall. You'd better hurry home. Hurry!"

About a minute later, the Mertzes burst though Lucy's door—Ricky obviously called them—and are surprised to find Lucy lounging on the couch. Asked what's going on, she relates the newspaper story and her hopes that Ricky would show up. Disappointed, she says, "I could have been murdered."

"You still might be!" threatens Fred. "I got better things to do." They both stalk out the door.

Lucy proceeds to trash the living room, knocking over furniture, then calls Ricky again, and this time tells him that the man is back in their apartment, as she screams into the receiver "No! No! Don't do that! Ahh! Ahhhhhh! Help!! RICKY!"

She chokes off her last words as if she's being strangled and hides in the closet. A few minutes later, Ethel saunters in the room. "C'mon, Lucy, Ricky knows you're just calling him to test him," says Ethel as she walks around to check out the premises. But when she can't find Lucy, she yells for Fred.

When Fred arrives, they widen the search, while Lucy climbs out of the bay window and onto the ledge. From her perch, she's able to hear everyone inside throughout the ensuing drama. Ethel calls Ricky in a panic, and when he flies through the door, Fred tells him he's checked with all the neighbors, and nobody has seen Lucy.

Ethel speculates that she might be hurt—"or she might even be ..." When the unthinkable hits her, she says through her tears, "I miss her already."

Fred joins in: "She was a good kid."

"If anything would happen to Lucy," mourns Ricky, "I just wouldn't

After Lucy reads an article about a husband who didn't come to his wife's help during a robbery, she wonders how Ricky would act if she were threatened.

She decides to put him to the test: Calling him at the club, she describes a man at the door with "long snaggly teeth and seven feet tall ..."

Minutes later, Fred and Ethel come to Lucy's "rescue." Fred's genuinely irritated when she explains her motives, and they both stalk out in disgust.

On her second call to Ricky, she really pours it on, telling him the man is now in the apartment—and she ends it by choking off her words as if she's being strangled.

Lucy proceeds to upend the furniture and throw some articles around the room before hiding in the living room closet.

Ethel wearily returns, but soon panics when she can't find Lucy and runs downstairs to get Fred. Meanwhile, Lucy climbs out onto the ledge.

After the Mertzes make a thorough search, Ricky finally arrives and Lucy hears him ask in deep concern: "Have you looked everywhere?"

Ethel's worry over Lucy's plight leads everyone to speculate the worst. "She was a good kid!" says Fred. Lucy's so convinced, she almost believes it herself.

The jig is up when a neighbor calls to tell Ricky that Lucy is out on the ledge, and Ethel asks: "Could I have that beautiful stole martin of hers?"

When Ricky says he's in no rush to report her missing because of the "bad publicity," Lucy almost falls off the ledge in shock and disbelief.

These tactics finally flush her off the ledge and into the apartment. Ricky explains about the neighbor's call and warns her about "crying wolf."

want to live!" Perched on her ledge, Lucy is beside herself with joy. Then the phone rings. A neighbor across the street calls to tell Ricky that Lucy is sitting on the ledge.

As he hangs up, Ricky writes a note to the Mertzes, who immediately catch on. Fred asks him if he's going to call the police, but he says the news of her disappearance would be "bad publicity." Lucy practically falls off the ledge in shock. "If she's gone, she's gone," he adds.

Says Fred, "You can always get a parrot and make it nag you and throw your money away." Ricky says he'll just have to get her out of his mind and throw away everything that reminds him of her. He offers Ethel her clothes, and Fred says they could use Lucy's mink stole for a bath mat. The trio are almost doubled over in silent laughter. When Ricky says he'll wait ten days— a "respectable amount of time"—to get remarried, Lucy can't stand it anymore. She climbs in through the window, and they tell her about the neighbor's call.

Later, while Ricky, Fred and Ethel are playing canasta, Lucy walks in. They needle her about the "prowlers and cutthroats" until she's had enough, marching defiantly out the front door, convinced that no one cares.

After a while, Ricky peeks into the hall to check on her. She's sitting in the stairwell, moping. A moment later, two real burglars creep down the stairs and grab Lucy, who screams. Our canasta players inside the apartment comment on her effective performance, admiring how she covers her mouth while screaming with a "fading effect" as she "pretends" to be carried away. "She's got a lot more talent than I give her credit for," Ricky concludes.

A short time later, when Ricky opens the door, he's confronted with a completely bound and gagged Lucy. Everyone gives her a round of applause, and Ricky hands her a statue from the mantle, announcing: "It's my great pleasure to present to you this statuette for the best performance of the year." After they remove the gag on her mouth, she hops around the room, still tied up, and tries to convince everyone what really happened, but no one believes her.

Later that evening, while everyone sits down to play canasta, Lucy persists in trying to convince everyone that there was an intruder.

After she goes out of the front door and sits in the stairwell pouting, real burglers grab Lucy and tie her up.

The canasta players hear a bump at the door, and Ricky opens it to find Lucy bound and gagged. Ricky hands her a statuette for "best performance."

Lucy tries desperately to persuade everyone that she was telling the truth, but they've heard too many stories and no one's buying it.

"CALIFORNIA, HERE WE COME"

The Ricardos are about to set out on a trip to Hollywood for Ricky's screen test for *Don Juan*, but logistical complications threaten to derail the journey.

With road maps strewn over the coffee table, Lucy's doing the last-minute planning of their Hollywood itinerary. When she shows Ethel the zigzag route she's outlined on the map, it seems to guarantee they won't make it in this century.

With deep dismay, Lucy reads Ethel a letter from her mother, who has decided to accompany them on the trip. There's only one solution, says Lucy: she'll tell Ricky that her mother is coming, and then jump out of the window. Ethel goads her into taking a firmer stand, and tells her to rehearse the bad news. She repeats it several times, and she's running down the entire speech with her back to the door just as Ricky walks in.

As he starts to yell at her in Spanish, the dreaded mother-in-law marches in behind him, and hears the heated exchange. His lame explanation that they're rehearsing his role for the movie draws an icy, unbelieving stare.

After her mother leaves, Ricky reminds Lucy that at first the trip was supposed to include only them and the baby. "Then everybody we've ever known is coming with us," he says. "First the Mertzes horn in," he says, unaware that Ethel has just walked in and can hear the whole thing. She stalks out.

A few minutes later, the Mertzes march into the Ricardos' living room to announce that they're not going to Hollywood. Lucy and Ricky ask them what the matter is. "Nothing's the matter," they say with sarcasm. "Don't forget to drop a postcard to Mr. and Mrs. Fred 'Horn-in-ski' or, as we are more commonly known, 'The Tag-Along Mertzes.'" With that they walk out of the door.

Lucy blames Ricky, and Ricky is blaming Lucy's mother just as the lady herself walks through the front door with Little Ricky. Mom then plays the martyr, telling them that she's to blame for everything and declaring that she won't go. Lucy argues with her, but Ricky says, "If she's made up her mind, don't force her," trying to hide his

The Ricardos and the Mertzes are about ready to leave on their trip to California when Lucy finds out her mother's expecting to accompany them.

Ethel gives Lucy a pep talk, telling her to take a real firm stand with Ricky, insisting that her mother accompany them on the trip.

Lucy dreads Ricky's reaction and after he finds out, he goes crazy. A quarrel begins with everyone involved—including the Mertzes. But reason finally prevails and the travelers resume their plans.

While Ricky and Fred pack the trunk, Lucy, her mother and Ethel drag seemingly every possession they own out onto the sidewalk.

Ricky and Fred close the trunk, thinking they've got the packing problem solved. Then they turn around and spot what's waiting on the curb.

Fred's packing job looks like something out of The Grapes of Wrath.

The magpies begin to argue until Ricky suggests that almost everything could be sent ahead. And Lucy's mother decides to take Little Ricky on the plane.

elation. When Lucy proclaims that she won't go if her mother doesn't, Ricky shoots back, "Well, if you're not going, then *I'm* not going!"

Fred and Ethel stroll in with smiles: "We thought it over and realized you were upset and didn't mean what you said, so we decided we're going to go on the trip after all."

"Well, send us a postcard, because we're not going," says Ricky. This is followed by a lot of folded arms and clenched fists. Then everyone then goes through an "I'm not going because…" speech. In the end, everyone again agrees to go.

The next morning, Ricky and Fred are packing the car, unaware that the three women are bringing out an endless quantity of packages behind them. When they put the last suitcase in the trunk, the boys look with satisfaction at their work, then turn around to see more bundles piled on the pavement. Undaunted, Fred asks Ricky to get some rope, and waves the women back into the brownstone.

Fred soon ushers everyone out on the stoop, and they behold a vehicle resembling something from *The Grapes of Wrath*—suitcases, boxes and paraphernalia strung around the car like decorations on a Christmas tree. "Now I've seen everything,'" says a disheartened Ricky. He finally hits on the idea of sending most of the packages ahead.

Another problem is solved when Lucy's mother decides to fly on ahead with Little Ricky. Ricky is overjoyed, and everybody agrees.

Later that day, they finally fire up the Pontiac and depart, and as they move on down the turnpike, the quartet breaks out in song: "California, Here I Come!"

After the car's repacked, Lucy says goodbye to her mother and Little Ricky while our four travelers settle in for the trip.

The car pulls away as Lucy waves goodbye.

On the road, the Ricardos and the Mertzes sing "California, Here I Come!"

"FIRST STOP"

$\mathcal{E}$n route to California, the Ricardos and the Mertzes stop at a ramshackle diner/motel with overpriced, inedible food and a proprietor right out of a hillbilly novel.

Out on the interstate, our fearless foursome is lost on some forgotten byway, desperate for a meal. They finally land at a broken-down establishment, but they're willing to give it a try. Picking up the menu, with visions of steak sandwiches and French fries, they're beginning to look it over when the hayseed proprietor, Mr. Skinner, ambles in from the back. He resembles an unmade bed, in his rumpled suspenders, undershirt and a celluloid-billed cap.

When Skinner informs them calmly that there're no steak sandwiches—or anything else they asked for—Lucy says, "Well, why don't you tell us what you *do* have?"

"How 'bout the specialty of the house? A cheese sandwich."

Skinner goes behind the counter and pulls out four bagged sandwiches, and deals them out like a hand of poker. When Lucy tries to take a bite, the piece of cheese slips out of the bread and dangles from Lucy's mouth. Lucy tries to fold it in half and put it between the slices of bread, but it's so rubbery that it causes the bread to flip off.

That's the last straw, and everyone gets up to leave. Back in the car with Lucy at the wheel, they drive for a while, and finally pull up—back in front of Skinner's roadside diner.

"Welcome back, folks," says Skinner, "I was waitin' for ya. That sign I put up really works. Takes you right around in circles!"

They're too weary to travel any farther, and decide to bed down for the night. Skinner ushers them into a room that looks more like the inside of a garage than a guest cabin. Lucy flops on the bed, and almost disappears into it. "This isn't a bed, this is a canoe," she says.

Then an advancing freight train whistle is heard, followed by a dreadful rumbling that shakes the cabin like a matchbox. Ethel, who had gone into the bathroom, reenters with trails of toothpaste all over her face and hair.

Weary from the road, the Ricardos and the Mertzes are ready for a meal, even at a dive like this one. The proprietor, Mr. Skinner, describes a menu that offers everything but edible food.

The cheese in the sandwiches at Skinner's is as rubbery as an inner tube.

Adding insult to injury, Skinner "entertains," then charges them for it. That's the last straw for everyone, especially Ricky, who piles everyone into the car.

*W*ith Lucy behind the wheel and everyone else asleep, she's finally able to find a place to lodge, but when everyone gets out, they're back at Skinner's.

*L*ying in wait for our group, a smug Skinner greets everyone: "That sign works!" It's too late, so the weary travelers resign themselves to a night at Skinner's.

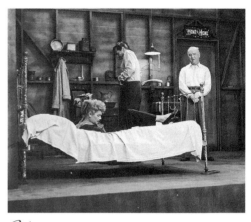

*Y*ou won't find Skinner's garage-like accommodations listed in a guide. Lucy sinks onto a mattress so saggy that she says, "This isn't a bed, it's a canoe."

*T*hen a passing freight train shakes their cabin to the rafters . . .

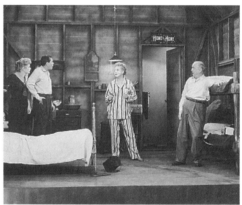

. . . and Ethel walks out afterward with a faceful of toothpaste.

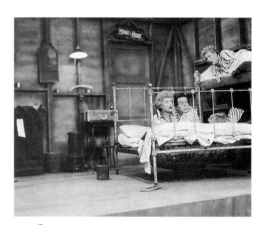

*A*nother train bounces the Ricardos' bed across the room, then another pushes them back. Lucy: "I wonder if this bed stops in Chicago?"

*A*fter switching beds with the Mertzes, then getting chased all over the room by the train-propelled bed, Ricky's had enough and suggests they hightail it.

Another train soon comes barreling by, and this time the vibration slides Lucy's and Ricky's bed clear across to the other side of the room, alongside the Mertzes' bunk. Fred wakes up to see Ricky staring him in the face. Another train from the opposite direction shakes the bed back from whence it came. "I wonder if this bed stops in Chicago," quips Lucy.

The couples decide to trade sleeping accommodations, with the Mertzes in the sagging double bed and the Ricardos giving the bunk a try. Another passing train proves too much: Ricky says he's leaving and vows that he's not paying a single cent for renting the cabin.

At the car, he discovers a string tied to the door handle. As he yanks it off, all hell breaks loose—alarms, buzzers, flashing lights all go off. Ignoring the ruckus, they crawl into the car and discover that the steering wheel is missing. Skinner appears and Lucy accuses him of taking the wheel just to keep them there. He says that people are always trying to sneak out on him, but there are no hard feelings—he'll let them go without paying. He also tells them he can help them with their steering wheel problem. It just so happens that he has one just like it on his porch and he's willing to sell it to them—for the same price as the room rental.

The gang tries to sneak out, but Skinner's ear-splitting car-alarm system goes off—and to top it all off, the steering wheel is missing.

Skinner says they don't have to pay for their room, but he'll sell them a steering wheel like the one they're "missing"—for the price of a room.

"L.A. AT LAST!"

Thrilled to be in Los Angeles, Lucy winds up celebrity hunting at the Brown Derby, and bags some big game: William Holden.

While Ricky is off to the studio, Lucy, Ethel and Fred decide to go stargazing at the Brown Derby. Even before the menus arrive, the girls and Fred begin pointing out various celebrities. Fred has more practical things in mind, like eating and berating the two for acting like tourists.

Then in strides William Holden, who sits down in the booth immediately behind Lucy. Ethel silently mouths his name to Lucy, who uses her compact mirror to spy on him in the reflection. When Holden catches her and stares back, Lucy shuts the mirror quickly and drops it in her lap.

Their order arrives—spaghetti and meatballs—and Lucy asks Fred to move over in the U-shaped booth so she can get a better look at Holden, but she keeps sliding until Fred pushes Ethel onto the floor.

Holden, who's aware of the drama unfolding next to him, slides around in the booth so that his back is to Lucy, as the waiter places a potted plant on the ledge between the booths to give him more privacy. While Holden is studying the menu, Lucy parts the foliage in the planter and he gets the uneasy sensation that he's being stared at. Musing to the waiter, he says he's going to turn the tables this time and stare back at a fan for a change. He turns around, kneels on the seat, slides the planter out of the way and props himself on his elbows on the ledge between the booths.

Lucy has her back to him and hasn't noticed his new position. She turns around, expecting the planter again, and winds up nose to nose with William Holden. Staring at him like a deity, she melts beneath his gaze, and when he gives her a grand wink, she flinches magnificently.

Lucy slides meekly back in front of her plate, rattled beyond belief. She reaches for the knife, and butters the palm of her hand. Eating her plate of spaghetti gracefully is impossible as Holden continues to stare at her with smiling pity. Her eyes widen in a cross between embarrassment and panic, as she takes in too many noodles. Ethel comes to the rescue, cutting them off with a pair of scissors.

With Ricky off to the studio, Lucy and Ethel decide to go star-hunting at the Brown Derby, and their eyes glaze over in ecstasy at the star-studded parade.

When superstar William Holden sits down in the next booth, Lucy tries to sneak a peek at him in her compact mirror.

Lucy moves in while Holden catches her in the act.

*H*olden turns the tables on Lucy while she tries to eat a plate of spaghetti . . .

. . . but when she bites off more than she can chew, Ethel comes to her rescue.

*L*ucy decides to leave, but while passing a waiter en route to the door, she knocks into his trayful of desserts—and Holden gets a faceful.

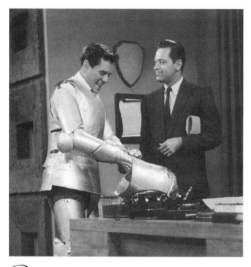

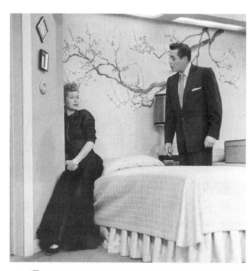

*B*ack at the studio and in costume, Ricky meets Holden, who offers him a ride back to the hotel.

*R*icky tells Holden his wife's "just dying to meet you," and goes in the other room to get Lucy. She says she's sick, then she swears she's shy.

*G*iving up, she agrees to meet him. But, "At least," she tells Ricky, "let me fix my face first"—and she puts on a putty nose to disguise herself.

*C*onfused by Lucy's new nose, Ricky introduces her to Holden. "I've seen you so many times I feel that I know you," she tells him.

"*I* have a funny feeling I know you, too," he replies.

"*M*y nose itches," says Lucy, reaching up and brushing it with her hand. Crossing her eyes, she notices that she's bent it out of shape.

Lucy can't stand this torture anymore and signals to Fred and Ethel that she wants to leave. As Lucy walks in front of Holden's booth, a waiter with a plate of dessert passes between them and she bumps into him, launching his tray straight into Holden's face. Whipped cream splatters sublimely all over him and over the wall, as Fred and Ethel grab Lucy and hustle her out the door.

Back at the studio, Ricky has been trying on costumes and runs into Holden, who offers him a ride to his hotel. Ricky asks if he has a few minutes to stop by: "My wife is just dying to meet you!"

At their hotel suite, Ricky leaves Holden in the living room and finds Lucy in the bedroom. He tells her he brought William Holden by to meet her, but he's mystified by her reaction when she drums up a variety of excuses not to go into the other room. She says she needs to "fix her face first."

Finally Lucy walks in to the living room wearing glasses, and her nose has taken on a Pinocchio appearance—it's grotesquely long. Ricky can't believe his eyes.

The putty nose Lucy has affixed to her face begins to itch, and she starts to wiggle it. "Anything wrong?" Holden asks.

"My nose itches," she says as she rubs her hand across it, causing the end to become misshapen. She turns away to realign it, but when she turns back it looks even worse than before. Picking up a cigarette case, she offers one to Holden, who lights one for her—and the fake nose catches fire. Both men look on with astonishment as Lucy crosses her eyes, watching her nose go up in flames. Everyone stands up as she blows on it to put it out and finally dunks it in a nearby cup of coffee.

Lucy comes clean as she peels off the remaining putty, admitting that she was at the Brown Derby that day. Gentleman that he is, Holden explains that he asked the head waiter who the beautiful redhead was. "I wanted to tell her that she should be in movies. But you left too soon," he says, with an epic wink that Ricky can't see. Lucy plants a big smack on Holden's lips. Exclaiming, "I KISSED BILL HOLDEN!" she falls backward into his arms, dreamy-eyed.

Lucy tries desperately to ignore her changing nose by offering a cigarette to Holden and taking one herself. Holden brings the lighter up to Lucy's face but her "nose" goes up in flames. Holden and Ricky are appalled, and she dunks it in her coffee cup. The jig is up and she comes clean, telling Holden that she was at the Brown Derby.

With a knowing wink, Holden tells Lucy he tried to get her name because he says he thought she should be in pictures. Lucy's so thrilled that he "covered" for her that she plants a big kiss on his lips.

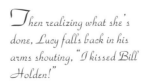

Then realizing what she's done, Lucy falls back in his arms shouting, "I kissed Bill Holden!"

"LUCY GETS IN PICTURES"

*L*ucy makes her Hollywood film debut as a Ziegfeld-type showgirl whose trip down a staircase is steered by an enormous headdress with a mind of its own.

It's just not fair: Ricky's starring in a Hollywood movie, Fred and Ethel have both been cast in a film as well. Hurt and jealous, Lucy wants to be in pictures, too. At the hotel where the Ricardos are staying, a sympathetic bellhop suggests that she go out to get herself "discovered," like Lana Turner did at the soda fountain in Schwab's. When Lucy's all-day trip to the famous drugstore leaves her still undiscovered, Ricky offers to talk to a director friend of his at MGM who might give her a little part in his new movie.

Lucy's dream comes true: she's going to play a showgirl who, during the big musical number, gets shot and dies. On the movie set, gorgeously gowned in ruffles and sequins, Lucy is being told by the director, "You're at the top of the staircase," flanked by four other beautiful showgirls. She's supposed to make her way down the steps, "a shot will ring out, you clutch your heart and you drop." Lucy nods confidently—she's ready for her big scene. Just then, a stagehand rushes over with the rest of her costume—a huge headdress covered with flopping feathers, draped with beaded necklaces and clusters of fat jewels. It's obviously top-heavy and impossible to balance, but she gamely assures the director she has everything under control. The moment the stagehand perches it on top of her head, however, Lucy is immediately tilted backward, and topples over. Getting unsteadily to her feet, she tipsily climbs the staircase, swaying like a huge palm tree in the breeze.

The director calls for a quick run-through as the music plays "A Pretty Girl Is Like a Melody," and Lucy, as the centerpiece, begins walking down the staircase. Listing from side to side, she reaches the bottom much too soon, and starts back up again, having as much trouble as she did coming down. She's about to fall over, but a stagehand rushes to her rescue, and keeps her upright. By now the director's patience is ebbing fast. The music begins again, the descent commences, and Lucy manages to remain graceful for the first two steps. Then the floor-length train attached to her headdress gets caught on a nail, and down she goes. As stagehands unhook her and prop her up,

The Mertzes are excited about upcoming movie roles they got through an old vaudeville contact. And as they leave to go to the studio, Lucy's crushed.

Ricky also leaves to go to the studio, and since he's the one who's discouraged her from trying to get into pictures, she's doubly distressed and sinks into a blue funk.

When Bobby the bellhop comes in to tell her he's got a movie part, Lucy cries—not at his performance, but because she's the only one around without a movie role.

When everyone returns home, Lucy explains that she spent the afternoon trying in vain to get "discovered" at Schwab's Drugstore.

Ricky finally can't stand it anymore and tells her he'll talk to a director he knows at MGM to see if the director can get her a small role in his latest production. Lucy is ecstatic.

Ricky manages to get her a part—as a showgirl who's shot onstage in the middle of a number. Ricky gives Lucy a good-luck kiss before leaving.

But her huge headdress weighs a ton. After a stage-hand sets it on her head and asks, "Can I let go?" Lucy sags below the weight, almost falling down.

Lucy starts down the stairs, but the headdress has a mind of its own, leading her down the staircase until she catches the train on a nail and takes a spill.

The director exchanges her big headdress for a smaller one—and a role to match—but Lucy's upset now that she's lost the opportunity to die on camera.

The director wants a faster run-through. This time Lucy falls against the balustrade, sliding all the way down on her forearms, winding up face to face with the director.

The death scene finally arrives and when the shot rings out, Lucy's so involved that she goes ahead with her screen death and clutches her chest.

Wobbling down the steps, she caroms off the sides of the staircase until she finally lands grandly at the foot of the stairs, dying in epic fashion.

the director orders a loudly protesting Lucy to switch head-dresses with one of the other showgirls—and with it goes her coveted death scene. But her high heels do her in on the next trip, and she ends up sliding down the wide, curved bannister. "Are you sure you don't want me to be the girl who gets killed?" she asks the director. "Don't tempt me," he responds through clenched teeth.

The run-throughs are over. Cameras now roll, and the big musical number begins. The center showgirl starts down first, the fatal shot rings out, she clutches her heart and falls. To the director's horror, so does Lucy, who continues dying all over the staircase, reeling, slipping and flailing her way down, landing in a dra-matic heap at the bottom. The director thinks it's time for another concept. He decides Lucy should already be dead when the scene opens. And he wants her lying face down. But she makes a prima donna demand to be face up, "into the camera." The director compro-mises—she can be face up, but she'll be lying on a stretcher that two orderlies will quickly carry out. But when she's unexpectedly covered with a sheet, leaving only her high-heeled shoes exposed, Lucy jumps off the stretcher, tells the director she'll be right back, and runs off the set. When she returns, Ricky's there, and he watches proudly as his wife "plays dead." Relieved and happy, the director yells, "Cut and print." But then an assistant whispers something in his ear that turns him angrily toward Lucy, demanding to see the bottom of her shoes. Smiling innocently, but with a touch of guilt, she props up her feet, dis-playing the soles of her high-heeled shoes. In big white letters, one sole reads "LUCY" and the other "RICARDO."

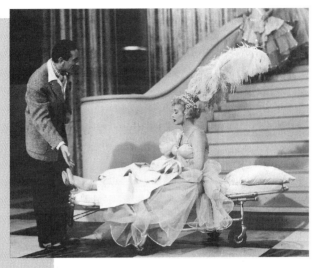

The director's had enough, so he agrees that he'll have her dead, covered in a sheet, lying on a gurney. Lucy: "How will people recognize me?" Director: "Your feet."

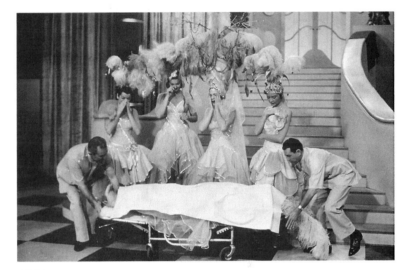

When she returns after "powdering her nose," Lucy dutifully lies down, is covered and the filming begins. When she's wheeled off the set, the director yells, "Cut!"

With the scene over, Lucy's ready to leave when the director demands, "Let me see your feet." Lifting them, her soles have "LUCY RICAR-DO" painted on them.

EPISODE
124

"HARPO MARX"

*L*ucy impersonates celebrities to impress a visiting friend, when a visit from the real Harpo Marx brings him together with Lucy's "Harpo Marx," in a classic turn at vaudeville pantomime.

*L*ucy's and Ethel's New York acquaintance Carolyn Appleby decides to take Lucy up on her invitation to stop over in Los Angeles to meet all the stars she says she's been schmoozing with. As usual, Lucy's exaggerated most of her socializing, but she wants to make an impression, so she's come up with a way to fool Carolyn.

Her friend has poor eyesight, so Lucy plans to masquerade as a variety of famous people. When Carolyn arrives, Lucy rattles off her roster of famous people.

Lucy and Ethel manage to hide her glasses, and while Ethel tries to "help" her find them, Lucy uses some lifelike masks to fool Carolyn. A short while later, "Gary Cooper" ambles in the door with a litany of "yups" and "nopes." After he leaves, the bell rings again and this time "Clark Gable" comes in, followed by "Walter Pidgeon" and "Bing Crosby."

Down at the pool, Ricky and Fred are talking but Fred's too busy watching the bathing suits by the pool to pay much attention. Then the stillness is shattered by two screaming beauties being chased by the real Harpo Marx. As Harpo passes by, he stops in his tracks, recognizing Ricky.

Then, in pantomime, he explains that he's here for a Women's Club Benefit—"Bend-Knee-Feet." Ricky asks Harpo if he'll go up to his room and impress Lucy, Ethel and Carolyn with a visit from a genuine movie star.

Back in the room after "Jimmy Durante" leaves, Ethel opens the door and finds the real Harpo Marx: She thinks it's really Lucy.

Carolyn mentions his woman-chasing bit: "You don't really do that, do you?" He gives Carolyn "that look" and starts to chase her around the room. "You didn't bring your harp, did you?" says Carolyn. He whistles in the affirmative and goes to get it.

The doorbell rings again and this time Lucy bursts in as "Harpo," scuttling across the room. She stops when she doesn't see Carolyn, and asks Ethel where she is. Ethel tells Lucy that Carolyn left to freshen up her makeup. Just when they begin to realize that the real

*T*o impress her myopic friend Carolyn about her close relationship with film stars, Lucy tests her eyesight while Ethel grabs her glasses. Nearly blind without them, Lucy can fool her by wearing movie-star masks.

*W*hen "Gary Cooper" makes an appearance, Lucy has Carolyn fooled with a Cooperesque string of monosyllabic "yups" and "nopes."

*M*eanwhile, down at the pool, Ricky's feeling bad about how he's treated Lucy, but Fred's more interested in checking out the "scenery."

Harpo Marx appears chasing the bathing beauties, but he stops to greet Ricky and explains—via pantomime—that he's there for a Women's Club Benefit.

Harpo squeezes Ricky's face to help him form the word benefit: "Bend-Knee-Feet." Afterward, Ricky asks if he'll surprise Lucy with a visit.

By this time, other "stars" have dropped in—including "Jimmy Durante"—and Carolyn is beside herself at the parade.

The next visitor is Harpo Marx—the real one—and Carolyn asks if he brought his harp. Thinking it's really Lucy, Ethel says "no," but he runs to get it.

While Carolyn is in the bathroom, Lucy arrives as "Harpo," and Ethel realizes that the real Harpo has just left.

With another knock, Harpo enters and Lucy hides behind the doorway to the kitchenette.

Ethel and Carolyn hear Harpo's rendition of "Take Me Out to the Ball Game."

After the recital Harpo picks up Carolyn and carries her out of the room.

Harpo was in the room, the doorbell rings.

Lucy hides in the kitchenette, as Harpo walks in with his harp. After he sets it down, Carolyn comes back in and he plays "Take Me Out to the Ball Game." Afterwards, he chases the two girls out of the room and catches sight of what appears to be his double: Lucy peeking around the folding kitchenette door. He stalks slowly over and plants his foot in the archway of the door. Lucy does the same. The two Harpos perform the same mirror image pantomime, with the real Harpo taking the lead and Lucy's Harpo matching his every move.

Facing each other, the two put hands on hips, reach out, touch hands, rub the imaginary mirror, breathe on it, rub again…hands back on hips…drop hands from hips—first slow, then fast—then up high, down again slowly…synchronized clapping…then the final clap. Back behind the door.

Harpo is more than bewildered—he's amazed! Snapping his fingers, he figures he'll fool his alter ego on the other side by making one of his famous faces—but he's bowled over to see his image staring back at him with the same puff-mouthed expression.

Finally, he decides to give it one more shot. The two Harpos reach out to take off their hats in a sweeping move. Harpo makes a gesture to drop his hat, but doesn't. Neither does his double. On the third time he lets it go, and so does his double, but with one trick left up his sleeve: Harpo has tied the hat onto an elastic band causing it to yo-yo back into his waiting hands.

Harpo explains in pantomime that Ricky put him up to this whole visit—just as Ricky and Fred walk in—as Groucho and Chico. Ricky asks which of the two Harpos is the real one. Holding hands, they both stroll over to the couch, sit down, each crossing their legs over each other, followed by their arms, and finally the two nest their heads together—pantomime pals.

Sneaking back into the room to chase Ethel, he sees his double peeking around the door. Flabbergasted, he stalks over and steps out in front of the archway.

Standing face-to-face with "Harpo," Harpo tries some pantomimic tricks to expose the impostor…

…beginning with a series of complicated hand gestures…

…then a series of his famous "faces"—but Lucy apes him move for move.

Finally Harpo launches his old retrieve-the-hat-with-the-elastic-band gimmick, and he wins in a final gesture of one-upsmanship. He's almost met his match.

"THE TOUR"

*R*icky refuses to bring Lucy to lunch with Richard Widmark, so Lucy and Ethel take a movie star tour, and Lucy winds up trapped on the star's Beverly Hills estate.

Ricky is set to have lunch with Richard Widmark, and Lucy wants to join in. He adamantly refuses: "If I as much as see your face, I'll wrap you up in brown paper and mail you back to New York."

Ethel suggests that a bus tour of the stars' homes would be a good way to get closer to them. Lucy argues that she'd rather see them in person, but they decide to give the tour a try anyway.

By the time the bus reaches Beverly Hills, the driver has had enough of Lucy's antics. When they pull up in front of the home of Richard Widmark, she launches into a boastful proclamation that her husband is having lunch with the star at that very moment.

"Nooo!" mocks the driver. "Wait'll I tell Lana at dinner tonight!"

Lucy persists, but no one is buying her story. Gazing at Widmark's house, she spots a grapefruit tree in his backyard. "Gee, I'd like to have a Richard Widmark grapefruit to go with my Robert Taylor orange!"

At Widmark's backyard wall, Lucy finds the prospect of scaling it far more daunting than at first glance. Ethel gives her a boost and, perched on the top, Lucy reaches too far and falls into the backyard. "I got one!!" she yells from the other side. "Gee, is it beautiful. A swimming pool…a tennis court…and a barbecue pit…and a doghouse [yelling] *and a dog!!*"

The dog seems to have taken a shine to Lucy, and begins to drag her back down from the wall. After it grabs her shoe, she hollers to Ethel that there's no way to get back over the wall, and Lucy tells her to go around to the front door—she'll try to sneak through the house.

Lucy is making her way down the hallway when the maid answers the phone, forcing Lucy to duck into a den filled with animal trophies. The call is for the maid, who begins a long-winded gossip session, blocking Lucy's exit.

After waiting an hour for Lucy, Ethel rushes to a nearby pay

Ricky's sprucing up for lunch with Richard Widmark and Lucy wants to join in, but Ricky refuses to have her "within pie-throwing distance."

So Lucy and Ethel take a bus tour through the streets of Beverly Hills.

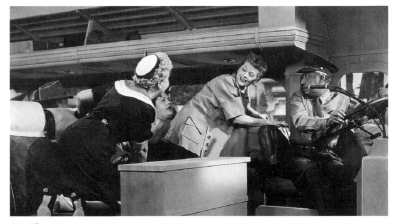

As the driver points out Shirley Temple's "dollhouse," Lucy's all over the bus. He says: "Your ticket entitles you to one seat. Will you please stay in it?"

Lucy's running commentary about Ava Gardner's lingerie irritates the driver who pokes the PA microphone at her just as she's saying "black lace lingerie."

After Lucy and Ethel leave the bus to take a grapefruit from a tree at Richard Widmark's house, Lucy falls into the backyard.

As Lucy tries to get through the house, she finds herself in Widmark's trophy room mugging at a bear's head mounted on the wall.

By the time she's got a chance to escape, Widmark comes home with Ricky, so Lucy tries to blend in with the decor.

When Widmark's dog saunters in and sits on the bearskin rug, the two men notice that the rug has come to life, and the star goes for his gun.

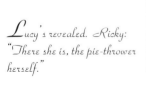

Lucy's revealed. Ricky: "There she is, the pie-thrower herself."

phone and calls Fred for reinforcements. To make matters worse, she just saw Ricky pull up with Widmark—there will be hell to pay.

Widmark gives Ricky a tour of his estate. While they're admiring his animal trophy displays in the den, the bearskin rug on the floor comes to life. They don't notice, and Ricky's tour continues, while Widmark's dog—a huge St. Bernard named Cap—trots in and lies down on the rug, with Lucy trapped beneath.

As Widmark is showing Ricky his elephant gun over the mantle, the bear comes to life again, this time in full view of the two. Widmark points his gun at the bear and Ricky walks slowly over, knowing already exactly who's underneath the rug.

Ricky pulls off the rug and there she is. "The pie-thrower herself," he says.

As Lucy stumbles to explain, she asks Widmark to lower the gun.

"Well, I don't know about that," says Widmark. "It would be such a public service."

"Go ahead, 'splain," says Ricky.

Lucy begins by blaming Widmark: if his walls weren't so high, she wouldn't have gotten trapped trying to grab one of his grapefruits.

"It sort of makes sense—in a crazy mixed-up way," concludes Widmark.

The maid announces that some people from the mental hospital have arrived, and when Fred and Ethel enter in white uniforms, Ricky buries his head in embarrassment. They advance on Lucy with a net, but Ricky informs them that the jig is up.

"You must lead a very interesting life," says Widmark.

"Well, you know everybody has a problem," explains Ricky. "There are some people that have financial problems, and then there are people that have health problems, everybody has something." In a grand gesture, he wraps it up: "Well, there it is. It's my problem. But I love her."

Lucy stares back at Ricky with a sick, silly little smile. "Oh, isn't he wonderful," says Lucy, walking over and giving Ricky a big hug.

Lucy: "I can explain how this all happened." Holding his gun, Widmark says getting rid of her "would be a public service."

Posing as a mental hospital team, Fred and Ethel try to snag Lucy with a net.

After Ricky explains everything to the Mertzes, he says, "Everybody has a problem. Well, there it is. It's my problem. But I love her."

Lucy won't give up, though. With the chutzpah only she could muster, she asks Widmark to sign the grapefruit she stole from his backyard.

THE FIFTH SEASON
♥ 1955 to 1956 ♥

#129
"Lucy and John Wayne"
October 10, 1955

#130
"Lucy and the Dummy"
October 17, 1955

#132
"The Great Train Robbery"
October 31, 1955

#140
"Bon Voyage"
January 16, 1956

#145
"Paris at Last!"
February 27, 1956

#146
"Lucy Meets Charles Boyer"
March 5, 1956

#150
"Lucy's Italian Movie"
April 16, 1956

EPISODE 129

"LUCY AND JOHN WAYNE"

*R*icky is trying his best to patch up the damage Lucy has caused by trying to "borrow" John Wayne's footprints from Grauman's Chinese Theater. Wayne does his best to help, but no one reckons on Lucy's ability to escalate her campaign of calamity.

Lucy is in hot water with the manager of the Chinese Theater for shattering the slab of cement containing John Wayne's footprints. But Ricky comes up with a brilliant idea: he tells Fred that he'll go to the Duke and ask him for another print. Wayne agrees. Visiting the Ricardos' hotel room, Wayne says he's "flattered" that Lucy is such a fan, and asks if she's around. "I've heard a lot about her from Bill Holden." Ricky winces at the reference.

Wayne sits down in front of the wet slab of cement on the floor, makes his foot impressions, and then signs his autograph with a stick. Ricky figures he is home free, and they both leave. A moment later, Lucy and Ethel return from their hair appointments and see the redone imprints. Assuming it's Ricky's and Fred's work, Lucy says, "Nice try, but they'll never get away with it." She picks up the trowel and obliterates Wayne's work.

Fred bursts into the room and shows Ethel the signature he received from Wayne when he was there a few minutes ago. Ricky comes back and confirms that Wayne was in the room. As a matter of fact, "he's down in the lobby getting his boots shined. He got them all dirty when he..." His eyes fall on the slab of cement, and he becomes furious when he sees what Lucy has done to Wayne's work. Lucy babbles her remorse, and suggests he go back downstairs to get Wayne for a "retake." He leaves the room, murmuring Latinisms.

At the moment Wayne walks in the girls realize their hair is still in curlers, and they go into a flurry of hand and arm movements to hide their heads. Lucy finally dumps out the contents of her purse and puts it over her head. Amazed at what's unfolding before him, Wayne says, "I'm afraid I owe Bill Holden an apology!"

Lucy and Ethel fawn over him, while he sticks his feet back in the cement, and they continue to make fools of themselves until Wayne leaves. As the group is occupied at the door, Little Ricky crawls into the cement and completely demolishes the footprints all over again.

Ricky is with Wayne later at the studio when he steps out of his boots after doing the footprints for the third time. Brimming over

After Lucy steals John Wayne's footprints from the Chinese Theater, Ricky tries to keep the manager from turning her over to the police if they bring it back. Unfortunately, it's shattered in a thousand pieces.

When Fred's bogus replacement doesn't make the grade, Ricky decides to call "the Duke" to ask for a new set—and Wayne agrees.

Twisting Wayne's legs in the process, Ricky and Fred manage to get the impression.

When Lucy sees the new prints, she thinks it's another poor attempt by the boys and erases it with a trowel. They're going to have to get another set.

Ricky snags the Duke for a second sitting, but this time he has to contend with Lucy's equally sticky fawning over him. Unfortunately, after Wayne leaves, Little Ricky crawls on the cement, and they'll have to get still another print.

After making another set of footprints in the studio dressing room, Ricky removes Wayne's boots to clean them one last time.

with apologies, Ricky tells Wayne that, just to keep matters uncomplicated, he didn't tell Lucy he was coming. Wayne is called to the set, and Ricky is preparing to leave—while Lucy and Ethel are dragging their own cement slab into position right in front of the dressing room steps in hopes of getting Wayne to step on it for a new set of footprints.

Wrestling with his own slab, Ricky comes out the door, down the steps and into the wet cement. He loses his footing and the slab he's carrying lands on top of his head, smearing its contents all over his face before it drops on the floor beside him.

When Ricky realizes what's happened, he can only utter a primal moan, and scurry off the soundstage like a wounded animal. Lucy decides to borrow Wayne's shoes for still another impression, and breaks into the dressing room to find them. She's still there when Wayne comes back into the dressing room, and she ducks into the closet.

After he flops face down on his massage table, Lucy tries to sneak out, but Wayne catches her in mid-step. "George?" He doesn't look up. "Let's get on with the rubdown."

Lucy puts one hand over her face, opens one eye between her fingers, looks down, nods approval, and dives in for the rubdown.

"You heard any good stories, George? I heard a beaut in the steam room the other day."

Distress creeps over her face as Wayne begins his "Farmer's Daughter" tale. Just as the story gets close to the raunchy part, Wayne is called onto the set. As he gets up, Lucy throws his robe over his head and scampers out of the door.

Back at the hotel, as Lucy is telling Ricky and Fred that she left Ethel behind at the studio, Ethel saunters in with Wayne in tow, carrying another finished slab. Almost knocking Ricky over, Lucy runs over to Wayne, promising that they'll take good care of it.

"I took care of that," he says. "Come on in, boys. I brought you a six-month's supply."

A team of bellboys carry in three more slabs, as Wayne picks up Lucy and Ethel by the waist. They plant big kisses on his cheeks.

Lucy and *Ethel* have dragged another slab to the stairs outside *Wayne*'s dressing room, and *Ricky* steps in it on his way out, ruining both slabs.

When Ricky realizes that *Lucy*'s done it again, he's only able to utter a primal moan and shuffles off the set, a broken man.

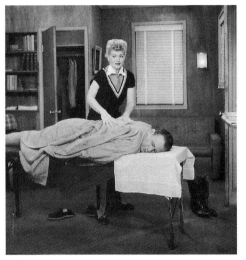

While Lucy's in the dressing room to borrow *Wayne*'s boots for a new impression, he comes in and plops on the massage table, thinking she's his masseur.

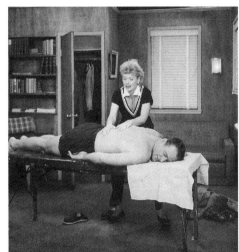

"*Heard* any good stories, *George*?" says *Wayne*. "*I* heard a beaut in the steam room the other day. *Seems* there was this farmer's daughter . . ." *Just* as the tale gets too racy, *Lucy* throws a robe on his head and sprints out the door.

Lucy's ecstatic when *Wayne* shows up at their hotel with "a six-month's supply" of footprints—four brand-new signed slabs.

The girls let him sweep them up in both arms for a tandem kiss.

"LUCY AND THE DUMMY"

*L*ucy's dance number with a life-sized dummy of Ricky is such a huge hit at an MGM studio party that she is offered a fantastic movie contract that Ricky has to talk her out of.

Ricky brings Lucy a souvenir from the Hollywood movie he just starred in—it's a life-sized mannequin head of him that was used for trick shots, and it looks amazingly real. Right now, Ricky is happy that he's finished the film and is going on a two-day, deep-sea fishing trip. Even when MGM calls to ask if he's available to entertain at a party for the studio executives tomorrow night, he refuses to cancel his trip. Without Ricky knowing it, Lucy tells MGM that both Mr. and Mrs. Ricardo—"a great undiscovered talent"—will be happy to perform their song-and-dance number for the studio show. How she will pull this one off, with Ricky out of town, suddenly becomes clear to Lucy as she studies the dummy's head.

The next morning, after Ricky leaves, Lucy invites Ethel and Fred to preview her performance. As the Mertzes watch, and with a recording of Ricky singing "I Get Ideas" in the background, Lucy comes tangoing out of the bedroom with a life-sized dummy in a gaudy gaucho costume, its feet attached to her shoes, and the mannequin head of Ricky on top. Ethel thinks she might fool the audience, if only for a few seconds, and that's all Lucy needs to hear. She plans to come out dancing with "Ricky," then pretend he's suddenly taken ill, dance him offstage, come back, and finish the number herself.

That night at the studio gala, the emcee announces the Ricardos' act, and the curtains part. Clad in a Spanish costume and dark wig, with a mantilla atop her head and a long, black, lace veil, Lucy dances onstage with the dummy attached to her, as she lip-syncs "I Get Ideas." After a few gracefully executed tango turns, she suddenly lets "Ricky" drop as if he's collapsing against her chest. She tells the audience that "something's the matter with Mr. Ricardo," but not to be alarmed—the show must go on—and she'll be right back. She dashes into the wings, where the waiting Mertzes start detaching her from the dummy. Lucy comes gliding out again, trailing her long veil, but when she's halfway across the stage, it yanks her backward.

Ricky brings home a life-size mannequin head of himself made by the studio for special effects.

While Ricky's in the shower, the studio calls to invite him to entertain at a party. She accepts for him, but Ricky's decided to go fishing.

With Ricky packed off on his fishing trip, she's still excited about performing in front of show-business elite. She takes another look at the head and gets an idea.

When the Mertzes return later, Lucy's put Ricky's head on a dummy and tells them about her plan to perform a tango number and pass off the dummy as Ricky.

At the party, Lucy dances onstage with the dummy of Ricky attached to her feet.

All goes well until the dummy slips, caught in her mantilla. Lucy apologizes, explaining that Ricky's fallen ill.

Taking the dummy backstage and dropping it off with the Mertzes for repairs, she hurries back onstage—but the dummy's still attached, pulling on her mantilla.

As she moves across the stage absorbed in her song, the dummy follows. Turning finally, she looks down and exclaims, "What a trouper!"

She tugs hard on it, starts gliding again, and the end of the veil emerges with the dummy still attached to it, on its stomach, face down—it couldn't look more like a dead body if it was one. "What a trooper," Lucy says to the audience, and rushes offstage, where the Mertzes again work frantically to separate the dummy from the veil. When Lucy reappears onstage once more, she pulls the veil too hard and it comes flying at her with "Ricky" in tow, knocking her down and into a sitting position on top of him. Up again, she continues singing, lifts the dummy into her arms—his legs flying over her right shoulder—and, realizing she'll never extricate herself from him, keeps on singing while holding "Ricky" in her arms like a baby. Her finale is a bow so deep that Lucy accidentally knocks off his head, which rolls around on the stage as she gives it several kicks, and one that finally sends it into the wings.

The next day, Ricky returns to find Ethel and Fred in his hotel room, but no Lucy. Ethel explains that last night's performance was considered such a great comedy act that MGM has offered Lucy a fabulous, one-year movie deal. She's at the studio, going over the contract right now. When Lucy comes in with her exciting news, Ricky says he's thrilled for her, but he, Little Ricky and the Mertzes are headed back to New York—he has nightclub commitments, and Fred and Ethel have an apartment building to run. Ricky tells her, "You can come and visit us every Christmas, and I'll show Little Ricky your picture every night so he won't forget his mommy." Lucy's miserable, torn between career and personal life. That night, alone in the living room, she pantomimes having become a big star, signing autographs, accepting her sixth Oscar—and then hears Little Ricky crying in the distance. She returns to reality, and runs into his room. A few moments later, the Ricardos are in each other's arms, and a long, loving kiss clinches the only deal Lucy really wants.

Picking it up, she continues the song, finally heading back to the Mertzes.

She keeps singing, poking her head from behind the curtain.

They can't detach it, so she carries it back on stage—but as she finishes the song, the head falls off the body. Desperate, she kicks it offstage.

When Ricky returns and learns that the studio offered Lucy a contract, he urges her to pursue her new showbiz career. "You can come and visit us every Christmas."

After trying to imagine a future without her family, Lucy realizes at last how happy she is with Ricky and Little Ricky.

EPISODE 132

"THE GREAT TRAIN ROBBERY"

On the train back to New York after their visit to Hollywood, Lucy thinks a dangerous jewel thief is on board, but this mistaken identity leads her into trouble with a real jewel thief.

The Ricardos and the Mertzes are on their way back home from Hollywood. As the train is about ready to leave, Lucy remembers she left her purse in the station. After Ricky steps off the train to find her purse, the train starts to leave, so she pulls the emergency cord, stopping the train with a jolt. Fred and Ethel, who have been in the dining car, walk in covered with food.

While Lucy and Ricky join the Mertzes in the dining car, back at the compartment the conductor moves Lucy's mother and Little Ricky into another compartment because of a ticket mix-up.

Holding the right ticket, a Mr. Estes moves into Mom's former compartment. The conductor spots a gun in his shoulder holster and quips: "Jewelry business must be successful if you have to wear that, Mr. Estes!"

Lucy, meanwhile, returns with a sandwich for her mother, and when Estes answers the door—holster and all—Lucy freaks out. Convinced that he has done something to her mother and her child, she flails her way down the hall, yanks the emergency cord, and again the train grinds to a halt.

When Ethel, Fred and Ricky walk in from the dining car, covered from head to toe in splattered food, the conductor is explaining to Lucy that he moved her mother and Little Ricky to another compartment.

Later, a detective knocks on the door and asks for their identification, explaining that there's been a jewel robbery, and he's checking out the passengers. Lucy warns him about the man in the next compartment, who's carrying a gun.

Ricky reminds her that they haven't eaten and heads for the door. As he walks down the aisle, Lucy tells him to go on ahead, she'll be along. Back in the compartment, she opens the adjoining door and sees Estes examining some jewelry. He spots her, pulls out his gun and says he wants to talk with her. She slams the door on him as Ricky comes back into the compartment. When she tells him what just happened, he says that the police have already talked with the man

On their way home by train, Lucy's left her purse in the station and Ricky rushes to fetch it. The train starts to leave so she pulls the emergency brake to get him back on.

After the train stops abruptly, the Mertzes appear—their clothes spattered with dinner. Soon after, Ricky returns relating how he ran into the end of the train.

Finally, the conductor emerges, his hat crumpled. "Did you stop the train by pulling that handle?" he says. "I didn't do it by dragging my foot," she retorts.

After spotting a man with a gun in the next compartment, Lucy thinks he's the jewel thief who's rumored to be on the train and tries to convince a dubious Ricky.

In the lounge car, Lucy tells Ethel about the thief while a man nearby shows interest. Ethel's worried about her jewelry, so she leaves to check on it.

When Lucy claims the jewel thief is in the compartment next to theirs, the man explains he's a "special agent" and recruits her to help him.

In the compartment, he tells her to lure the thief in—vamp style. Lucy gyrates her hips and sneers. "That's great!" says the man. "Pretend you're sick."

Holding her stomach, Lucy moans, and when the man next door—a genuine jeweler—bursts into the room, the "agent" hits him over the head.

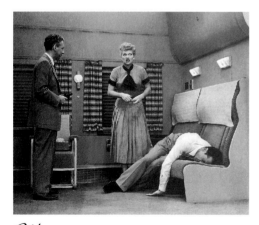

When the "agent" turns his gun on her, it dawns on Lucy that he just might not be who he claims to be. "Yeeeeooooouuugh!" she cries.

The man takes her hostage, but Lucy eludes him and ducks into the men's room, emerging disguised with shaving cream. She again pulls the emergency cord.

After Ricky subdues the thief, the Mertzes appear with their clothes once again a food fresco. As they glare at Lucy with loathing, she tries to explain.

and don't consider him a suspect—case closed. He pulls her out of the door, and ushers her toward the dining car.

In the dining car, while Lucy tells Ethel about what's been going on, a man sitting next to them is eavesdropping from behind a newspaper. When Ethel leaves to make sure her own jewelry is safe, the man convinces Lucy that he's a "special agent," and orders her to help him apprehend this criminal.

Back in the compartment, he instructs Lucy to lure Estes in, and he'll take care of the rest. When she pounds on the door and moans, Estes barges into the room and the "special agent" knocks him out. Flushed with excitement, Lucy jumps up and down shouting, "Let's put the cuffs on him!"

The man turns slowly to point the gun at Lucy and she says with alarm: "I made a boo boo? He's not the man the police are looking for? You? Yeeeeoooouuugh," says Lucy in her spider voice.

Poking the gun in Lucy's rib cage and sneering, the man says, "We're gonna walk out of here and stop between the next two cars."

As they move down the aisle, a cluster of people come between Lucy and the gunman, and she slips into the men's room. A moment later, she comes out in a stolen robe and a bowler hat, applying shaving cream to her face with a brush.

As she walks down the aisle, she passes Ricky and screams, pointing at her pursuer: "He's the real jewel thief! He's got a gun!" As the man advances on them, Lucy pulls the emergency cord again, and the train lurches to a stop. Ricky wrestles the man to the floor and grabs the gun away from him.

In the aftermath, a reporter and his photographer question Lucy about her heroics. In reenacting the drama, of course, she accidentally pulls the emergency cord again. Moments later the Mertzes come in again, covered with food—but this time they're wearing raincoats.

But Lucy's the heroine as a newspaperman interviews her in the hallway where it all happened, and a news photographer sets up for a reenactment.

But in trying to reconstruct the action, Lucy pulls the cord again, sending everyone to the floor, including a woman who leaps from her berth brandishing an umbrella.

Before the woman can use it on Lucy, Fred and Ethel come sauntering back—but this time they were ready—fully clad in rain gear.

"BON VOYAGE"

The Ricardos and the Mertzes are about to shove off on their long-awaited trip to Europe—but Lucy almost misses the boat.

*L*ucy wants to give Little Ricky one last kiss before leaving on their transatlantic trip, so she debarks, and after a long goodbye, her dress is caught up in a bicycle wheel and she can't get back on the ship. Lucy, Lucy's mother, the babysitter Mrs. Trumbull and the distraught owner of the bicycle try to extricate Lucy from the gears while the ship gives one last toot.

Meanwhile Ricky, who doesn't know that Lucy's not on the ship, is up on the deck waving goodbye: "Goodbye Little Ricky, goodbye Mrs. Trumbull, goodbye Mother, goodbye Lucy. LUCY?!"

Ricky's eyes pop out of his head when he sees her on the dock, and he runs down to the gangplank entrance below. Panicked, Lucy picks up the bicycle she's attached to, but the owner won't let her take it on board. After a struggle, she finally gives up and takes off her skirt, but while she's running up the gangplank, a hoist removes it from the ship. Standing in the entranceway, Ricky yells at her to jump, but the ship is already in motion and too far away to risk a try at it. The ship pulls away from the dock, on its way into the harbor.

Ricky runs upstairs and explains what happened to one of the ship's officers, who tells him Lucy can be brought out on a pilot boat by calling the dock agent, who's down with Lucy. Rushing to his cabin, Ricky regresses to Spanish in talking to the ship's operator, but manages to collect himself, and is finally patched through to the dock agent. "Say, Doc," he says, "please page Mrs. Ricky Ricardo." She gets on the phone and lapses into one of her crying jags, until Ricky explains that she can still get to the ship on the pilot boat. She hangs up, asks the dock agent what to do, and he

*T*he Ricardos and the Mertzes are about to set sail for Europe, and tearful goodbyes are the order of the day as the ship's PA system announces the "all ashore" warning.

*W*aving goodbye to her mother and Little Ricky, Lucy experiences one last homesick pang and decides to run down the gangplank for a final kiss.

*L*ucy manages to get down on the dock and after one more goodbye she's about to run toward the gangplank when she catches her dress in the gears of a bicycle.

On the deck, Ricky blithely waves goodbye to Little Ricky, his mother-in-law, Mrs. Trumbull and Lucy. "Lucy?" he yells as she struggles with the bicycle.

Ricky calls the dock agent, who puts a weeping Lucy on the phone. He tells her that a pilot boat can take her out to the ocean liner.

A bedraggled Lucy returns several minutes later: "Have you got a pilot boat that goes to the pilot boat?" She then explains how she ran to the end of the pier . . .

. . . and landed "kerplunk on the deck. That boat was on the way in, and by the time I noticed my mistake the outgoing boat had already left."

The dock agent suggests Lucy catch the ship by helicopter, so she hightails it to Idlewild airport, but the 'copter's already left to pick her up at the pier.

Once on the aircraft, the pilot tells her to enjoy the view, but Lucy points out a cigar on the water. "That cigar is your ship," he says. "That dinky little thing?" she declares.

As it starts getting closer, the pilot informs her that they're going to lower her down in a harness. Lucy: "You're going to lower who in a what?"

"Put your legs over the side and jump out," the pilot instructs. "Jump out?" She seems glued to her seat until he gives her a push.

explains that she needs to catch a pilot boat at the end of the pier. She runs out and then runs back in a few minutes later. The dock agent doesn't understand why she missed the boat. She explains that when she reached the end of the pier, she saw that one pilot boat had just left, so she jumped onto another one, but it was on the way in. By the time she realized her mistake, it was too late.

She doesn't know what to do, until the agent suggests she can try hiring a helicopter from Idlewild [now Kennedy] airport. Lucy treks all the way to the airport and hires a pilot.

When the pilot boat reaches the liner and they find out that Lucy missed that one, too, Ricky can't understand why. But Fred has the answer: "Because she's Lucy."

Just when Ricky and the Mertzes have given up, they receive word that Lucy is on her way by helicopter. Tethered to the end of a rescue line, she's having second thoughts about the whole thing, but after several passes, she finally lands on the deck, and clings to Ricky. Bon Voyage!

After dropping like a rock and then bobbing up and down several times, she finally lands safely on the deck. "There's nothing to it," she tells them breezily.

Whereupon, crossing her eyes, she falls into Ricky's arms in a dead faint.

"PARIS AT LAST!"

*L*ucy's misadventures in Paris get everyone in hot water with the *gendarmes* for passing counterfeit French francs and bogus paintings.

While heading into the foreign exchange office to convert some American dollars into French francs, Lucy meets a man who says he can give Lucy a better exchange rate than the one she can get inside. "I work out of doors, no overhead—no building, you see."

"That makes sense," says Lucy. The man yanks her money away, hands her his currency and beats a hasty retreat around the corner. Within seconds a *gendarme* strolls by, followed by Fred and Ethel.

Lucy reveals her stroke of luck, and gives Fred some of her money so that he can cash in on the bargain. While the Mertzes enter the exchange building to pick up their mail, she spies an artist down the block who sells her his painting for a thousand francs, proclaiming, "This picture is my life—it took me three years to paint." As soon as she's out of sight, of course, he takes out a copy of the same painting and sets it up on his easel for the next sucker.

As Lucy soaks up the sights of Paris, she stops at a sidewalk café and manages a fairly convincing masquerade as a French woman while placing an order. A few minutes later, when the waiter returns with a plateful of *escargot*, she reverts rapidly back to her native tongue: "Waiter, this food has snails in it!"

"Oui, *escargot*. Mmmmmmm!" he says with delight.

"I'm supposed to eat this?"

"Oui, *mange*," he says, repeating her gesture. He hands her a pair of tongs.

In a quandary about their use, she places them over her nose. Startled, the waiter deftly removes the tongs from her nostrils and demonstrates their proper use. Lucy picks gingerly at the shell, and finally asks: "Maybe if I had some catsup...?"

He leaves and, a moment later, the serenity of the café is shattered when the chef comes out to find out who's desecrating his cuisine. Sputtering a string of French phrases and brandishing a bottle of catsup, he blasts Lucy.

In Paris, Lucy's on her way to exchange dollars to francs when she's stopped by a man who says he can give her a better rate. She goes for it.

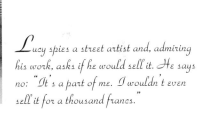

Lucy feels she's made a deal and passes some of her new francs to Fred Mertz.

Lucy spies a street artist and, admiring his work, asks if he would sell it. He says no: "It's a part of me. I wouldn't even sell it for a thousand francs."

"A thousand francs?" she repeats. "I'll take it," he says, grabbing her money and handing her the painting.

*L*ucy sits down at a sidewalk café and unwittingly orders escargot. When the order arrives, she complains, "*Waiter, this food has snails in it.*" "*Mmmm!*" he replies.

*S*he picks up a pair of tongs and—looking around as if to see what others might be doing with theirs—clamps them on her nose.

*A*fter the waiter demonstrates their proper use, Lucy pantomimes an order for catsup.

*T*he waiter returns with the chef, who's apoplectic over this desecration.

*L*ucy's had enough, asks for the check and hands the waiter her remaining francs. Before she can get very far, the waiter and the chef shout, "*Contrefait.*"

*C*alling her husband from the police station, Lucy cries, "*Ricky, I'm in the Bastille.*"

*L*ucy explains to Ricky how she was handed counterfeit money by a street-side sharpster. A jailed drunken Spaniard who speaks German is dragged in to trans-late.

*T*he exasperated sergeant says he'll let her go if she'll pay the restaurant bill. Hearing this, she says "*Hooray!*" Ricky says "*Olé!*" the Spaniard says "*Wunderbar!*" and the *gendarme* turns to the sergeant, kissing him with a hearty "*Très bien!*"

Lucy's had enough French culture and asks for the check. Handing the waiter the money, she tells him to keep the change, and gets up. She doesn't even reach the sidewalk when the waiter and the chef run after her, grab her and yell. Lucy complains, "Since when is it a crime to put catsup on snails?"

All she can hear them say is the word, "*Contrefait!*" She finally realizes what the word means, but a *gendarme* swoops down on the fracas and hauls her off to the station.

Lucy does her best to communicate in broken French to the desk officer that she wants to call her husband, and tries to make him understand his celebrity status. "A sort of Spanish Maurice Chevalier," she says. She finally gets him on the phone.

Ricky runs into the station and Lucy explains as only she can, ending with the observation that no one at the station speaks English: "They're all foreigners!"

They don't speak Spanish either, he learns, when he tries to make himself understood. So the desk officer trots out a drunken Spaniard they've just arrested, who happens to speak German, and what follows is an attempt to translate from Lucy in English on one end through Ricky in Spanish to the drunk, from the drunk to the French *gendarme* in German, and finally from the *gendarme* to the desk officer in French.

Through the five-person translation chain, Lucy is finally able to convince her captors that she's innocent. If she pays the bill—in real cash—they'll let her go.

As Ricky digs into his pocket, Fred and Ethel walk into the station with their tour guide, who accuses the Mertzes of the same con game, and when Fred spots Lucy, he's quick to say: "There's the brains behind the whole thing!"

Later at their hotel, the matter all cleared up, Ricky says he bought Lucy a painting. Lucy chimes in with the same statement, and so do the Mertzes. They all head for their respective rooms and return with the same painting. So much for French culture.

Just as the whole mess gets cleared up, a tour guide hauls Fred and Ethel into the station screaming, "Contrefait!" The madness begins again.

Back in the hotel, Ricky tells Lucy he bought her a painting. When she replies that she did, too, they both produce the exact same reproduction.

EPISODE 146

"LUCY MEETS CHARLES BOYER"

Trying to spare Charles Boyer from meeting Lucy, Ricky sets the stage for a charade that inadvertently places the suave actor at her mercy.

The Ricardos and the Mertzes are sitting at a sidewalk café in Paris while Lucy and Ethel ogle Charles Boyer, who's perched at a nearby table. Lucy and Ethel leave for the powder room to plot a meeting, and Ricky goes over to warn Boyer about Lucy, telling him to deny who he is when she finally approaches him.

When the girls return, they wend their way over to Boyer's table, and the moment they introduce themselves, he slams his newspaper down on the table and exclaims: "It's happened again!" He's annoyed because he's always being mistaken for the famous actor. Disappointed, Lucy and Ethel return to their hotel room.

While moping, Lucy reads a news item in a Paris newspaper announcing that Ricky Ricardo and Charles Boyer are meeting to discuss an upcoming American television special, so she asks Ricky if she can go along. He says, "No!" But when she insists that Boyer is her romantic idol, Ricky bellows that he is insanely jealous. "You're mine, mine, all mine!!" he says dramatically, playing it to the hilt, then grabs her, bends her over backward and kisses her passionately. He strides out the door with a melodramatic "Goodbye, my sweet," and leaves.

When Ethel arrives, Lucy is still reeling, and says she has to convince Ricky that Boyer doesn't mean a thing to her. She comes up with the idea of enlisting the services of that Boyer look-alike whom they met at the café to pose as the actor and make a pass at her right in front of Ricky. She vows she won't pay a bit of attention to him, and Ricky will realize "he has nothing to be jealous about."

Lucy returns to the sidewalk café and sits down with the man she thinks is the Boyer look-alike. She explains Ricky's tirade and her plan to reassure him of her loyalty. Playing along, Boyer agrees to help her out. After she leaves, the actor meets Ricky for their lun-

The Ricardos and the Mertzes are having lunch at a sidewalk café, and when Lucy spies Charles Boyer, she vows to get his autograph.

While she goes off to freshen up with Ethel, Ricky walks over to Boyer's table and warns him about Lucy. "Play it safe and tell her you're not Charles Boyer."

Lucy introduces herself and Ethel. "It's happened again!" he exclaims, lamenting over being mistaken for Boyer. "I'm Maurice DuBois," he insists.

To keep her away from Boyer, Ricky puts on an act to make Lucy think he's jealous of the actor. Grabbing Lucy, he roars, "You're mine!"

*L*ucy approaches "Maurice DuBois" to have him pretend to romance her as Boyer in front of Ricky—only she'll ignore his overtures.

*A*fter she leaves, Boyer tells Ricky about Lucy's plan to stage a blasé act to reassure him of her loyalty. Ricky says he's not jealous, but Boyer thinks it'll be "fun."

*L*ucy invites Boyer/DuBois back to her hotel room to coach him on learning how to act like the French actor. She's unimpressed with his hand-kissing technique.

*S*he teaches him the famous Boyer sneer . . .

. . . which he tries to duplicate for a derisive Lucy.

*W*hen Boyer shows up at the appointed hour, a "glowering" Ricky stands by as the actor begins to compliment Lucy on how beautiful she is. She yawns . . .

. . . and while he continues his romantic discourse, Lucy feigns indifference by munching on hors d'oeuvres.

*B*ut Lucy ignores Boyer even after receiving a call from Ethel . . .

. . . until Ethel reveals Ricky's collusion with Boyer.

cheon and tells him about the visit from Lucy. Ricky warns: "Don't do it!" But Boyer sees it as a lot of fun, and unveils the details.

Later on, Lucy coaches Boyer on how to romance her, and she reminds him to be in her room at five o'clock.

At the appointed hour, Boyer comes to the Ricardos' room, and Ricky orders Lucy to leave, but she refuses, saying she's going to prove to him that Boyer means nothing to her. With Ricky looking on, Boyer begins to flirt with Lucy. Hamming it up, Ricky barks at Boyer to stop. Meanwhile, Lucy is acting bored as Boyer kisses up and down her arm while she munches on table snacks.

In the midst of all this, Ethel calls and tells her Ricky is playing a trick on her: the man who is slobbering on her arm is the real Charles Boyer.

As Boyer advances on her, she's beside herself—and both Ricky and Boyer break out in laughter. Ethel runs in, and the girls hound Boyer for his autograph, but when she takes out the fountain pen, it squirts a trail of ink all over the front of his shirt. As the two girls fight over who'll help him into his overcoat, they rip it in two and—in a final indignity—Lucy opens the door, hitting him on the head as he desperately tries to make a safe exit.

"*Au revoir*," says Lucy as he waves goodbye.

"No, don't say *au revoir*," he tells her. "Say goodbye."

She recoils as Boyer advances on her, but Ricky stops the charade, wise to the fact that the phone call has alerted Lucy.

Asking for his autograph, Lucy produces a pen that squirts ink all over his white shirt—but they're not finished with him.

As the girls fight over the privilege of helping him into his overcoat, it rips in two. But the mayhem doesn't stop there as Lucy opens the door into his face. "Au revoir," says Lucy. Boyer retorts: "Just say goodbye!"

"LUCY'S ITALIAN MOVIE"

*L*ucy soaks up some local color in a wine vat to add some "flavor" to her role in an Italian movie. Grape-stomping will never be the same again.

On a train trip to Rome, Lucy is "discovered" by Vittorio Phillipe, the famous Italian producer, who needs her for his newest film.

After he leaves, she begins to emote, Roman-style, spouting Italian and tousling her hair with her hands.

In their hotel room, Lucy has her head buried in an Italian movie magazine article about Phillipe and his new picture, entitled *Grappulo Pungente*, which translates to "Bitter Grapes."

Lucy surmises that she needs to learn about the grape vineyards and how the whole process works. The bellhop tells her that the town of Turo is a good place to start. Ricky warns Lucy that he doesn't want to have to worry about her "lousing up the entire grape industry."

"All I want to do," she assures him, "is soak up a little culture."

In Turo, Lucy walks into an old-fashioned, Mediterranean-looking winery, complete with a grape-pressing vat designed for human feet. Lucy saunters in wearing traditional peasant clothes, and joins the other women. They soon begin to make fun of her, but the mocking ends and the bickering begins when the winemaster assigns Lucy and another woman to work in the vat, apparently a choice job. He justifies his decision by pointing out the size of Lucy's feet, "like large pizzas." As the other woman looks at Lucy, her apprehension is apparent as she looks down in the vat. Lucy finally succumbs, and gingerly sets her bare feet into the sea of grapes. She reacts as if she just stepped into a vat of eyeballs.

Meanwhile, the other woman has already settled into a marching dance step, which Lucy finally begins to pick up, along with her confidence. Pretty soon she's jogging with joy, flapping her arms as she circumnavigates the vat. She then tries hooking her partner's arm square-dance style, but the woman is in no mood to do that, and barks at her.

By now Lucy has expended more energy than her counterpart. She sits down on the edge of the vat for a rest. "I'ma pooped," she says. The woman grabs her arm, and as Lucy tries to extricate her-

On a train to Rome, the noted Italian producer Vittorio Phillipe says Lucy is the perfect type for a new picture, and she begins to emote, Italian style, to prove he's right.

In Rome, reading up on the Italian film world, Lucy discovers that Phillipe's next picture is entitled Grappulo Pungente, *which translates to "Bitter Grapes."*

Lucy tells Ethel she's going to locate a vineyard to find out about grapes, demonstrating her ability to communicate with Italians through universal gestures.

At an old-fashioned winery in the town of Turo, Lucy perches demurely on top of a vat while two professional grape pressers eye her suspiciously.

As her feet hit the grapes, she looks as if she's stepped into a vat of eyeballs.

But soon she begins to get a perverse pleasure out of the chore . . .

. . . and falls into the rhythm, merrily jogging within the circumference of the vat . . .

. . . until her stomping partner gets tired of Lucy's technique and yells at her.

When Lucy declares, "I'ma pooped," the woman tries to pull Lucy back into the action. After the woman throws a handful of grapes into Lucy's face, they face off . . .

. . . and Lucy returns the favor . . . Mayhem ensues . . .

. . . and the two disappear into the juice with limbs thrashing in every direction.

self, the woman falls on her backside. Frustrated, the woman picks up a bunch of grapes from the vat and flings it into Lucy's face. Lucy gives her the "don't mess with me" look and, reaching down, returns the favor—followed by another volley from the woman.

Lucy reaches down into the mire, marches over to the woman and rubs more grapes into her face. As the woman lets loose a string of Italian epithets, she charges at Lucy. Mocking the woman's speech, she sidesteps the assault like a matador, and as the woman passes her, launches a kick at her rear—and slips down in the process. The woman leaps headfirst at Lucy, and the confrontation turns into a free-for-all with arms, legs and grapes flying in all directions.

Vittorio Phillipe is ready to leave the hotel when Lucy walks in on Ricky and the Mertzes, her figure bathed from head to toe in crushed grape leavings. "Boy, when it comes to soaking up local color, you don't mess around," quips Fred.

Phillipe explains that the title is symbolic, and has nothing to do with grapes. Lucy would be cast as an American tourist—but considering the state she's in, there won't be enough time for the stains to come out of her skin. As he's walking out of the door, he takes notice of Ethel, and offers her the job instead. As Ethel goes into a state of euphoria and carries on about her role, tousling her hair and emitting a string of "*Arrivedercis*"—Lucy sinks into unbridled jealousy. Advancing on her, Lucy begins mouthing a string of epithets, but the word "censored" appears in a subtitle.

With Phillipe waiting for her, Lucy walks in stained purple from head to toe: "I was just looking for atmosphere for working in your picture." Phillipe tells Lucy that she won't be able to play the scene while she's stained purple. "Couldn't I play a typical American tourist who fell in a wine vat?" she pleads.

As he bids her goodbye, Lucy hasn't given up: "I'll shave my head and wear a mask."

When Phillipe asks Ethel, "Would you be interested in playing the part?" she begins to emote in an Italian vein, sputtering "Arrivedercis." Lucy looks at Ethel with dagger eyes, and she advances threateningly.

THE SIXTH SEASON
❤ 1956 TO 1957 ❤

#154
"LUCY MEETS BOB HOPE"
October 1, 1956

#155
"LUCY MEETS ORSON WELLES"
October 15, 1956

#158
"VISITOR FROM ITALY"
October 29, 1956

#164
"LUCY AND THE LOVING CUP"
January 7, 1957

#166
"LUCY AND SUPERMAN"
January 14, 1957

#171
"LUCY RAISES CHICKENS"
March 4, 1957

#172
"LUCY DOES THE TANGO"
March 11, 1957

"LUCY MEETS BOB HOPE"

A determined Lucy will do whatever it takes to get Bob Hope as the guest star for the opening night of Ricky's Club Babalu. But first she has to get Hope's attention.

Lucy, Little Ricky and the Mertzes are at Yankee Stadium for a game between the New York team and the Cleveland Indians. But Lucy can't concentrate on baseball—she's too worried about the opening night of Ricky's Club Babalu. Since Bob Hope, the much-sought-after guest star for this big event, hasn't been heard from, Lucy thinks it's all her fault. "I'm a jinx," she tells Ethel. "Every time I go near a celebrity, there's trouble." What's more, Ricky agrees with her.

When Hope arrives at the stadium—he's part owner of the Indians—and takes his box seat, Lucy sees her golden opportunity to talk him into appearing at the club, but a security guard prevents her from getting near the star. Spotting a hot dog vendor, Lucy's eyes light up with the brilliant plan she's hatched.

At Club Babalu, as workmen are frantically getting the place ready for opening night, an agitated Ricky is convinced nothing will be finished in time. He simmers down just a bit when the club manager tells him that Bob Hope is at Yankee Stadium and waiting to talk to him about the show.

But Lucy gets to Hope first. Disguised as a hot dog vendor, complete with moustache and her bad imitation of a male voice, Lucy maneuvers her way to Hope's box seat. When he refuses to buy a hot dog, she keeps trying to talk to him while hawking her frankfurters to the people around them. Caught in the middle of Lucy's enterprise—he's now passing hot dogs to customers, making change and trying to get rid of Lucy—a distracted Hope is suddenly hit on the head by a foul ball that knocks him out cold. Lucy realizes her jinx is still working.

As Hope sits in the Indians' locker room with an icebag on his head, telling Ricky about the "weirdo" who caused all this trouble, in struts Lucy—disguised as a Cleveland pitcher.

Fred turns a sympathetic ear as Ricky grapples with a way to keep Lucy away from Bob Hope, whom he wants as a guest star for opening night at his Club Babalu.

Fred takes Lucy and Ethel to Yankee Stadium for a game between New York and Cleveland, and they're sitting down when Hope arrives to watch from his box seat.

Seeing an opportunity to talk Hope into appearing at the club, Lucy tries to worm her way past an usher, saying she's Mrs. Ricky Ricardo. It doesn't work.

She comes out a few minutes later disguised as a hot dog vendor and sidesteps over to Hope, but he's not buying. Another spectator wants a frankfurter, though.

Hope winds up passing hot dogs and money back and forth between Lucy and her other patrons.

When Lucy inadvertently slathers his finger with catsup, he quips, "Will you put a bun around this finger? It looks delicious."

Just then, while she's distracting him with her inane chatter, a foul ball arcs through the air and lands squarely on Hope's noggin.

Lucy finds out Hope's in the locker room and tries to bribe an attendant. No sale.

Ricky's inside with Hope, talking about the show when a rather effeminate baseball player strolls in. They both know it's Lucy and though the jig is up, she plays on.

They ask her to demonstrate her pitching style, but she claims a chaw of tobacco would help. Ricky produces a plug, hands it to her and she takes a big bite. Yuck!

"Lucy, who do you think you're fooling?" says Ricky. Hope slaps Lucy on the back, which jars the plug from her mouth and down her gullet.

Afterward, Ricky and Hope discuss the show, but there's a spot left open for a song-and-dance routine and Lucy blubbers to Hope about her performing aspirations.

Ricky and Hope are immediately on to her but go along with "the new rookie from Indianapolis" whose pitching style looks as if she's tossing bon-bons. Lucy defends herself by saying she pitches better with chewing tobacco in her mouth. Ricky finds some in a locker, and she's forced to begin chewing. Her rubber-faced grimaces tell us every-thing, but even when Hope slaps her on the back, causing her to swallow the sickening wad, Lucy doesn't give up—or throw up. Babbling a mile a minute, she apologizes profusely for Hope's getting clobbered—and his probably not wanting to appear at the club—and almost misses his announcement that he will be there. And he has a musical baseball number that he'd love to do, but it requires three people. Ricky volunteers, leaving a vacancy Lucy is desperate to fill. "You mean the kiss of death can sing and dance?" Hope asks Ricky, who assures him that they'll get someone else.

It works, and the comedian insists that Ricky use her in the song, a whimsical baseball ditty entitled "Nobody Loves the Ump."

The moment Ricky leaves the locker room, Lucy cries on Hope's shoulder, whining "you have no idea how talented I am," claiming it's Ricky's professional jealousy that keeps him from letting her perform. Increasingly sympathetic, Hope listens as she confides that she's only trying to be a good wife and help her husband. By the time Ricky returns to the locker room, an irate Hope calls him a "Cuban heel" and threatens not to appear at the club unless Lucy is in the act with them.

It's opening night at Club Babalu and the trio is onstage, dressed as baseball umpires, singing "Nobody Loves the Ump." Despite Lucy's off-key warbling and getting her spike shoes stuck in the floor tiles, she sings and clumsily taps her way to momentary stardom. All three end the show with Hope's classic, "Thanks for the Memories," singing personalized lyrics written just for this happy occasion.

She nearly torpedoes the entire number, but Hope rescues the act with a trio rendition of his theme song, "Thanks for the Memories."

"LUCY MEETS ORSON WELLES"

*L*ucy's embarrassing high school performance in Shakespeare's *Romeo and Juliet* makes an even more humiliating comeback—opposite a hapless Orson Welles.

Ricky wants Lucy to buy whatever she'll need for a trip to Florida, and she's on a shopping spree. When she and Ethel come across snorkeling equipment in a department store, Lucy decides to take up skin-diving. Ethel asks, "Don't you get into enough trouble on dry land?" But Lucy's not deterred, heading for a dressing room to try on the diving gear. A moment later, Ethel yells for her to hurry out because Orson Welles has just arrived at the store to autograph his new Shakespearean record album. Wearing flippers, webbed gloves and a huge goggle mask with dangling rubber hoses, Lucy pushes through the crowd of adoring fans to get to Welles. Eying her ridiculous outfit, he says, "The *Man From Mars* broadcast was eighteen years ago. What kept you?"

Lucy brags about her high-school days playing Shakespeare, but Welles caustically remarks that every actress he's met thinks her Juliet was played "to an audience practically awash with overactive tear ducts," and goes back to autographing albums. Asked to write "To Lucy Ricardo" on her record, Welles realizes she's Ricky's wife, and reveals that he's doing a charity benefit at her husband's nightclub. Not only that—he's sorry she's not going to help him with his act because Ricky told him she was going to Florida. Furious that she's been double-crossed by "that conniving Cuban," Lucy begs Welles to let her have the job of assisting him. As she recites the parting lines from *Romeo and Juliet*, it's all Welles can do not to roll his eyes upward.

Elated, Lucy calls to invite Miss Hanna, her old high-school dramatic teacher, to watch her Shakespearean performance opposite Orson Welles. "What class was he in, dear?" asks Miss Hanna, and explains that, though she wishes she could attend, she has to substitute for a sick student in an all-male *Caine Mutiny Court Martial*.

Ricky feigns innocence when his wife accuses him of trying to get rid of her until Welles leaves town, insisting he didn't want her to be hurt when she learned that the great actor only needed her assistance

Ricky finances Lucy's trip to the department store to keep her away from Orson Welles, who will be performing at the club. But the actor is signing albums at the store.

Lucy's in skin-diving gear when Welles strides in and sits down. Upon seeing Lucy, he quips: "The *Man from Mars* broadcast was eighteen years ago. What kept you?"

As Ethel tells him how to autograph her album, Lucy relates her experiences playing Juliet in high school to a long-suffering Welles.

When he finds out she's Ricky's wife, he tells her he's sorry she couldn't be in his act. She asks if her part is filled. He says, "No. And please take your flippers off me."

Walking on air, she starts to emote: "Farewell, parting is such sweet sorrow." Welles: "So we'll just charge these albums and send them out tomorrow."

Reeling from the thought of her upcoming debut with Welles, she assumes she's going to play Shakespeare and calls to inform her high-school dramatic teacher.

In costume at the club, Lucy rehearses the final speech from Romeo and Juliet.

Welles endures Lucy's dramatics while Ricky—feigning amusement—tries to distract him with refreshments.

Lucy starts to butter up Welles about his Shakespearean prowess, hoping that he'll do a scene with her. He then performs Romeo's death scene while Lucy watches raptly.

Backstage, Lucy's teacher appears, telling her that she came with her class to see her perform. So Lucy's determined not to let her down.

Welles begins the act: "From the mysterious East, the inscrutable princess Loo-Cee." After Lucy walks out, he places two brooms under her arms and puts her into a "trance."

Welles then removes one of the brooms, lifts her legs in the air, lets go, and she remains suspended.

in a magic act. Lucy doesn't buy any of it, posing the logical question to Ethel, "Would he send me all the way to Florida just to keep me from handing Orson Welles a hatful of rabbits?"

That afternoon, at Club Babalu, as Welles and Ricky discuss the show, Lucy enters reciting Juliet's famous soliloquy, or rather, demolishing it. Welles explains that he'll be performing only as a magician, but Lucy keeps telling him that he's "the greatest Shakespearean actor who ever lived" until his mellifluous Romeo finally takes over. When "Juliet" can't remember her lines or cues, however, he decides to stick with the magic act.

On the night of the benefit, Lucy's paid a surprise visit by Miss Hanna, who has brought her whole acting class to see the show. Lucy can't admit it's going to be a levitation trick, not Shakespeare's tragic love story.

Curtain up: Welles brings out the "mysterious Princess Loo-Cee" in Chinese mandarin garb, positions her on a small stool, places two upside-down brooms under her armpits, and immediately puts her into a "trance." Removing the stool and one broom—leaving her suspended in the air with one armpit barely resting on the other broom—the master magician slowly turns Lucy's "levitated" body. But trance or no, she can't resist doing her Juliet, to Miss Hanna's delight and Welles' horror. Apologizing to his audience—"there just wasn't enough trance"—he rotates Lucy again, promising that now the princess will feel nothing, "and definitely speak nothing." Undaunted and unstoppable, Lucy cries out, "Romeo, Romeo, wherefore art thou...?" as Welles gives up in disgust and walks offstage, leaving his "assistant" still turning in mid-air, and yelling after him, "Romeo, Romeo, get me down from here!"

As Welles warns the audience not to make a sound "Loo-Cee's" eyes open wide.

"Apparently the princess is not in a deep trance," says Welles. Passing a hoop over her he says, "The princess will feel nothing, and definitely speak nothing . . ."

. . . which prompts "Loo-Cee" to start her monologue. Disgusted, Welles walks off the stage and she's left spinning in a circle reciting desperately, "Wherefore art thou Romeo? Romeo, get me down from here!"

"VISITOR FROM ITALY"

Lucy's desire to help an Italian houseguest earn some money puts her center stage at a pizza parlor where her dough-spinning technique earns her no applause—and no dough.

The Ricardos and the Mertzes receive a surprise visit from Mario, a little Italian in whose gondola they rode on the Grand Canal in Venice. He's in New York to see his brother Dominick, but has just learned, via a note on Dominick's door, that he's visiting "Sam Francesco." Assuming this is Mario's fractured English for "San Francisco," the foursome explain that he still has three thousand miles to go. He's not going to make it on the ten dollars he has left, but he's too proud to accept a loan, so he says he'll get a job to earn the money. When he finds out there's not much call for gondoliers in New York City, Ricky hires him as a busboy at the Club Babalu for a few nights.

After only one night and numerous near-disasters, Ricky has had it with the new busboy. He gives Lucy a check for him and tells her to send him to San Francisco—immediately—but she doesn't do it, knowing that Mario won't accept the money. In fact, he's already gotten another job, at Martinelli's Pizza Parlor. But according to the immigration official who comes to see Lucy, he's in big trouble because he doesn't have a work permit. One more day on the job will mean deportation.

Lucy goes to the pizza parlor to collect Mario's earnings for him, only to find out that he owes Martinelli another day's work—or no salary at all. She bravely offers to fill in and instantly receives a crash course in pizza-making. Lucy watches in awe—and terror—as the pizza man spins the dough, tosses and twirls it, even flips it behind his back, all with the speed and dexterity of a juggler. Then, with lightning speed, he spreads the sauce, sprinkles on the cheese, shoves it into the oven and ends his shift.

Donning an apron and chef's hat, Lucy tries desperately to act nonchalant as she heads for the worktable. Grabbing a ball of dough, she tosses it from hand to hand like a baseball, then runs it quickly through the kneading machine, which spits out a small, round piece of dough. Confidently, Lucy spins and tosses it into the air. Not only

Mario from Italy shows up at the Ricardos' front door. Lucy and Ricky are trying to place him; all they know is that he remembers them from their European trip.

Finally Mario reminisces about the wonderful time they had in his gondola in Venice. He's here to visit his brother, but he's gone to see "Sam Francesco."

He doesn't have enough money to get to San Francisco, so everyone tells him they'll chip in. He insists on working for it, so Lucy suggests Ricky hire him as a busboy.

Ricky tells Lucy about Mario's disastrous night as a busboy dropping trays and worse. Handing Lucy a check, he tells her to give it to Mario and put him on the bus. A proud Mario refuses the charitable gesture.

Lucy gets him a job at a pizza parlor, but an immigration official threatens to deport him if he shows up at work again. Lucy tries to get him to quit, but Mario's adamant.

To keep him from returning where the immigration man threatens to show up, Lucy makes up a story about a new labor law: "You work two days and get the third day off, with pay." Mario's thrilled as he prepares for his San Francisco trip.

Lucy goes to the pizzeria to pick up his pay for the days he's worked, but Martinelli says Mario gets no pay if he doesn't show. Lucy proposes to substitute for him.

The man leaves his shift as Lucy has to fend for herself.

Tossing the dough into the air several times . . .

. . . she finally flings it up into the cooking vent, where it disappears.

When Ricky shows up unexpectedly, she flops one huge round of dough over her head, forming two perfect holes for her eyes and her mouth.

"What are you doing?" asks Ricky. "No speaka de English," she replies.

does it come down in a rectangle, it has also gotten smaller. Amazed, she dangles it in front of her like a wet towel. Another toss, another fiasco—this time the dough splits and ends up looking like a long strap hanging over her wrist. Martinelli is not a happy man as he watches while impatient customers call for their pizzas in the background.

When the owner of the pizzeria fires Lucy, calling her "stupido," that sets Ricky off and Lucy has to intervene.

Panicking, Lucy sends the next twirl of dough flying over her shoulder and onto the floor behind her. Kicking it out of the way, she starts again. Her next aerial spin boomerangs, coming back at her rolled into a ball again. Just to get rid of it, she throws it into the oven. The next whirl of dough goes so high up that it completely disappears from sight, into the cooling vent, eventually plopping back down on the floor in front of her worktable. She also flings this failure into the oven. Finally, and frantically, Lucy takes a little piece of dough from the kneading machine and fashions it into the world's smallest pizza, but at least it goes into the oven with all the ingredients on top.

Having just discovered that Mario is being stowed away in the Mertzes' apartment, Ricky goes to the pizza parlor to confront his wife. The moment she spots him, Lucy slaps a circle of dough on her head, where it falls like a curtain down her face. He starts yelling at her in Spanish, Martinelli starts yelling at him in Italian and the oven begins spewing out black smoke from the burning lumps of dough. Lucy's pizza-making days are over.

After they've packed Mario off on a bus, a man turns up and says he's looking for him. Lucy says: "He's going to San Francisco to find his brother." "I'm his brother Dominick," says the man.

Mario has finally been sent off to San Francisco, and Fred Mertz is adding up the damage that the little gondolier has wrought, when Dominick arrives at the Ricardos' door. Upset to learn that his brother is halfway across the country, Dominick says he wasn't in San Francisco at all—he's just been uptown, visiting a sick friend named Sam Francesco.

"I no mova to San Francisco," he says. "I justa beena witha my sick friend, Sam Francesco." Everyone in the room moans. It's another fiasco.

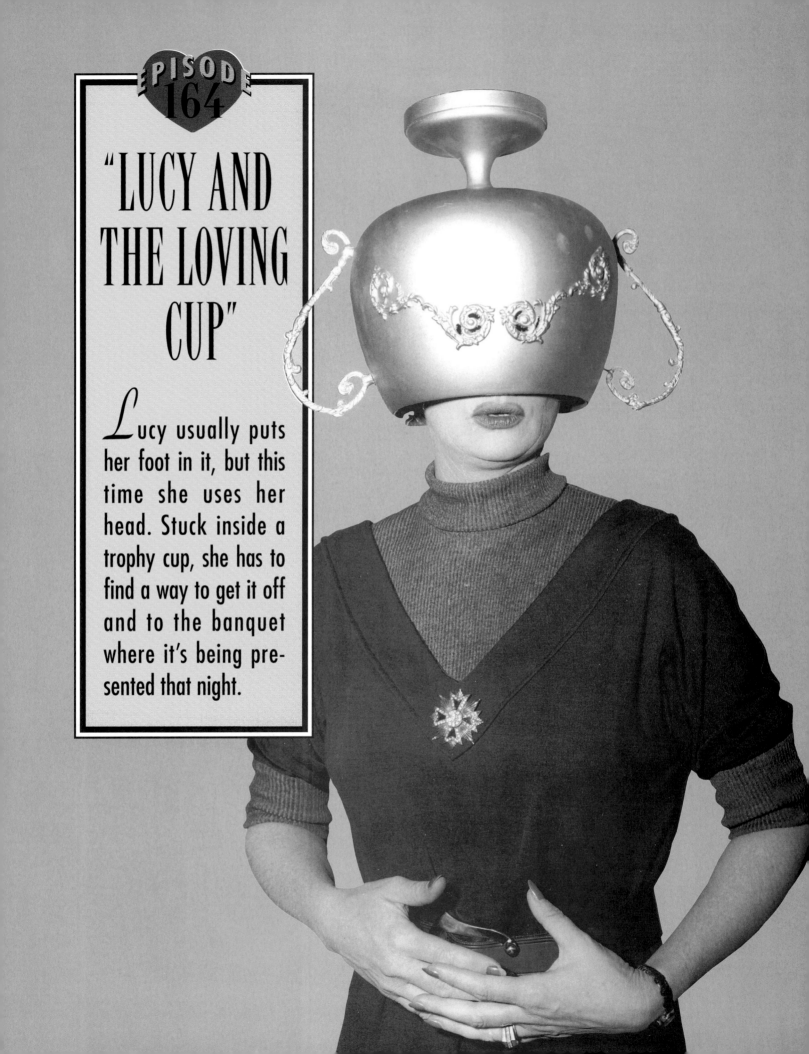

"LUCY AND THE LOVING CUP"

*L*ucy usually puts her foot in it, but this time she uses her head. Stuck inside a trophy cup, she has to find a way to get it off and to the banquet where it's being presented that night.

Ricky and Fred think Lucy's new hat—the latest from Paris—is hilarious. Their jokes not only hurt her feelings but make her even more determined to wear it to the banquet she and Ricky are attending that night in honor of Johnny Longden, "the world's winningest jockey." When Ricky protests that anything would look better than that ridiculous hat—even the loving cup that he'll be presenting to Longden—Lucy gets so mad that she takes the big, round trophy by its handles and plops it over her head. Ricky laughs at her little gag as he leaves the apartment, but Lucy tells Ethel she'd almost like to wear the cup just to get back at Ricky.

Reaching to lift it off her head, Lucy discovers that it won't budge—she's stuck in it. "We could butter your head," Ethel suggests, but Lucy is not amused. After a few futile attempts to remove it, Ethel takes Fred's suggestion to contact a silversmith who'll blowtorch it off—but he doesn't make house calls and is closing his shop in half an hour. Since Lucy can't see, can barely hear and has only her mouth and chin exposed, Ethel offers to go with her.

A taxi will never get them there on time, so they opt for the subway. As they sit on the train, having done their best to camouflage the trophy under a coolie-style hat and a huge veil, Ethel tries to reassure Lucy that no one is staring at her even though she now looks like "a beekeeper." Arriving at their station, Ethel maneuvers Lucy off the crowded train, only to lose her among the shoving passengers, and ends up watching horrified from the platform as the train pulls out with Lucy on it. Stumbling through the lurching train—with the loving cup no longer disguised—Lucy falls into people's laps, knocks others in the head, and finally slides against a pole to the floor in search of a seat. At the next stop, Lucy thinks she's worked her way onto the platform, but when

Ricky breaks into paroxysms of laughter when Lucy models the hat she plans to wear at an awards ceremony he's hosting for the winningest jockey, Johnny Longden.

"You'd look better wearing that trophy on your head," he says, indicating the loving cup that's to be presented to Longden at the ceremony.

Lucy puts the cup on her head to tease Ricky, but after he leaves it's no laughing matter: Ethel gives it a valiant try, but she can't get it off.

"This could only happen to you," says Ethel, but Lucy doesn't hear her. Shouting, Ethel's voice finally carries into the cup, but it echoes so loudly that Lucy's head rings.

After attempting to extricate herself, she ponders her predicament with Ethel.

Fred suggests Lucy go to a silversmith, but there's no time before the show.

On the subway en route to the show, they try to be inconspicuous, but this spectacle draws stares even in New York, and Ethel jeers at an onlooker.

As they're about to debark, an onrush of people separates them and the subway rumbles off with Ethel on the platform and Lucy still on the train.

Wandering the aisle alone, she tries to find a seat but keeps bumping into everything in her path and even loses her veil in another mob rush.

When she discovers her head is completely exposed, she tries to act casual and covers up with a newspaper. The passengers enjoy the show.

Finally off the subway, she corners a man and asks: "Can you tell me where I am?" "Yeah," he says, "you're on earth."

When a cop stops her to ask if a policeman could help, she says, "No, they're nothing but trouble."

she asks a passerby where the stairs are, he suggests she get off the train first. "I am off," she replies. "You're telling me!" he says and runs from her.

Back in a seat, Lucy realizes she's lost her veil and, sensing the stares and snickers of the other passengers, grabs a nearby newspaper, opens it with a flourish, and pretends to read, but embarrassment takes over, and she throws the paper onto her head.

Off the train at last, but having wound up all the way in Brooklyn, Lucy grabs a woman and asks her to call Ricky to "tell Johnny Longden to hold his horses"—pausing long enough to laugh at her own pun—and say that she's on her way back to the city. Naturally, the woman thinks Lucy is a certified loony, and calls a cop instead. "Sir, you're not going to believe this..." Lucy says as the officer nods in agreement.

Ricky fumbles through his banquet speech, trying to delay the loving cup presentation—"the trophy should be here shortly"—as he praises the jockey's remarkable career. Just as he's run out of excuses, in walks the cop, escorting the trophy-headed Lucy. More chagrined than ever, Ricky introduces both his wife and her headgear to the audience. "I'm sure it'll look good in my trophy collection, but what am I gonna do with your wife?" Longden asks. Ricky answers, "That's been my problem for fifteen years. Johnny, now it's yours!"

After she explains what happened, the cop accompanies her to the banquet, where an anxious Ricky has been killing time waiting for the trophy—and Lucy.

Ricky tilts Lucy's head down to try reading the inscription to the guest of honor.

Longden thanks Ricky but asks, "What am I going to do with your wife?" Ricky: "That's been my problem for fifteen years. Johnny, now it's yours!"

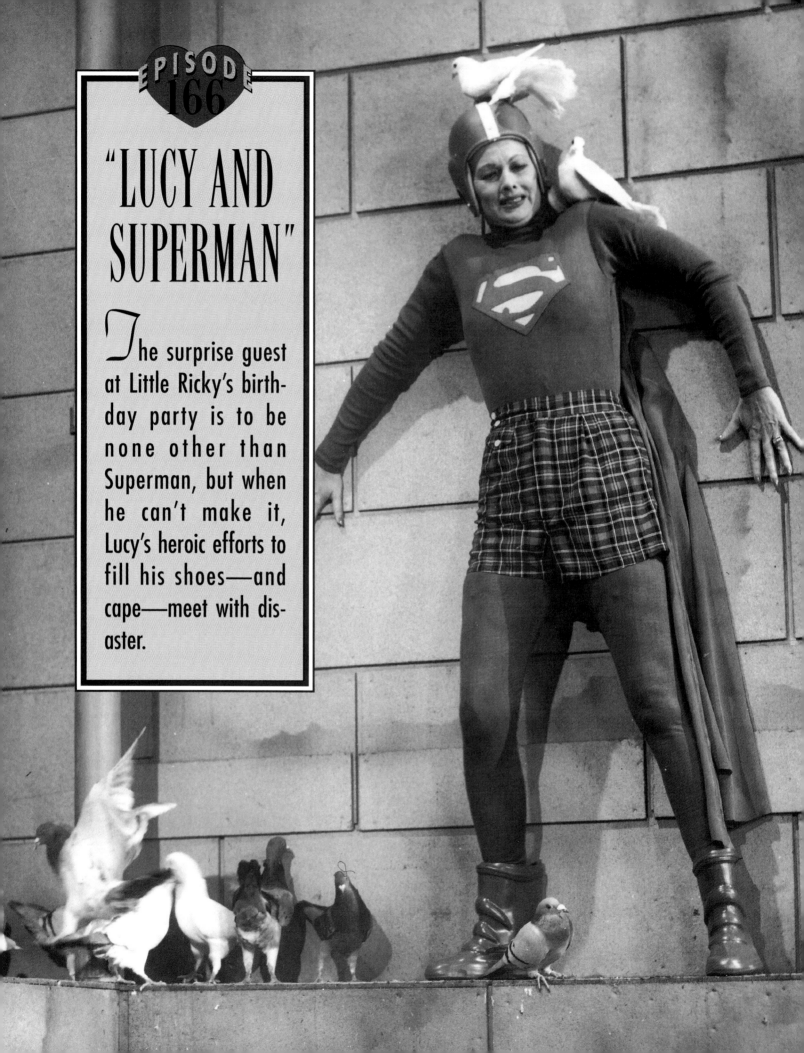

"LUCY AND SUPERMAN"

The surprise guest at Little Ricky's birthday party is to be none other than Superman, but when he can't make it, Lucy's heroic efforts to fill his shoes—and cape—meet with disaster.

When Caroline Appleby and Lucy Ricardo discover they're both throwing a party for their sons' fifth birthdays on the same Saturday, they agree that one of them has to change the date. But a nasty stalemate ensues when both stubbornly refuse.

Lucy complains to Ethel that since Little Ricky and Stevie Appleby are inviting the same children, and since Caroline has hired a magician, a clown and a puppet show, all the kids will surely go to Stevie's party. Unless, of course, she can top the entertainment. As Little Ricky dashes through the living room in his Superman costume, Lucy gets her inspiration. The Ricardos met television's man of steel when they were in Hollywood, and he just happens to be in New York that week, and Lucy is sure Ricky can get him to come to the birthday event. So sure, in fact, that she calls Caroline to gloat, and when little Stevie hears the fabulous news, his mother is forced to concede defeat.

But bad news is not far behind for Lucy either. Ricky tells her that Superman is leaving town early Saturday morning and scolds his wife for counting on something before it's set: "Lucy, you shouldn't cross your bridges before they're hatched."

Determined not to disappoint the kids, she gets her second bright idea—she'll impersonate Superman herself. Instructing Ethel to rush to the window at some point during the festivities and announce Superman's arrival, Ethel responds, "You're not going to fly in here?!" Lucy explains that she'll use the vacant apartment next door, walk out on the ledge to her own apartment window and then jump in. The fact that it's three stories up terrifies Ethel, but not the heroic redhead.

While the Mertzes play party games with the children, Lucy runs into the empty apartment and begins her transformation. Ethel has to interrupt her party chores long enough to show the vacancy to prospective tenants, but Lucy has already gotten herself onto the ledge, wearing a long-sleeved turtleneck with the Superman emblem, tights, bright plaid shorts, cape, rain boots and a helmet to conceal her

It's Little Ricky's birthday and Lucy promised everyone that Superman would appear at the party. But his personal appearance schedule conflicts with party day.

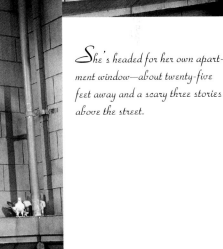

Lucy doesn't want to disappoint the kids, so she dons the caped crusader's togs, climbs out of an empty apartment window and onto the ledge.

She's headed for her own apartment window—about twenty-five feet away and a scary three stories above the street.

*W*hen a battery of pigeons lands on her, she implores, "Why don't you go to Central Park? There's a million statues over there."

*A*s she reaches her window, she sees the real Superman make his surprise entrance, jumping through the alcove from the kitchen, followed by "Yay!" from the kids.

*W*ith Superman on the scene, Lucy heads back to the empty apartment to rejoin the party, but on her way around a corner, she slips and pulls the downspout with her.

*P*rospective tenants have conniptions as she tries entering the apartment.

*J*ust then it starts to rain, one of the prospective tenants locks the window.

*H*eading back to her apartment, she gets her costume tangled in the downspout.

*B*ack at the party, Ricky is thanking Superman for stopping by, and the caped crusader says that he regrets not having met Lucy. "She's on the ledge," says Ethel.

Superman comes to the rescue, unhooking her and leading her back to the window.

hair. Discovering she's not alone on that ledge—a dozen pigeons are strutting around noisily—Lucy orders them to: "Go deliver your messages!" but instead, three white pigeons park right on top of her, one on each shoulder, another on top of her helmet. "Why don't you go to Central Park, there's a million statues there," she yells. They keep fluttering around and making her mission even more dangerous as she begins inching her way precariously along the ledge.

Ricky arrives at the party and excitedly tells the children to get ready for a terrific surprise. Suddenly the kitchen's shutters fling open and the real Superman bursts in, to the squealing delight of a dozen five-year-olds. Apparently he just couldn't let them down after all. From outside the window, Lucy takes all this in, greatly relieved that her impersonation won't be needed. Working her way back toward the vacant apartment, she slips and grabs onto a drainpipe which comes loose from its moorings, almost sending her off the ledge. Shakily, she arrives at her destination just as a thunderstorm begins, only to find that the window is locked. Lucy is stranded outside, the pigeons have commandeered the corner alcove for shelter, her cape is caught in the broken drainpipe—and she's getting drenched.

Little Ricky's party is over, the kids are leaving, and Superman says he wishes he could have met Lucy. Lucy! Everyone rushes to the window. Ricky starts screaming at her as Superman swings gallantly out onto the ledge in the torrential downpour. As he unhinges Lucy from the drainpipe, she asks, "When you're flying around, do you ever have cape trouble?"

Ricky shouts that this is the craziest stunt she's ever pulled in fifteen years! "You mean you've been married to her for fifteen years?" Superman asks, dumbfounded. When Ricky nods, the television hero says, "And they call me Superman!"

As they come through the window, Superman says, "You've been married to her for fifteen years?" "Yeah," says Ricky. Superman: "And they call me Superman!"

"LUCY RAISES CHICKENS"

*L*ucy is sure she can make some badly needed extra income by becoming a chicken farmer. That is, until five hundred baby chicks take over home and hearth.

When the Ricardos' new country home in Connecticut is chosen for a feature layout in *House & Garden* magazine, Ricky's unable to share his wife's excitement—he's too worried about how much their new home is costing them. As he gloomily contemplates a pile of unpaid bills, Lucy cheerily proposes that they should "make the country work for us—we could raise things." When she suggests fruit orchards and a herd of cattle, Ricky reminds her that two acres isn't adequate space, but her next idea does interest him: raising chickens. He wants to know what the " 'spenses" would be and Lucy figures it wouldn't cost more than fifty cents for each sack of grain. "That's chicken feed" she says, cackling loudly at her own joke. Ricky's all for the venture—they can sell the eggs, market the chickens, and if business gets bad, they can always eat the inventory.

Fred and Ethel strongly urge the Ricardos to get help with their new enterprise, hiring someone who'll work for a share of the profits and can live in the little guest house on the property. Lucy and Ricky agree that they'll need an extra hand or two, so they place an ad in the paper, and who should answer it but the Mertzes! They've given this a great deal of thought and absolutely want to do it, mainly because they miss Ricky and Lucy so much, ever since they moved out of the apartment in New York. And Fred says he was raised on a farm with a lot of chickens. Besides, he's especially qualified for this line of work because, as he tells Ricky, "for the past twenty-five years I've been henpecked!"

The Mertzes move in, and Fred gets started immediately, painting and plastering the henhouse while Lucy and Ethel go out shopping. They return with good news: they stopped by a local hatchery and, well, they just couldn't resist...so Fred watches as they lug in huge boxes filled with chirping baby chicks—five hundred of them! Fred is aghast—the henhouse isn't ready, it's much too cold, and the chicks will "freeze their fuzz off!" He tells Lucy to call the hatchery and have them send over two brooders, the heating equipment to keep the

Finally settled in their new Connecticut home, Lucy wants to "raise things." Ricky's reply: "How 'bout money to pay for the house?" Lucy: "How about chickens?"

Lucy and Ricky bounce the chicken idea off the Mertzes. Ricky figures they can make a nice piece of change marketing the birds and selling the eggs.

Fred suggests they run an ad in the local paper to find some hired help, and soon there's an unusual application in the mail.

The letter instructs Ricky to open the front door. The Mertzes walk in and reveal that they've decided to move and would like to work with Lucy and Ricky.

Fred's resting after working on the hen house when the girls come home and inform him that they've brought home five hundred baby chicks and put them in the coop.

He's practically apoplectic, explaining that baby chicks must be in a room of at least ninety degrees, so they bring them inside the house.

The thermostat is up to ninety degrees, and it's feeding time in the den as Lucy flings chicken feed around the room with abandon.

The three sit down for a snack. When Little Ricky comes in with a chick, they dash to the living room to find it overrun with baby chicks.

Fighting the heat and fatigue, they're finally able to find all but sixty-five chicks.

chicks warm, but the place is already closed. Fred decides they'll have to use the den and turn up the heat to ninety degrees. "I want to raise chickens, not roast them," Lucy protests, as she and Ethel prepare the room.

When it comes time to feed the adorable little critters, Lucy spreads paper all over the den floor, tosses grain everywhere, and releases them from their boxes. The den is instantly covered with cheeping chicks running in all directions.

Feeding time is over and the chicks are all finally boxed, but when Little Ricky comes home from school and discovers them, he thinks they deserve the run of the house, and lets them out again. Once more, it's roundup time for his mother and the Mertzes, as Lucy shouts above the peeping din, "To the rear, march!" Once corralled at last, and returned to their sweltering den, Lucy makes a head count and finds that sixty-five chicks are still at large. Just as the chicken farmers begin searching the rest of the house, Ricky walks in. What he sees makes him wish he lived next door, but Lucy hasn't got time to explain what's going on.

Ethel shouts from the laundry room that she just found the chicks under the clothes dryer, and Lucy says she'll get them out by "pretending to be their mother." She starts strutting around, flapping and clucking, and pretty soon there's a little parade of chicks following her across the living room. In the midst of all this pandemonium, the front door opens, and there stand several people from *House & Garden* magazine. They take one quick but very distasteful look at the scene before them and instantly cancel the Ricardos' featured layout. As they leave, Lucy starts crying, but Ricky comforts her: "Don't worry, honey, maybe we'll make the next issue of the *Chicken Breeders' Gazette*."

Wearing summer clothes, Fred's made some lemonade and everyone sits down for a well-deserved rest while pondering where to find the remaining chicks.

Ricky comes home to the commotion, and while the others explain, he's shedding his own clothes to beat the heat.

Lucy comes up with the idea of mimicking a mother hen. When she begins shuffling across the floor in a hen-like waddle, a flock of chicks follows. After she finds out that she's blown a possible home photo spread when House & Garden magazine editors see her waddling and squawking, she begins to cry.

"LUCY DOES THE TANGO"

Lucy's attempt to save the floundering Ricardo-Mertz chicken business backfires when she has to hide dozens of eggs from Ricky—inside her blouse—then dance a tango with him.

As the Ricardos rehearse the sexy tango number they're going to perform at a PTA event, Ethel comes in to announce that their chicken business coventure should be producing eggs very soon. Lucy and Ricky stop dancing and start congratulating themselves on the smart move they made teaming up with the Mertzes and becoming chicken farmers. According to Lucy, "if all the hens are conscientious," there'll be five hundred eggs a day. But a moment later their hopes are dashed when Fred arrives and admits that he made a small miscalculation—it'll be another six months, not six weeks, before the hens start laying. And Fred says that since he is managing the business, and there won't be any profit-sharing for quite a while, he deserves a salary in the meantime. "Wrong!" Ricky shoots back. As a matter of fact, he thinks the Mertzes should start paying rent, because they're only supposed to live in the guest house rent free if there's a chicken business to run. Insulted and incensed, Ricky and Fred are just about to square off when Lucy offers the perfect solution to save both their friendship and their investment: they can trade their five hundred chicks for two hundred egg-producing hens.

Two weeks later, this terrific idea lays an egg of its own: it took two hundred hens to produce six measly eggs. So Ricky gives the chickens an ultimatum: twenty-four more hours to start laying, or the business is out of business. Lucy decides to motivate the hens by putting store-bought eggs in their nests "just to show them what they're supposed to do." Ricky and Fred mustn't know about this, so she and Ethel plan to sneak the eggs into the henhouse undercover—that is, under blouses and in pants' pockets. Ethel's back pockets are bulging with eggs, and Lucy begins gingerly placing three dozen more inside the front of her denim shirt, creating a huge, lumpy, sagging mass. Just then Ricky appears, insisting on another tango rehearsal—and this is the only time he can do it.

While the Ricardos are rehearsing a tango number for a PTA function, Lucy scolds Ricky for not being "sultry" enough and shows him how to do it.

After watching the Ricardos cut a rug, Ethel shows off her "FRESH EGGS FOR SALE" sign. The excitement's growing as their egg business is just weeks away from starting.

When they discover the chickens are still six months away from laying, Ricky and Fred get into an argument about the financial setback—each blaming the other.

Lucy comes up with the idea of trading the baby chicks for ready-to-lay hens. In the meantime, to prevent more fighting, the girls buy eggs to plant in the hen house.

They need to bypass Fred through the yard, so Lucy stashes several dozen eggs in her blouse . . .

. . . while Ethel loads a couple dozen in her pants pockets.

As they're about to leave, Ricky stops them at the door. He wants to rehearse the tango again. As they start to dance, Lucy manages to keep Ricky at arm's length . . .

. . . until the final moment when, after a whirling spin, he spins her around and into his arms for a big, crushing embrace. Splat!

Lucy takes off her woolen shirt and fumbles with the gooey mess while Ricky asks, "Why?" "I was trying to hatch 'em?" she says tentatively.

While all this is going on, Ethel tries to slip out the back, but Fred opens the kitchen door behind her, smashing the eggs she's carrying.

After the broken-egg fiasco, Ricky wants to sell off everything and get out of the chicken business, but the chickens suddenly disappear. He accuses Fred of thievery after discovering chicken feathers in the guest house.

Fred's anger escalates as he says: "I defy you to find one in my house."

Wide-eyed with terror, Lucy lets him swing her around, spin her out, and pull her back while she's trying to push him away and prevent him from discovering her hidden treasures. But she's an accident waiting to happen, and a quick turn sends her pirouetting away from Ricky and then back to him, his arms pulling her into a tight, egg-crushing squeeze. Ethel watches, grimacing in the background, as a dumbstruck Ricky stares at his wife, who's pretending that nothing has happened, while simultaneously trying to stem the messy tide that's pouring out of her shirt. Finally giving up, she crosses her arms over the sodden bulge, and smiles contritely. Ricky bellows at Ethel just as she's about to sneak out of the door, forcing her to turn around at the very moment that Fred opens the door, rear-ending his wife's stash of eggs. Ricky's had it! He puts the hens back on twenty-four-hour notice: produce or go to market.

The next day, the hens are nowhere to be found, thanks to Little Ricky and his friend Bruce, who have managed to hide them all over the house and guest cottage. As a poultry man waits to buy the chickens, Ricky frantically goes in search of them, and when he discovers chicken feathers in the Mertzes' living room, he self-righteously accuses Fred of stealing. Fred cries "foul" himself and indignantly quits his job, declaring that he and Ethel are moving back to New York. With that, a clucking hen emerges from a hatbox and another from a closet, confirming Ricky's suspicions. He promises not to "prosecute" if all the chickens are immediately returned. Back in his own house, Lucy and Ethel are finding hens in closets, basement, everywhere.

Still feuding, Fred and Ricky enter, and now the accusations really start flying, along with the chicken feathers. Lucy and Ethel are just as mad as their husbands, and just as they're all on the verge of clobbering one another, Bruce's mother calls to say that her son's room is overrun with chickens. After Little Ricky is called in to do some fast explaining, the Ricardos and Mertzes make up, as Bruce opens the front door and lugs in a huge basketful of eggs. The Ricardo-Mertz chicken business has finally hatched.

But a cackling noise leads Ricky to a closetful of birds. When Ricky gives him an ultimatum—return the chickens and he won't prosecute—Fred blows a gasket.

The arguing spreads to the girls as Ethel defends Fred. Then suspicion spreads to Lucy, and she asks: "How did a chicken get into your closet?"

The mystery's solved when a neighbor's phone call reveals that Little Ricky and his playmate stashed the chickens because they'd grown fond of them. After everyone makes up, Little Ricky's friend shows up at the door with a basket. It seems that the chickens he hid in his closet laid some eggs. All is forgiven.

PART THREE

A TV-ography

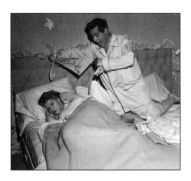

❤ **#1** (November 5, 1951)*
LUCY THINKS RICKY IS TRYING TO MURDER HER

Spooked by a whodunit she's reading, and misinterpreting a conversation she overhears, Lucy's convinced that Ricky's trying to bump her off. Armed with a "gun" and skillet, she confronts him at the Tropicana, where she's embarrassed to discover her mistake.

#2 (October 15, 1951)
THE GIRLS WANT TO GO TO A NIGHTCLUB

To celebrate the Mertzes' eighteenth anniversary, Ricky and Fred want to go to a fight, but Lucy and Ethel are determined to go to the Copa. They get a friend to arrange blind dates for them, which she does—but Ricky and Fred are the dates.

#3 (October 22, 1951)
BE A PAL

Afraid Ricky is losing interest in her, Lucy follows the advice in a book, *How to Keep the Honeymoon from Ending*, and ends up decorating their apartment to look like Cuba, and doing her impression of Carmen Miranda. Ricky can't help but love her for it.

#4 (October 29, 1951)
THE DIET

Desperate to lose twelve pounds in four days so she can replace one of the singers in Ricky's nightclub act, Lucy crash-diets and steams her way to svelteness. She's a big hit in the show, but winds up fainting afterward from hunger.

#5 (November 12, 1951)
THE QUIZ SHOW

In dire need of extra money, Lucy is willing to make a fool of herself to win a thousand dollars on a game show, even if it means introducing Ricky to a bogus "long-lost first husband." Lucy wins the jackpot, but ends up with fifty cents after paying her overdue bills.

❤ **#6** (November 19, 1951)
THE AUDITION

When Lucy begs Ricky to let her audition for a talent scout at the Tropicana, he says no. But she sneaks into the show anyway by replacing the club's ailing clown. The act nets her a contract which she declines, preferring her role as Mrs. Ricardo.

#7 (November 26, 1951)
THE SEANCE

When Lucy finds out that she shares a mutual interest in the occult with a theatrical producer, who is considering Ricky for a part in his show, she stages a seance for him, with Ethel as the medium. It's a success, spirit-wise, and Ricky gets the part.

#8 (December 3, 1951)
MEN ARE MESSY

Fed up with Ricky's sloppiness, Lucy divides their apartment into two halves: hers, neat; his, a mess. When a man comes to do a photo layout of Ricky at home, she thinks he's from a musician's journal. Unfortunately, he's a photographer for *Look* magazine.

*Please note: Episodes are in numerical sequence. Original airdates are in parentheses.

#9 (December 24, 1951)
DRAFTED
Ricky has been requested to appear at Fort Dix to entertain soldiers, but Lucy misconstrues the invitation as a notice that her husband is being drafted. When she starts knitting socks for him to take to boot camp, he mistakenly assumes she's pregnant.

#13 (January 7, 1952)
THE BENEFIT
Ethel wants Ricky to headline at her women's club benefit, but Lucy refuses to ask him unless she's part of the song-and-comedy act. Ethel relents. Then Lucy rewrites the material when she discovers that Ricky has all the punchlines.

#10 (December 10, 1951)
THE FUR COAT
Lucy thinks the mink coat Ricky brought home is her anniversary gift, but it's only rented for his nightclub act. Upon learning the truth, she decides to get even by substituting a fake fur, and cutting it up in front of a stunned Ricky.

#14 (January 14, 1952)
THE AMATEUR HOUR
Badly needing some extra money, Lucy takes on a baby-sitting job for two unruly, eight-year-old twin boys who just about do her in. But when she performs with them in a talent contest—and they win—the boys' mother gives Lucy the prize money.

#11 (December 17, 1951)
LUCY IS JEALOUS OF GIRL SINGER
Lucy's convinced that Ricky's being unfaithful to her with one of the pretty dancers at the Tropicana, so she sneaks her way into the chorus line to keep an eye on him and upstage her rival. Later, Ricky teases Lucy about that "terrible new chorus girl."

#15 (January 21, 1952)
LUCY PLAYS CUPID
Lucy tries to play "Cupid" between a local grocery man and a shy spinster, but it backfires when the grocery man thinks Lucy's the interested party. To discourage the man, Lucy invites him over to see her twenty-five children—and to meet the shy spinster for a look-see.

#12 (December 31, 1951)
THE ADAGIO
Before Lucy can perform an apache dance number at the Tropicana, she takes lessons from a Frenchman who's more interested in romance than dance. When Ricky discovers him hiding in a hall closet, the Parisian challenges the Cuban to a duel.

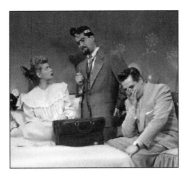

#16 (January 28, 1952)
LUCY FAKES ILLNESS
Since Ricky won't put Lucy in his new nightclub act, she fakes a nervous breakdown by developing multiple personalities—one of whom is Tallulah Bankhead. Ricky is on to the fakery, and calls in a phony doctor to scare Lucy back to sanity.

#17 (February 4, 1952)
LUCY WRITES A PLAY
Lucy has written a play about a Cuban tobacco picker for her women's club competition, but when she can't get Ricky to star in it, she rewrites it for Fred Mertz. Unaware of the change, Ricky decides to appear in the play after all.

#21 (March 3, 1952)
NEW NEIGHBORS
Lucy and Ethel overhear their new neighbors plotting tenants' murders, unaware that they're only actors rehearsing lines. To protect themselves, the Ricardos and Mertzes take the law into their own hands, and all four wind up in jail.

#18 (February 11, 1952)
BREAKING THE LEASE
The Ricardos' late-night singing and other noisy endeavors set off a feud with the Mertzes. Lucy and Ricky decide to break their lease by becoming totally undesirable tenants. They succeed, but on moving day the sentimental foursome make up.

#22 (March 10, 1952)
FRED AND ETHEL FIGHT
Lucy and Ricky succeed in patching up the sparring Mertzes, only to start fighting themselves. Ethel's advice to Lucy, and Fred's to Ricky, bring the Ricardos back together, but set the Mertzes off again.

❤ **#19** (February 18, 1952)
THE BALLET
Lucy fails miserably at ballet lessons but does much better learning a burlesque act. So when asked to replace a sick performer in Ricky's show, Lucy comes on as a pie-throwing, seltzer-squirting comic. But Ricky needed the ballet dancer.

#23 (March 17, 1952)
THE MOUSTACHE
Ricky grows a moustache for a movie role, but Lucy doesn't like it, and retaliates with a fake beard. The powerful glue she used makes it impossible to remove, and Lucy has to hide behind a harem veil when Ricky brings the producer home.

#20 (February 25, 1952)
THE YOUNG FANS
A teenage girl meets her favorite performer, Ricky Ricardo, and develops a crush on him, while her steady boyfriend falls in love with Lucy. But when the Ricardos start acting like ninety-year-olds, the teenagers quickly return to each other.

#24 (March 24, 1952)
THE GOSSIP
Ricky and Fred bet their wives that they can keep from gossiping longer. Then each one sets out to trick the other into gossiping first. Lucy and Ethel win the bet, but only because Lucy bribed the milkman into creating some phony gossip.

♥ #25 (March 31, 1952)
PIONEER WOMEN
Having been bet by their husbands that they can't do without modern conveniences, Lucy and Ethel churn butter and bake bread from scratch—an eighteen-foot loaf! But then Lucy demands Ricky start living as if it's the turn of the century for him, too.

♥ #29 (April 28, 1952)
THE FREEZER
To stock their new walk-in freezer, Lucy and Ethel buy enough beef for a cattle drive. Then Lucy gets locked in the freezer. She emerges dripping icicles, just as the meat she hid in an unlit furnace starts cooking because Fred turned on the heat.

#26 (April 7, 1952)
THE MARRIAGE LICENSE
Lucy thinks she and Ricky aren't legally married because his name was misspelled on their marriage license. So she wants them to renew their vows at the same place in Connecticut where Ricky first proposed to her. But they run out of gas getting there.

♥ #30 (May 5, 1952)
LUCY DOES A TV COMMERCIAL
Lucy schemes her way into doing a vitamin commercial on a TV show Ricky is hosting. Rehearsing her lines and sampling the liquid tonic, which is one-quarter alcohol, Lucy gets bombed, as she extols the product's virtues while barely staying upright.

#27 (April 14, 1952)
THE KLEPTOMANIAC
When Ricky finds a closetful of valuables that Lucy has collected for a bazaar, he mistakenly thinks she's become a kleptomaniac. He secretly calls in a doctor to hypnotize her, but Lucy is wise to them, and feigns recalling a notorious past.

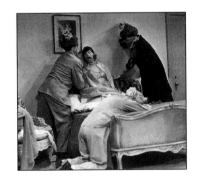

#31 (May 12, 1952)
THE PUBLICITY AGENT
Lucy dreams up some publicity to boost Ricky's career by posing as a Middle Eastern princess who's his biggest fan. The media thinks she's the real thing, and so does Ricky, until she shows up at the Tropicana and wants to hear twenty-five encores of "Babalu."

#28 (April 21, 1952)
CUBAN PALS
Ricky's former dance partner, the very sexy Renita, visits them from Cuba, and Lucy is immediately jealous. Enlisting Fred to drive the dancer to Philadelphia, Lucy takes over Renita's number at the club, and ends up in the wildest dance of her life.

#32 (May 19, 1952)
LUCY GETS RICKY ON THE RADIO
Lucy enters Ricky as a contestant on a radio quiz show, but he refuses to appear. In the producer's office, Lucy comes upon the answers for the show, memorizes them, and Ricky is a contestant again. But at airtime all the questions are switched.

#33 (May 26, 1952)
LUCY'S SCHEDULE
Lucy is habitually late, so Ricky puts her on a strict time schedule, then invites his boss over for dinner. Lucy gets back at her husband by serving each course of the meal for just a few seconds and then whisking it away again.

❤ **#37** (October 6, 1952)
THE HANDCUFFS
After Lucy snaps a pair of antique handcuffs on herself and Ricky, they realize there's no key. A locksmith is found, but not before the Ricardos go to bed handcuffed together, and Ricky has to do a TV show with his "attached" wife trying to upstage him.

#34 (June 2, 1952)
RICKY THINKS HE IS GETTING BALD
Ricky's so afraid he's losing his hair that Lucy invites a group of bald men over to reassure her husband he has nothing to worry about. When Ricky doesn't show up, Lucy concocts a bizarre hair-growth procedure to get him off his "balding" kick.

❤ **#38** (October 13, 1952)
THE OPERETTA
Lucy's women's club wants to stage an operetta, but they're completely broke. So she and Ethel write and star in the musical, but when their check bounces for the costumes and scenery, the rental company repossesses everything in mid-performance.

#35 (June 9, 1952)
RICKY ASKS FOR A RAISE
A new act is competing with Ricky's at the Tropicana, so Lucy makes dozens of bogus reservations, and appears at the club with the Mertzes in various quick-change outfits, pretending to be customers who only want to see Ricky Ricardo perform.

❤ **#39** (September 15, 1952)
JOB SWITCHING
Ricky wants Lucy to try working for a week, so she and Ethel get jobs in a candy factory, where they are totally inept, especially at wrapping—due to a speeding conveyor belt that has them stuffing chocolates into their mouths, blouses and hats.

#36 (September 29, 1952)
THE ANNIVERSARY PRESENT
Ricky's spending time with a neighbor who's helping him buy an anniversary gift for Lucy. But she is convinced he's having an affair with the neighbor. When she and Ethel are caught spying on the "lovers," an embarrassed Lucy finally learns the truth.

#40 (September 22, 1952)
THE SAXOPHONE
When Lucy fails her saxophone audition for Ricky's band, she tries to stop him from going on the road by pretending there's another man in her life. Ricky gets back at her by hiring several "lovers," and hiding them in Lucy's closet.

#41 (October 27, 1952)

VACATION FROM MARRIAGE

The Ricardos and Mertzes take a week off from their in-a-rut marriages. But each spouse misses the other too much, and despite a last-minute effort to make each other jealous, they'd all prefer being in a rut with their mates.

#45 (January 26, 1953)

SALES RESISTANCE

Convinced his wife is a sucker for a sales pitch, Ricky demands she return the vacuum cleaner she bought from a door-to-door salesman. Instead, she tries unsuccessfully to sell it. Ricky insists he'll return it—and ends up buying a refrigerator.

#42 (November 10, 1952)

THE COURTROOM

The Ricardos give the Mertzes a television set for their anniversary, but Ricky's zealous tuning causes it to blow up. Fred retaliates by breaking the Ricardos' set, and the foursome end up in court, where they manage to destroy the judge's TV.

#46 (February 2, 1953)

THE INFERIORITY COMPLEX

Lucy's equally dreadful jokes and bridge-playing leave her feeling depressed and inferior. Ricky arranges for a psychiatrist to flatter her back to mental health, but the doctor gets carried away with his too-ardent treatment.

#43 (November 24, 1952)

REDECORATING

Waiting to find out if she has won a home furnishing contest, Lucy won't leave the house, much to Ricky's annoyance. He tells Fred to call her and say that she won. Lucy immediately sells all the old furniture, which Ricky now has to try to buy back.

#47 (February 16, 1953)

THE CLUB ELECTION

Lucy and Ethel become embroiled in a women's club presidential election, running against each other for the top spot using any means necessary—bribery and other types of payola. After all the hoopla, though, they both wind up winning the election.

#44 (December 1, 1952)

RICKY LOSES HIS VOICE

Ricky's laryngitis makes it impossible for him to perform in a big reopening show at the Tropicana. So Lucy substitutes herself, the ex-vaudevillian Mertzes, and a chorus line of middle-aged showgirls from the Flapper Follies of 1927.

#48 (March 9, 1953)

THE BLACK EYE

Lucy misses catching a book tossed to her by Ricky, and winds up with a black eye which Fred Mertz is convinced was intended. Trying to patch things up for the Ricardos, Fred sends Lucy flowers, but inadvertently uses his own name instead of Ricky's.

#49 (March 30, 1953)
LUCY CHANGES HER MIND
Ricky is furious that his wife can't make up her mind and never finishes what she starts. So Lucy decides to pick up where she left off with an old boyfriend, but meeting her former beau after all these years turns into a major disappointment.

#53 (December 29, 1952)
LUCY HIRES AN ENGLISH TUTOR
Lucy hires a tutor to improve her English—she's given up on Ricky's. But in exchange for lessons, the teacher wants to sing at the Tropicana. Ricky promises to get the man recording auditions if he'll start speaking English like a Cuban.

♥ **#50** (December 8, 1952)
LUCY IS ENCEINTE
Upon learning she is pregnant, Lucy has to break the wonderful news to Ricky, hoping for the perfect moment to tell him. After a couple of failed attempts, she goes to the Tropicana and sends a note to him with a song request: "We're Having a Baby."

#54 (January 5, 1953)
RICKY HAS LABOR PAINS
After Lucy's friends give her a baby shower, Ricky becomes so jealous of all the attention she's getting, he develops morning sickness. Lucy suggests his friends give him a daddy shower, which Fred Mertz promptly turns into a stag party.

#51 (December 15, 1952)
PREGNANT WOMEN ARE UNPREDICTABLE
Lucy thinks Ricky cares more about the baby they're having than about her, especially after buying her presents like bonnets and rattles. But when he takes her out for a night on the town, she thinks he's lost interest in the baby.

#55 (January 12, 1953)
LUCY BECOMES A SCULPTRESS
With fifty pounds of clay and Fred posing as a discus thrower in his longjohns, Lucy proves she can't sculpt. To discourage her, Ricky brings home an art critic, and there's Lucy, her head covered in a thin coat of clay, pretending she's a "bust."

#52 (December 22, 1952)
LUCY'S SHOWBIZ SWAN SONG
Despite her pregnancy, Lucy wants to appear in Ricky's Gay Nineties revue at the Tropicana. After a disastrous audition, Lucy disguises herself and sneaks into the barbershop quartet number, then proceeds to ruin it.

♥ **#56** (January 19, 1953)
LUCY GOES TO THE HOSPITAL
As Ricky and the Mertzes rehearse their roles for taking Lucy to the hospital, she announces "This is it," sending the three into total hysteria and chaos. That's nothing compared to the chaos Ricky creates at the hospital as a voodoo witch doctor.

#57 (April 20, 1953)
No Children Allowed

When a cranky tenant threatens to move because of Little Ricky Ricardo's loud crying, Ethel makes it clear that her friendship with Lucy is more important than a rental agreement. But Ethel doesn't let the Ricardos forget her loyalty.

#58 (April 27, 1953)
Lucy Hires a Maid

Lucy's sleepless nights with the new baby are exhausting, so the Ricardos hire a maid. Unfortunately, she takes better care of herself than of Lucy or the apartment. Unable to fire her, Lucy wrecks the place, hoping it will make the maid quit.

#59 (May 4, 1953)
The Indian Show

Even the arrival of the baby hasn't dampened Lucy's showbiz aspirations. Wanting to get into the new Indian act at the Tropicana, Lucy pays off one of the performers and appears herself, carrying Little Ricky papoose-style on her back.

#60 (May 11, 1953)
Lucy's Last Birthday

Convinced everyone has forgotten her birthday, a forlorn Lucy sits on a park bench and meets up with a group of musical "lost souls." To embarrass Ricky, she brings them to the Tropicana, only to discover a surprise birthday party awaits her.

#61 (May 18, 1953)
The Ricardos Change Apartments

Now that they have Little Ricky, Lucy insists they need more room, and wants to exchange apartments with one of the other tenants. She convinces a reluctant Ricky by cluttering their apartment with baby things and assorted junk.

#62 (May 25, 1953)
Lucy Is Matchmaker

Lucy wants to fix up a friend of hers with a friend of the Mertzes who happens to be a lingerie salesman. But when she and Ethel wind up in his hotel room, trying on lingerie, and Fred and Ricky arrive, the girls have a lot of "'splainin'" to do.

#63 (June 1, 1953)
Lucy Wants New Furniture

Lucy tries to hide some new furniture she bought without Ricky's permission in the kitchen. Discovering his wife's extravagant purchase, Ricky insists that she pay for it with her allowance. But Lucy's forced economy brings disastrous results.

#64 (June 8, 1953)
The Camping Trip

Anxious to join Ricky on a camping trip in order to have more shared interests, Lucy hatches a plot, with Ethel's help, to prove she's as outdoorsy as her husband. Her plan backfires when Ethel throws an already-dead duck at her to shoot.

#65 (October 5, 1953)

RICKY'S LIFE STORY

After Ricky is featured in *Life* magazine, Lucy is more desperate than ever for a showbiz career. To prevent it, Ricky and Fred concoct an impossible dance routine for her. She gets back at them by upstaging Ricky in his own big number.

#69 (October 19, 1953)

LUCY AND ETHEL BUY THE SAME DRESS

Lucy and Ethel discover they've both bought the same gown to wear in their big musical number for their women's club talent show. Both promise to buy new gowns, but neither one does, which leads to a decidedly unfriendly performance of "Friendship."

#66 (June 22, 1953)

RICKY AND FRED ARE TV FANS

With Ricky and Fred glued to a TV fight, their wives go to a local cafe, where service is so slow that Lucy makes change for herself at the cash register and the girls are arrested. They finally get home to husbands who didn't know they were gone.

#70 (October 26, 1953)

EQUAL RIGHTS

Since Lucy and Ethel insist on equal treatment, their husbands oblige, and everyone gets separate checks at a restaurant. Because they have no money, the girls end up washing dishes, and get back at Ricky and Fred by pretending they've been robbed.

#67 (June 29, 1953)

NEVER DO BUSINESS WITH FRIENDS

The Ricardos sell their old washing machine to the Mertzes for thirty-five dollars. When it breaks down the next day, Fred and Ethel want out of the deal. A tug-of-war ensues, however, when the Mertzes want the machine back after a repairman offers them fifty dollars for it.

#71 (November 2, 1953)

BABY PICTURES

The Ricardos and the Applebys always brag to each other about their little sons. But when Lucy's and Caroline Appleby's exchanges turn hostile and sarcastic, Ricky worries that it will jeopardize a TV job that's been offered to him by Caroline's husband.

#68 (October 12, 1953)

THE GIRLS GO INTO BUSINESS

Lucy and Ethel buy a local dress shop, expecting to make millions. But when business is bad, they're happy to sell it for a few hundred more than they paid, only to find out it was sold again for a lot more money, to make way for a skyscraper.

#72 (November 9, 1953)

LUCY TELLS THE TRUTH

Ricky and the Mertzes bet Lucy that she can't go twenty-four hours without telling a lie. The outcome: she insults all her friends, and has to admit her real age and hair color. But she does get a part on a TV show by telling the truth, more or less.

#73 (November 16, 1953)
THE FRENCH REVUE

Ricky is planning a French revue for the club, and since Lucy is determined to be in it, she hires a Frenchman to coach her. When Ricky forbids her to come near the place, she tries various disguises, and finally succeeds as a chorus girl.

#74 (November 23, 1953)
REDECORATING THE MERTZES' APARTMENT

Lucy helps Ethel with repainting and refurbishing chores. But when Fred turns on a fan as Lucy is unstuffing a chair, the paint and feathers go flying. Lucy feels responsible for the ruined furniture, and gives Ethel her own living room set as a gift.

#75 (November 30, 1953)
TOO MANY CROOKS

Lucy sneaks into the Mertzes' apartment to borrow one of Fred's suits so she can order a custom-made one for his birthday gift. This leads Ethel to assume that Lucy is the notorious neighborhood burglar, and she goes spying on her friend to prove it.

#76 (December 7, 1953)
CHANGING THE BOYS' WARDROBE

Disgusted with their husbands' old clothes, Lucy and Ethel give them to a secondhand store, but the boys buy everything back. Then, dressed in new tuxedos, they call their wives to meet them at the club. The girls arrive in their grubbiest attire.

#77 (December 14, 1953)
LUCY HAS HER EYES EXAMINED

Lucy is about to audition for a movie in which she has to do a mean jitterbug. But on the day of the audition, she takes Ricky to the eye doctor, and winds up with drops in her eyes that blur her vision and seriously impair her dance.

#78 (December 21, 1953)
RICKY'S OLD GIRLFRIEND

A magazine marriage quiz prompts Lucy to tell Ricky about her old boyfriends. He gets even by inventing an old flame, but the name he uses is someone he once knew who is now appearing in town. Lucy's relieved to discover that the woman is fat and unattractive.

♥ **#79** (January 11, 1954)
THE MILLION-DOLLAR IDEA

After Lucy and Ethel promote their salad dressing product on TV—Lucy drank it to prove its great taste—Ricky shows them why they won't make a profit. So they go back on TV to "unsell" the dressing—tasting and hating it—but the orders pour in anyway.

#80 (January 18, 1954)
RICKY MINDS THE BABY

Ricky agrees to watch his son, but while Daddy is engrossed in a football game, Little Ricky wanders off. Lucy finds him in the hallway, and calls Ricky to ask where the baby is. Panicking, Ricky searches everywhere, before Lucy walks in with their son.

#81 (January 25, 1954)
THE CHARM SCHOOL

When one of Ricky's friends brings a gorgeous, attention-getting date to the Ricardos' party, Lucy and Ethel head straight for charm school. They emerge wearing too much makeup and outrageously sexy gowns, but their husbands aren't impressed.

#85 (February 22, 1954)
RICKY LOSES HIS TEMPER

Ricky explodes when Lucy buys an expensive hat. She offers to return it, and bets him that he'll lose his cool over something else before she buys another hat. But no matter what she does to provoke him, the hot-tempered Cuban remains unruffled.

#82 (February 1, 1954)
SENTIMENTAL ANNIVERSARY

The Ricardos want to spend their anniversary alone, but Ethel has planned a surprise party for them. So when the guests start arriving, Lucy and Ricky have to sneak out of their apartment and pretend to be surprised when they come back in.

#86 (March 1, 1954)
HOME MOVIES

Lucy and the Mertzes are so bored with Ricky's home movies that they make one of their own: a Western-musical-drama which they splice into a TV pilot Ricky's working on. Fortunately, the show's producer thinks the unintentional comedy is hilarious.

#83 (February 8, 1954)
FAN MAGAZINE INTERVIEW

An "average day in the life of" article is being written about the Ricardos. When the reporter arrives, it's anything but average when Lucy hits the roof after finding out about Ricky's "date" with another woman at the club. It's actually part of a publicity stunt, but Lucy's on the warpath.

❤ **#87** (March 8, 1954)
BONUS BUCKS

Ricky's contest-winning one-dollar bill—worth three hundred dollars—goes on a wild journey: from Lucy's purse to the grocery boy, to Ethel, to Ricky's pajamas, to the Speedy Laundry, where Lucy, attempting to retrieve the bonus buck, ends up in a vat of starch.

#84 (February 15, 1954)
OIL WELLS

When the Ricardos find out the Mertzes bought some oil stock that they, too, wanted in on, Fred sells them half his shares. Then the foursome mistakenly think they've been swindled and get their money back—just before the wells start gushing.

#88 (March 22, 1954)
RICKY'S HAWAIIAN VACATION

Hoping to go with Ricky on a Hawaiian concert tour, Lucy appears on a game show that gives away free airline tickets. Ricky is unexpectedly there, too, singing while Lucy is doused with water, sprayed with honey and pelted with eggs and pies.

#89 (March 29, 1954)
LUCY IS ENVIOUS
Lucy's past fibs to her rich and snotty ex-schoolmate are about to catch up with her when she unwittingly pledges five hundred dollars to a charity drive. In order to come up with the money, she and Ethel agree to a publicity stunt that puts them on top of the Empire State Building posing as women from Mars.

#93 (April 19, 1954)
THE BLACK WIG
Lucy is sure Ricky won't recognize her in a stylish black wig, so she plans to test his fidelity. When she flirts with him, he pretends not to know her. They make a dinner date to which Lucy brings Ethel, in disguise, and Ricky shows up with Fred.

#90 (April 5, 1954)
LUCY WRITES A NOVEL
Lucy is writing a novel she's sure will make a fortune. But when Ricky and the Mertzes find themselves in the book—a bit too thinly disguised—they burn it. There are, however, carbon copies, and even a publisher who's momentarily interested.

❤ **#94** (May 3, 1954)
TENNESSEE ERNIE VISITS
Hick cousin Tennessee Ernie Ford visits the Ricardos and becomes an unwelcome guest. His singing is too loud, his appetite is gargantuan, and he destroys Ricky's maracas. And Lucy's vamping—meant to scare him off—makes him want to stay longer.

#91 (April 12, 1954)
LUCY'S CLUB DANCE
As a fund-raiser for their women's group, Lucy and the others form a quintet, hoping to appear with Ricky at the club. Appalled by their lack of talent, he gets even more upset when a newspaper item suggests he's put together an "all-girl orchestra."

#95 (May 10, 1954)
TENNESSEE ERNIE HANGS ON
The Ricardos' houseguest, Tennessee Ernie Ford, has overstayed his welcome. To get rid of him, Lucy says they're too poor to buy food, so Ernie takes them and the Mertzes on a talent show, where their act wins a prize and a ticket home for Ernie.

#92 (April 26, 1954)
THE DINER
The Ricardos and Mertzes buy a diner together, but Fred and Ethel do all the work. So they divide the place in half—American and Cuban. When a price war and a pie fight ensue, the foursome are happy to sell it back to the original owner, cheap.

#96 (May 17, 1954)
THE GOLF GAME
Tired of being golf "widows," Lucy and Ethel take up the game themselves. To discourage their wives, Ricky and Fred invent some nutty new rules. When a golf pro sets the women straight, they enlist his help to teach the men a lesson.

#97 (May 24, 1954)
THE SUBLEASE

Since the Ricardos are off to Maine for two months, the Mertzes have to sublet the apartment. When they finally find a tenant they like, Ricky's summer booking falls through and the Ricardos have to move in with the Mertzes. It's hell all around.

#101 (November 1, 1954)
MR. AND MRS. TV SHOW

When Lucy learns Ricky tried to decline a TV appearance to keep her off the airwaves, she sabotages a "dress rehearsal" of the show in their apartment by making fun of the sponsor. The only problem: it's actually a live TV broadcast of "Breakfast with Lucy and Ricky."

♥ **#98** (October 18, 1954)
LUCY CRIES WOLF

To test Ricky's devotion, Lucy creates a few phony emergencies requiring him to rush to her side: she even pretends to have been kidnapped. He's wise to her, and acts indifferent. But when real burglars nab Lucy, he thinks she's still bluffing.

#102 (October 11, 1954)
MERTZ AND KURTZ

Fred's old vaudeville partner pays a visit, with tales of world travel and entertaining royalty, then finally admits he's just a cook in the Bronx. So to help the old trouper impress his grandson, Ricky stars him in a revue at the club.

#99 (October 25, 1954)
THE MATCHMAKER

Lucy invites two shy friends over for dinner, planning to show them how wonderful marriage is. But the dinner burns, the baby cries, Ricky is cranky and the Ricardos end up fighting. Still, all this marital bliss sends the shy couple to the altar.

#103 (November 8, 1954)
RICKY'S MOVIE OFFER

When the neighbors find out that a Hollywood agent is meeting with Ricky, they and their pets converge on the Ricardo apartment, hoping to audition—Lucy even has her god-awful Marilyn Monroe takeoff ready. Fortunately, Ricky and the agent meet at a hotel.

#100 (October 4, 1954)
THE BUSINESS MANAGER

Ricky hires a business manager to handle Lucy's hopeless household budget. Lucy gets back at them by buying groceries for the neighbors, pocketing the money, and charging everything to her new account—which all leads to a stock market tip that pays off.

#104 (November 15, 1954)
RICKY'S SCREEN TEST

According to showbiz gossip, Ricky's a sure bet for a Hollywood movie and Lucy is praying that her small role in his screen test will mean stardom for her, too. But despite all her valiant efforts, only the back of Lucy's head ends up on camera.

#105 (November 22, 1954)
LUCY'S MOTHER-IN-LAW
Lucy's attempts to impress Ricky's mother keep meeting with disaster. She even loses her in-law on the subway. Then, at a Spanish-speaking party, she hires a man to secretly translate for her, but when he departs suddenly, she's left tongue-tied.

#106 (November 29, 1954)
ETHEL'S BIRTHDAY
An argument over a birthday gift Lucy picked out for Ethel leads to a rift between them. Fred and Ricky mend it by arranging for the women to sit next to each other at the theater, where a sentimental play rekindles their friendship.

#107 (December 6, 1954)
RICKY'S CONTRACT
Ricky's so anxious for a phone call from Hollywood confirming a movie deal that Fred makes up a phony message saying the magic words. Lucy and Ethel then try to intercept it before it reaches Ricky—but he's already gotten the news for real.

#108 (December 13, 1954)
GETTING READY
The Ricardos plan to drive out to Hollywood for Ricky's film debut, and the Mertzes, who can't bear to say goodbye, are invited to come along. Fred buys a vintage Cadillac, but it's too old to make the trip, and Ricky's stuck with it.

#109 (January 3, 1955)
LUCY LEARNS TO DRIVE
Ricky has bought a new car for the trip to Hollywood, and Lucy insists he teach her how to drive. He gives up after the first lesson, but she thinks she's doing great, and offers to teach Ethel, which makes two accidents waiting to happen—and they do.

❤ **#110** (January 10, 1955)
CALIFORNIA, HERE WE COME
The day before the Ricardos and Mertzes leave for California, Lucy's mother decides to join them. The Mertzes back out, but when Lucy's mother decides to take Little Ricky and fly, Ethel and Fred decide to go again. Finally, all four head west.

❤ **#111** (January 17, 1955)
FIRST STOP
On the road, the Ricardos and Mertzes get lost in Ohio. Stopping at a run-down motel, they eat inedible food and rent a very shaky cabin. Meanwhile, their car's steering wheel is stolen, and the motel owner sells them a new one—or rather their own.

#112 (January 24, 1955)
TENNESSEE BOUND
The Ricardos and the Mertzes are arrested for speeding in cousin Tennessee Ernie Ford's hometown. After trying to help them escape from jail, Ernie offers to marry one of the sheriff's chubby daughters in exchange for his friends' release.

#113 (January 31, 1955)
ETHEL'S HOMETOWN

The foursome make a stop in Albuquerque, Ethel's hometown, where her recent letters have led everyone to assume she's the one heading for Hollywood stardom. Invited to perform at a local theater, she gets upstaged by Fred and the Ricardos.

#117 (February 28, 1955)
THE FASHION SHOW

Lucy talks her way into being one of the models at a Hollywood charity fashion show. Wanting to exchange her New York pallor for a California tan, she overdoes it, ending up lobster-red, and has to wear a scratchy tweed suit on the runway.

♥ **#114** (February 7, 1955)
L.A. AT LAST!

Starstruck Lucy spies William Holden at the Brown Derby, then accidentally knocks a tray of desserts into his lap. When Ricky brings Holden home from the studio to meet his biggest fan, the second encounter with Lucy tops the first by a nose.

#118 (March 14, 1955)
THE HEDDA HOPPER STORY

To get Hedda Hopper's attention, Ricky's publicity agent wants him to "save" Lucy from drowning in the hotel pool just as the famous columnist walks by. But when a bowl of fruit is mistaken for one of Hopper's hats, the stunt backfires.

#115 (February 14, 1955)
DON JUAN AND THE STARLETS

Ricky attends a movie premiere with four starlets, while Lucy falls asleep on the couch in their hotel suite. Seeing his bed made up the next morning, she assumes he never came home (he did, and went out again early) and is ready to sue for divorce.

#119 (March 21, 1955)
DON JUAN IS SHELVED

When Ricky's movie is canceled, Lucy hires a man to impersonate a producer and say great things about Ricky at a meeting he's having with the head of MGM. Unknowingly, Lucy has "hired" the studio chief himself, who plays along with her.

♥ **#116** (February 21, 1955)
LUCY GETS IN PICTURES

Thanks to a director friend of Ricky's, Lucy finally lands a part in a movie. She plays a Ziegfeld-type showgirl who gets shot during her descent down a huge staircase. But Lucy's top-heavy headdress does her in long before the gun goes off.

#120 (March 18, 1955)
BULLFIGHT DANCE

In order to avoid Lucy saying nasty things about him in a movie magazine article, Ricky has to let her appear on his TV benefit show. She's the bull to his matador in a Spanish dance number, only slightly revamped—Lucy does it as a dancing cow.

#121 (April 4, 1955)
HOLLYWOOD ANNIVERSARY
Lucy is mad because Ricky doesn't remember their anniversary date. When he tells her he's arranged a big celebration at Mocambo, she forgives him, until she finds out that he wired the county clerk's office where they were married to confirm the date.

#122 (April 18, 1955)
THE STAR UPSTAIRS
Lucy is so determined to get a look at Cornel Wilde—he's in the hotel suite above the Ricardos'—that she disguises herself as a bellhop and brings him a food cart. But leaving his suite isn't as easy: she gets herself locked out on his balcony.

#123 (April 25, 1955)
IN PALM SPRINGS
The boys and the girls need a break from each other, so the boys stay in L.A., and Lucy and Ethel go to Palm Springs. Secretly arranged by Ricky, the girls meet Rock Hudson, who tells them a touching story that sparks a happy reunion of the "odd couples."

❤ **#124** (May 9, 1955)
HARPO MARX
Hoping to impress Caroline Appleby, who is passing through L.A., Lucy invites her friend over to meet a few movie stars. Because Caroline's myopic, Lucy herself portrays Gable, Cooper, Crosby, even Harpo Marx. Then the real Harpo arrives.

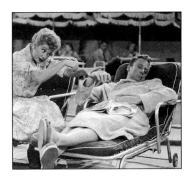

#125 (May 2, 1955)
THE DANCING STAR
Hoping to make Caroline Appleby jealous, Lucy says she and Van Johnson are dance partners. After picking him up at her hotel, Lucy begs him to go along with her charade. But when his regular partner is ill, Johnson actually asks Lucy to dance with him.

#126 (May 16, 1955)
RICKY NEEDS AN AGENT
To spur MGM into a movie deal for Ricky, Lucy pretends to be his agent, and tells the studio that he's been offered a Broadway musical. To her horror, the studio releases him. Now she has to convince MGM that a crazy woman was impersonating his agent.

❤ **#127** (May 30, 1955)
THE TOUR
Lucy will do anything to get Richard Widmark's autograph. She scales the walls of the actor's estate, gets past a dangerous dog, and winds up in Widmark's den disguised as a bearskin rug. Enter the star, Ricky and the dog.

#128 (October 3, 1955)
LUCY VISITS GRAUMAN'S
Lucy wants to go back to New York with the most incredible souvenir of Hollywood: the concrete block at Grauman's containing John Wayne's footprints. She and Ethel manage to steal the slab, but Ricky demands they return it. On the way back, they drop it.

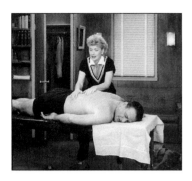

❤ **#129** (October 10, 1955)
LUCY AND JOHN WAYNE
Ricky arranges for the Duke to make a replacement of his cement footprints at Grauman's. The first one is mistaken for a forgery by Lucy and Ethel, and they erase it. Little Ricky messes up the second one. Finally, Wayne makes a six-month supply.

❤ **#130** (October 17, 1955)
LUCY AND THE DUMMY
At an MGM studio party, Lucy dances with a life-sized dummy of Ricky, hoping her talent will finally be "discovered." When "Ricky" apparently becomes permanently attached to her, the dance turns into a comedy act that leads to an MGM movie contract.

#131 (October 24, 1955)
RICKY SELLS THE CAR
Planning to return to New York by train, Ricky sells the car, which leaves the Mertzes hurt that they're not going back with the Ricardos. Fred buys an old motorcycle for the trip, but when he crashes it immediately, Ricky finally buys them train tickets.

❤ **#132** (October 31, 1955)
THE GREAT TRAIN ROBBERY
The Ricardos are on the train to New York when Lucy realizes she left the tickets in the station. So she pulls the emergency cord, stops the train and angers the conductor. But when she pulls it again to help catch a thief on board, she's a heroine.

#133 (November 7, 1955)
HOMECOMING
Once back in New York, Lucy's movie star husband has become something of a celebrity. Even she starts fawning all over him, and Ricky can't stand it. Hoping to get back his real wife, he begins treating Lucy like a slave until she finally rebels.

#134 (November 14, 1955)
THE RICARDOS ARE INTERVIEWED
A TV interview show plans to visit the Ricardos at home, but first Ricky's agent wants them to move to fancier digs. When Lucy says no, the Mertzes pick a fight with the Ricardos, hoping it will make them move. It doesn't work, and their fighting goes on.

#135 (November 28, 1955)
LUCY GOES TO A RODEO
Ricky can't perform in a Western-theme show at Fred's lodge—he thinks he has a radio booking—so Lucy and Ethel fill in. When Ricky learns it's a rodeo—not radio—show he's got to do, he hires Lucy and the Mertzes to perform their Western numbers.

#136 (December 5, 1955)
NURSERY SCHOOL
Lucy wants her son at home, but Daddy wants him in nursery school, so he's enrolled. Little Ricky loves it there until he needs a tonsillectomy that requires an overnight hospital stay. Lucy disguises herself as a nurse to spend the night with him.

#137 (December 12, 1955)
RICKY'S EUROPEAN BOOKING
Ricky's off to Europe but can't afford to take Lucy and Ethel, who decide to raise their trip money by raffling off a TV set. But threat of imprisonment for fraud halts the raffle. Luckily, Ricky gets free passage by ship for all of them.

#141 (January 23, 1956)
SECOND HONEYMOON
On the ship to Europe, the Mertzes are enjoying a second honeymoon. Lonely because Ricky's busy performing on board, Lucy "kidnaps" him for an evening, locking the stateroom and tossing the key out the porthole, then gets herself stuck through the porthole.

#138 (December 19, 1955)
THE PASSPORTS
Since Lucy can't produce her birth certificate to get a passport, she needs the signatures of two people who have known her from birth. A childhood baby-sitter and her family doctor try unsuccessfully to help. But finally Lucy's mother sends the certificate.

#142 (January 30, 1956)
LUCY MEETS THE QUEEN
Lucy dances in Ricky's London Palladium show just so that she can meet the Queen after the performance. But a leaping finale renders her unable to curtsy properly. The Queen, however, insists on meeting the girl who did that wonderful comedy dance.

#139 (January 2, 1956)
STATEN ISLAND FERRY
Fred's so afraid his seasickness will ruin the trip to Europe that Lucy takes him for a trial run on the Staten Island Ferry. Both of them take seasickness pills, fall asleep on deck and almost miss picking up their passports at the government office.

#143 (February 6, 1956)
THE FOX HUNT
Jealous of a British starlet's attention to Ricky, Lucy arranges a weekend at the estate of a famous movie producer, only to discover he's the starlet's father. Then, adding injury to insult, she takes part in a fox hunt and ends up in brambles.

❤ **#140** (January 16, 1956)
BON VOYAGE
The Ricardos and Mertzes sail for Europe but Lucy literally keeps missing the boat—first when she goes ashore for a last goodbye with Little Ricky, then when she misses the pilot boat to take her to the ship. Finally a helicopter drops her on board.

#144 (February 20, 1956)
LUCY GOES TO SCOTLAND
Lucy dreams that she's visiting her ancestral village in Scotland, arriving just in time to be sacrificed to a two-headed dragon. Ricky comes to rescue her, then backs out. Waking up, she hits him with a pillow and calls him a "coward!"

❤ **#145** (February 27, 1956)
PARIS AT LAST!
Lucy exchanges American money for French francs with a man on the streets of Paris and gets more than the going rate—a wad of counterfeit francs. Innocently trying to pay for lunch with the money, she's arrested and lands in jail.

❤ **#149** (April 9, 1956)
LUCY GETS HOMESICK IN ITALY
An Italian street urchin wins Lucy's heart by reminding her of Little Ricky, whom she misses terribly, especially since it's his birthday. So she throws a birthday party for her son in his absence, and makes the little Italian boy her guest of honor.

❤ **#146** (March 5, 1956)
LUCY MEETS CHARLES BOYER
Forewarned by Ricky, the great actor pretends he's someone who looks like Boyer in order to avoid the attentions of Lucy and Ethel. Hoping to make Ricky jealous, Lucy hires the fake Boyer to impersonate the real one, and muddled madness results.

❤ **#150** (April 16, 1956)
LUCY'S ITALIAN MOVIE
When an Italian director casts Lucy in his new film, she mistakenly thinks it's about wine-making. To prepare for the role, she goes to a vineyard, climbs into a grape-filled vat for some exuberant stomping, and ends up in a mushy grape-throwing fight.

#147 (March 19, 1956)
LUCY GETS A PARIS GOWN
Lucy pretends to be on a hunger strike until Ricky buys her a Paris gown. So he and Fred create burlap outfits for their wives with French labels sewn in. The women find out the gowns are not "originals," and force their husbands to buy them the real thing.

#151 (April 23, 1956)
LUCY'S BICYCLE TRIP
The Ricardos and the Mertzes bicycle from Italy to the French Riviera. At the border, Lucy realizes her passport is in the luggage that went ahead. While she's detained, the others pedal on to Nice—only to discover that the luggage key is back with Lucy.

#148 (March 26, 1956)
LUCY IN THE SWISS ALPS
Caught in an Alpine snowstorm, the Ricardos and Mertzes take refuge in a deserted cabin, where the famished foursome have a food fight over a sandwich, and end up confessing dark secrets. They're rescued by an "oompah" band playing "La Cucaracha."

#152 (May 7, 1956)
LUCY GOES TO MONTE CARLO
Lucy's roulette spin at a casino nets her almost a million francs. Hiding the money from Ricky in the Mertzes' luggage leads to false assumptions and accusations by the foursome. Lucy gambles the winnings away as quickly as she won them.

#153 (May 14, 1956)
RETURN HOME FROM EUROPE
Lucy flies home with a giant hunk of Italian cheese disguised as a baby to avoid excess baggage fees. When she finds out that there's a small charge for a baby, Lucy eats half the cheese and stashes the rest among Ricky's band's musical instruments.

❤ **#154** (October 1, 1956)
LUCY MEETS BOB HOPE
Bent on convincing Bob Hope to perform at Ricky's club, Lucy accosts him at the ballpark, disguised as a hot dog vendor. After a fly ball hits him on the head—thanks to Lucy—she catches up with him in the locker room while posing as a tobacco-chewing pitcher.

❤ **#155** (October 15, 1956)
LUCY MEETS ORSON WELLES
When Lucy learns that Orson Welles is doing a benefit show at Ricky's club, she desperately wants into the act as Juliet to Welles's Romeo, but Welles isn't doing Shakespeare. Instead he uses Lucy as his "levitating" assistant in a magic act.

#156 (October 22, 1956)
LITTLE RICKY GETS STAGE FRIGHT
Little Ricky is too terrified to debut in a school recital, but his father manages to persuade him to appear at the club instead. When the ukelele player gets sick and Lucy fills in at the last minute, the result is a delightful mother and son duet.

#157 (October 8, 1956)
LITTLE RICKY LEARNS TO PLAY THE DRUMS
After days of noisy, nonstop drum playing by Little Ricky, the Mertzes threaten to evict the Ricardos, turning off their water, heat and electricity. The foursome keep fighting even after the little tyke's finally asleep, exhausted from drumming.

❤ **#158** (October 29, 1956)
VISITOR FROM ITALY
The Ricardos' Italian houseguest needs some extra money, so he gets a job as a pizza-maker. Threatened with deportation, he has to stop working, so Lucy fills in for him at the pizza parlor, where her dough-tossing and spinning fall flatter than...a pizza.

#159 (November 12, 1956)
OFF TO FLORIDA
Off to meet their husbands in Miami, Lucy and Ethel share a car ride to Florida with an eccentric lady whom they mistakenly think is an ax murderess fleeing the law. But she thinks they're the wanted criminals, and ditches them.

#160 (November 19, 1956)
DEEP-SEA FISHING
On a deep-sea fishing trip with their wives, Ricky and Fred bet the women that they'll catch bigger fish. Then both buy huge tunas and pretend that they've caught them. But Lucy lands the biggest fish when Ricky falls overboard, and she manages to reel him in.

#161 (November 26, 1956)
DESERT ISLAND

To prevent their husbands from getting ashore to judge a beauty contest, Lucy and Ethel make sure the boat they're all on runs out of gas. They find an almost deserted island where Ricky, Fred and an actor in war paint teach the girls a lesson.

#165 (January 21, 1957)
LITTLE RICKY GETS A DOG

Little Ricky brings home an adorable puppy whom everyone falls in love with—except for a new tenant who complains about the barking. Telling the man to move, landlord Fred says he prefers the doggie (who, incidentally, has been named "Fred").

#162 (December 3, 1956)
THE RICARDOS VISIT CUBA

Trying to impress Ricky's family, Lucy ends up saying and doing everything wrong. After destroying Uncle Alberto's cigars, she goes to a tobacco store, but when Alberto arrives, she disguises herself as a cigar-roller, and creates a foot-long stogie.

♥ **#166** (January 14, 1957)
LUCY AND SUPERMAN

For Little Ricky's fifth birthday party, Lucy invites TV's Superman to surprise the kids. When he can't make it, she decides to impersonate him. In costume, Lucy gets trapped on a building ledge with pigeons and has to be rescued by Superman himself, who makes a last-minute appearance.

#163 (December 17, 1956)
LITTLE RICKY'S SCHOOL PAGEANT

When extra cast members are needed for Little Ricky's class play, Lucy signs on as the witch, Ricky plays a hollow tree, Ethel, a fairy princess and Fred, a frog. Although the lead, Little Ricky, forgets a few lines, the play's a big hit.

#167 (January 28, 1957)
LUCY WANTS TO MOVE TO THE COUNTRY

Lucy is desperate to get out of the city, but when she finds out that Ricky's made a deposit on a Connecticut home, she can't bear to leave the Mertzes. After an attempt to sabotage the sale, Lucy sees the house, and can't live without it.

♥ **#164** (January 7, 1957)
LUCY AND THE LOVING CUP

To get back at Ricky for making fun of her new hat, Lucy plops a huge trophy cup on her head, then gets stuck in it. On the way to a silversmith who'll blow-torch it off, Lucy rides a subway train, scaring passengers and embarrassing herself.

#168 (February 4, 1957)
LUCY HATES TO LEAVE

Before moving to Connecticut, the Ricardos agree to vacate their apartment a few days early so the new tenants can move in. They bunk with the Mertzes, which is hard enough, but then Lucy and Ricky learn their home won't be ready for another two weeks.

#169 (February 11, 1957)
LUCY MISSES THE MERTZES
Having just moved to Connecticut, the Ricardos already miss the Mertzes, and head to the city to visit them. But Ethel and Fred are on their way to see the Ricardos. When Lucy and Ricky get back to their home, they mistake the Mertzes for burglars.

#170 (February 18, 1957)
LUCY GETS CHUMMY WITH THE NEIGHBORS
After Lucy spends a fortune on new furniture, Ricky demands she return most of it. Their neighbor, Betty Ramsey, is insulted because she helped Lucy make the purchase at a discount. Fortunately, Ralph Ramsey offers Ricky a TV job, which pays for everything.

♥ **#171** (March 4, 1957)
LUCY RAISES CHICKENS
The Ricardos lay an egg as chicken farmers: Lucy buys five hundred baby chicks and has to put them in the den with the heat turned up to ninety degrees. Then Little Ricky gives them the run of the house and Lucy can't round them up. Ricky comes home to all this.

♥ **#172** (March 11, 1957)
LUCY DOES THE TANGO
Lucy buys a few dozen eggs to put under her unproductive laying hens, in hopes of inspiring them. Hiding the eggs from Ricky, she stuffs them into her blouse, then has to rehearse a tango with him that ends in a jumbo egg-smashing collision.

#173 (March 18, 1957)
RAGTIME BAND
Lucy has volunteered Ricky's services at a Westport benefit, but he refuses to appear. Undaunted, she organizes her own orchestra, featuring Little Ricky and the Mertzes. They're so bad that Ricky has to step back in to save his reputation.

#174 (March 25, 1957)
LUCY'S NIGHT IN TOWN
Lucy's Broadway show tickets for a night out with the Mertzes were for the matinee, so Ricky buys the two remaining box seats: the girls will see Act One, the boys Act Two. But Lucy and Ethel end up on their husbands' laps for the second half.

#175 (April 1, 1957)
HOUSEWARMING
Ethel and Lucy are jealous of each other's new friendship with Betty Ramsey. But Lucy feels better when she thinks the other two are planning a surprise party. Ethel, realizing her friend's mistake, has to hastily organize a real party.

#176 (April 8, 1957)
BUILDING A BARBECUE
When Lucy thinks her wedding ring fell into the wet cement used to build the backyard barbecue, she enlists Ethel's help in taking it apart, brick by brick. Putting it back together again results in a disaster that resembles the leaning tower of Pisa.

#177 (April 22, 1957)
COUNTRY CLUB DANCE
Disgusted with their husbands' attentions to a neighbor's pretty cousin at the country club, Lucy, Ethel and Betty decide to compete with her at a party. The men are extra nice to their wives, and admit the girl was just too immature for them.

#2 (December 3, 1957)
THE CELEBRITY NEXT DOOR
Lucy invites neighbor Tallulah Bankhead to dinner and asks the great actress to appear in a PTA benefit. The meal's a fiasco, but Tallulah gamely agrees to do the show. When Lucy accidentally spray-paints her, they have a falling out that ends with Lucy trying to upstage the star.

#178 (April 29, 1957)
LUCY RAISES TULIPS
Readying her garden for a flower judging, Lucy rides a power lawn mower that levels her tulip bed and takes her on a terrifying trip through town. Lucy replaces the tulips with wax ones, but on competition day the hot sun causes a meltdown.

#3 (January 3, 1958)
LUCY HUNTS URANIUM
Ricky brings everyone to Las Vegas, where he's performing. Lucy enlists movie star Fred MacMurray to help her prospect for uranium in the desert. Then she has a phony newspaper printed announcing a big uranium strike, and hundreds get into the doomed-to-fail prospecting venture.

#179 (May 6, 1957)
THE RICARDOS DEDICATE A STATUE
Ricky's set to dedicate a statue of a Revolutionary War hero, but Lucy accidentally demolishes it with her car. So she does the next best thing: she becomes the statue. But at the ceremony, when a dog starts licking her face, she comes to wide-eyed life.

#4 (February 3, 1958)
LUCY WINS A RACEHORSE
Lucy tries to win a horse for her son, and sends in entries under the Mertzes' name. Fred wins the horse and gives it to Lucy, over Ricky's objections. With the help of Betty Grable and Harry James, Lucy enters her steed in a harness race where she becomes the reluctant jockey.

THE *LUCY-DESI* COMEDY HOURS

#1 (November 6, 1957)
LUCY TAKES A CRUISE TO HAVANA
Flashback to twenty years ago: Lucy and Ann Sothern are on a cruise to Cuba, hoping to meet eligible men. Instead, they meet the honeymooning Mertzes and Rudy Vallee. But in Havana, Lucy and Ricky discover each other and fall in love. Then she pesters Vallee into giving Ricky a job with his band.

#5 (April 14, 1958)
LUCY GOES TO SUN VALLEY
The Ricardos' "second honeymoon" in Sun Valley is canceled because Ricky has to do a TV show, but Lucy and Ethel go anyway. When the girls meet Fernando Lamas, Lucy plots to make Ricky jealous. It starts with an unintentional ski ride on Lamas's shoulders and ends with a pair of black eyes.

#6 (October 6, 1958)
LUCY GOES TO MEXICO
Lucy and the Mertzes go shopping in Tijuana and a run-in with U.S. Customs forces Ricky and Maurice Chevalier to rescue them. But when the Frenchman can't get back into the States, Lucy goes in search of the American consul, who's at a bullfight. Lucy dresses as a matador, and winds up in the ring.

#7 (December 1, 1958)
LUCY MAKES ROOM FOR DANNY
Off to Hollywood to make a movie, the Ricardos rent their house to Danny Thomas's TV family, the Williamses. Unfortunately, the film is canceled, so Ricky and Lucy want their house back, but the Williamses refuse. The Ricardos bunk with the Mertzes, but it all ends in a fight and a day in court .

#8 (February 9, 1959)
LUCY GOES TO ALASKA
The Ricardos and Mertzes are in Alaska for Ricky's appearance on a Red Skelton TV show. Ricky and Fred discover that some land they bought is frozen tundra. Lucy takes Skelton to inspect it, hoping for a sale but gets caught in a blizzard, and they take a plane back to Nome, flying it themselves.

#9 (April 13, 1959)
LUCY WANTS A CAREER
Lucy's morning job as TV sidekick to actor Paul Douglas conflicts with Ricky's late-night club hours. Douglas offers to drop her contract, and Lucy takes a sleeping pill to avoid waking up at 4 A.M. The sponsors insist she appear but she falls asleep in a bowl of their cereal.

#10 (June 8, 1959)
LUCY'S SUMMER VACATION
The Ricardos meet Howard Duff and Ida Lupino at a Vermont lodge. When Ricky and Duff spend most of the time fishing, the wives get even by drilling holes in their husbands' rowboat. The men finally take Lucy and Ida for a romantic moonlit ride, but it turns into a sinking and bailing expedition.

#11 (September 25, 1959)
MILTON BERLE HIDES OUT AT THE RICARDOS
Lucy offers Milton Berle the daytime use of her home so he can finish writing his book in peace. Ricky learns about a mysterious stranger and he storms in to find Milton trying to escape—in drag. Lucy pursues Berle to New York, where she makes her way to his office window via a construction crane.

#12 (November 27, 1959)
THE RICARDOS GO TO JAPAN
In Tokyo for Ricky's band date, Lucy gets Robert Cummings to help her buy pearls—that she can't afford. To get to Cummings before he completes the transaction, Lucy and Ethel wind up in a geisha house, in full costume. Cummings is there, but so are Ricky and Fred!

#13 (April 1, 1960)
LUCY MEETS THE MOUSTACHE
Lucy invites over Ernie Kovacs and his wife, Edie Adams, to get Ricky on his TV show. Instead, the comedian offers a job to Little Ricky. Undaunted, Lucy disguises herself as the comedian's chauffeur, but when she picks him up at the station, Ricky's with him, and the two have fun at her expense.

BIBLIOGRAPHY

Andrews, Bart, and Thomas J. Watson. *Loving Lucy*. St. Martin's Press, 1980. A pictorial tribute to the life and career of Lucille Ball.

Andrews, Bart. *The "I Love Lucy" Book* (revision of *Lucy, Ricky, Fred and Ethel*). Doubleday, 1985. A backstage history of *I Love Lucy* with capsule synopses of all episodes.

Arnaz, Desi. *A Book*. Morrow, 1976. A very personal autobiography of Desi Arnaz, ending at the time he and Lucy dissolved their marriage.

Barnouw, Erik. *Tube of Plenty*. Oxford University Press, 1990. A panoramic study of the birth and development of American television.

Bianculli, David. Teleliteracy: *Taking Television Seriously*. The Continuum Publishing Company, 1992. A groundbreaking work on television as a medium of cultural importance.

Blesh, Rudi. *Keaton*. The Macmillan Company, 1966. The definitive biography of the legendary screen comedian Buster Keaton—one of Lucy's comedy mentors.

Bowers, Ronald L. *Films in Review* (article), National Board of Review of Motion Pictures, 1971. A profile on Lucille Ball with her complete filmography.

Brady, Kathleen. *Lucille*. Hyperion, 1994. A comprehensive biography of Lucille Ball.

Brooks, Tim, and Earle Marsh. *The Complete Directory to Prime Time Network TV Shows*. Ballantine Books, 1979. The ultimate one-volume reference work on television.

Brown, Les. *Television: The Business Behind the Box*. Harcourt, Brace, Jovanovich, Inc., 1971. A penetrating study of how the networks function.

Gregory, James. *The Lucille Ball Story*. Signet, 1974. A Lucille Ball biography.

Harris, Eleanor. *The Real Story of Lucille Ball*. Ballantine, 1974. A Lucille Ball biography.

Harris, Jay S. *TV Guide: The First 25 Years*. Simon & Schuster, 1978. A collection of the best *TV Guide* features.

Harris, Warren G. *Lucy and Desi*. Simon & Schuster, 1991. An examination of the relationship of Lucille Ball and Desi Arnaz.

Higham, Charles. *Lucy: The Real Life of Lucille Ball*. St. Martin's Press, 1986. A Lucille Ball biography by one of the best-known personality biographers.

Jones, Gerard. *Honey, I'm Home! Sitcoms: Selling the American Dream*. Grove Weidenfeld, 1992. An analysis of the American television situation comedy.

Jones, Landon Y. *Great Expectations*. Ballantine Books, 1980. The book that coined the term "boomers." An absorbing examination of the first generation raised on television entertainment.

Lasky, Betty. *RKO: The Biggest Little Major of Them All*. Prentice Hall, 1984. An insider's look at the studio Lucy and Desi bought.

McNeil, Alex. *Total Television*. Penguin Books, 1991. A highly readable directory of television programs from 1948 to the present.

Michael, Paul, and Robert Parish. *The Emmy Awards: A Pictorial History*. Crown, 1970. A visual retrospective of the Emmy Awards.

Morella, Joseph, and Epstein Edward. *Forever Lucy*. (revision of *Lucy: The Bittersweet Life of Lucille Ball*) Edward, Lyle Stuart, 1986. A Lucille Ball biography.

Sanders, Coyne Steven, and Tom Gilbert. *The Desilu Story*. Morrow, 1993. An exhaustive study of Lucille Ball, Desi Arnaz and how they created Desilu.

Shulman, Arthur, and Roger Youman. *How Sweet It Was*. Bonanza, 1966. The best pictorial look at television ever published.

Taylor, Ella. *Prime Time Families: Television Culture in Postwar America*. University of California Press, 1989. A sociological look at the effect of television on the American family.

Thibodeaux, Keith, with Audrey T. Hingley. *Life After Lucy*, New Leaf Press, 1994. Autobiography of *I Love Lucy*'s "Little Ricky."

Wilk, Max. *The Golden Age of Television*. Delacorte Press, 1976. An anecdotal retrospective of the birth and early growth of television.

ACKNOWLEDGMENTS

Writing this book is the end of a very long journey and many people were there along the way to help me through some very challenging times—and still are.

First, I want to thank Lucie Arnaz and Desi Arnaz, Jr., for their wholehearted cooperation throughout the writing of this book. Their encouragement and enthusiasm set the stage for much of the progress that followed.

I would also like to extend my thanks to those who worked at Desilu: special thanks to writers Bob Carroll, Jr., and Madelyn Pugh-Davis, without whom I would have never understood the dynamics of the special creative collaboration that resulted in the show; and to writer Bob Schiller, who offered me unique insight into the direction of the show's changing creative growth. Many thanks to Gregg Oppenheimer, who brought me into his father's world: the late Jess Oppenheimer, without whose genius the show would not have had the creative cohesion that made it a classic.

Personal thanks to Dann Cahn for his perceptive technical and artistic understanding of how the show was produced; and to Elois Jenssen for her detailed reflections on how she designed Lucy's wardrobe—both personal and professional.

A major debt of gratitude to director Bill Asher for his keen analysis of the complex partnership between Desi Arnaz, Jess Oppenheimer and Lucille Ball; to Maury Thompson, whose humorous anecdotes and understanding of production matters strengthened the book's credibility; to Emily Daniels, who gave forth a wealth of information about the early days and the important contribution of her husband, director Marc Daniels; to Mercedes Manzanares and Johny Aitchison for their candid insight on how Desi Arnaz and Jess Oppenheimer ran their daily business; and to Hal King, Lucy's makeup artist for nearly three decades, who graciously gave me his informative backstage impressions.

I wish to express my sincere thanks to Oscar Katz for his detailed insight into the CBS/Desilu connection; to Martin Leeds, whose razor-sharp recall added depth and dimension to the Desilu phenomenon; and to Art Manella, who gave me a wealth of information on the inner workings of the Desilu empire. Thanks to all the other people from Desilu with whom I have shared my life. Thank you one and all!

My everlasting gratitude to Bernie Weitzman, agent and guide, who's been a solid supporter of my various causes for more than thirty-five years, a gracious human being who defines the word integrity; and to one of the most considerate people I have ever known, Wanda Clark-Stamatovich, Lucy's loyal secretary for nearly thirty years, whose quiet humor and gentle disposition during some diffi-

cult times has been a comfort to my family.

Thanks to the following, who provided materials and services: Tom Watson, president of We Love Lucy Fan Club, who helped verify facts and supply photos; and to Knight Harris—his broad and deep knowledge of the photo business, his thirty-year association with Desilu and Lucille Ball Productions, and his professional friendship added much to the making of this book.

For their wide-ranging support, I owe much to the following people who were there when I needed them: Don Garrett, Wally MacGalliard, Bill Sampson, James Gill, Jerry Suiter, John Tedeschi, Evan Smith, Steve Ibay, Teresa E. Victor, Joanne Reeves, Lisa Benadom and Marc Wanamaker.

An important note of appreciation to the following special people: to Tom Gilbert, who, among countless other generosities, gave me critical access to his *I Love Lucy* video collection—the primary reason I was able to complete the "Classic Episodes" section of the book; to Ron Rose, a true friend, who gave unblinking help along the way; to Rodney Buchser, a man of substance and integrity who was there when I needed him; to Michael Frydrych, who put up with my stream of questions and who encouraged me for years to get this project going; to Lloyd Richmond, whose faith in my abilities gave me the means to move closer to my goals; to Ann Fisher, who was there to provide me with some very important editorial assistance as well as some heartfelt advice and companionship; to Steve Rosenberg (and Ida), my friend and partner who has endured some very difficult and jubilant times over our twelve-year association; and finally to the late Clifford Palmeter, whose encouragement and faith in my ability to bring this off gave me the determination to finish it.

In addition, I express my sincere gratitude to Martin Silverstein of CBS Photos and Martin Garcia of CBS Entertainment, whose cooperation paved the way for this book.

How do you thank someone through whose efforts a dream of a lifetime is finally realized? My literary agent, Arthur Shimkin—whose sage advice and rock-solid support gave me the strength to endure—has been a guide through some rather treacherous territory. I owe a lot to Arthur, whose faith in my project was unwavering long before any accolades began.

Special thanks to others directly responsible for making this book happen: to Kathleen Clinton, a real friend whose faith and help started the ball rolling, I thank you. A singularly special note of appreciation to Mike Hamilburg, who opened numerous publishing doors at the beginning of this project. And finally, to

Warner Books's Mel Parker, whose "above and beyond the call of duty" help and timely input added a vital dimension to this project, which would have been a much less fully realized work without him; and to his editorial assistant, Sharon Krassney, who was a godsend during the critical stages of preparation.

To my two families, thank you for everything. Thanks to Paul, Donna, Jeffrey and Mary; to Kathy and particularly Elizabeth—my brave youngest sister. And especially to my dear mother, Barbara McClay, who came through at a time when all else failed, and who imbued in me the principles which have given me the courage to persevere. Special and heartfelt thanks to my aunts, Esther Whiting and Annie Zaharis, who gave of themselves without question. And to my second family, Dean M. and Melba Gaffner, Mark Gaffner, Chuck and Nora Underwood, and especially to I. Dean and Lenora Gaffner, my dear mother- and father-in-law, who have given their unwavering support and encouragement over many years. I thank you. And to my "other family" John and Mary Catherine Grady, who have been a beacon of hope and cheer to all of the McClays for over fifty years.

A special thanks to our longtime friends, Ann and Dan Christensen, Susan Malerstein-Watkins and David Watkins, Debbie and Pat Quick, who have shared our hopes, dreams and fears over the years. Thank you all for being who you are.

Space cannot allow for the superlatives I would like to list for my personal editor, Murray Fisher. Murray is a friend of long standing whose honesty and truth has seen me through some challenging times. But he has never allowed his friendship for me to get in the way of his sharp, objective editorial eye. The narrative flow and finished language between these covers are due to a large extent to his input. Thank you, Murray—and Sarah.

And finally, my special appreciation to my lifelong friend, companion, confidant, supporter, champion and soul-mate: my beloved wife, Deanna, whose patience, help, understanding and comfort have nourished me and given me the fortitude to persist and overcome all obstacles. This project would have perished long ago were it not for her sacrifice and precious time given over the years. I love you, dear. *Fide et amore.*